Advance Praise for

The Margins of Journalism

"This book offers a fine-grained examination into the struggles and successes of local newspaper journalists adjusting to a digital era. It demonstrates how shining a light on their unique - often underexplored - practices can provide broader learnings for the future of journalism. While the book appeals to emerging and experienced scholars alike, it also offers practical wisdom in understanding the post-socialist and post transitional media environment within the Czech Republic. This makes it a refreshing contribution of knowledge beyond a western-centric gaze. Anyone building a collection of seminal literature on local media should add this to their library."
—Professor Kristy Hess, Deakin University, Australia.

"Grounded in robust primary data, collected through a rigorous mixed-method research design and guided by Bourdieu's theory of action, this book provides fresh understanding of the dynamics of the periphery and what it means to be on the margins of journalism. Unveiling layers of periphery within the context of a post-socialist and post-transitional media system, often overlooked in dominant Westernised study of journalism, this book provides a fresh and insightful perspective. This rich and insightful contribution directs our attention to the important but often under researched margins of journalism, and as such it contributes to a wider understanding of what it means to be a journalist."
—Professor Agnes Gulyas, Canterbury Christ Church University, UK.

The Margins of Journalism

Frontiers in Journalism Studies

Scott A. Eldridge II
Series Editor

Vol. 1

Lenka Waschková Císařová

The Margins of Journalism

PETER LANG

New York · Berlin · Bruxelles · Chennai · Lausanne · Oxford

Library of Congress Cataloging-in-Publication Data

Names: Waschková Císařová, Lenka, author.
Title: The margins of journalism / Lenka Waschková Císařová.
Description: New York : Peter Lang, 2025. |
Series: Frontiers in journalism studies; 1 | Includes bibliographical references and index.
Identifiers: LCCN 2024028816 (print) | LCCN 2024028817 (ebook) | ISBN 9781636674605 (hardback) | ISBN 9783034351669 (paperback) | ISBN 9781636674612 (ebook) | ISBN 9781636674629 (epub)
Subjects: LCSH: Journalism–Czech Republic. | Journalism, Regional–Czech Republic. | Local mass media–Czech Republic.
Classification: LCC PN5355.C95 C57 2025 (print) | LCC PN5355.C95 (ebook) | DDC 070.92–dc23/eng/20240624
LC record available at https://lccn.loc.gov/2024028816
LC ebook record available at https://lccn.loc.gov/2024028817
DOI 10.3726/b22154

Bibliographic information published by the Deutsche Nationalbibliothek.
The German National Library lists this publication in the German National Bibliography; detailed bibliographic data is available on the Internet at http://dnb.d-nb.de.

Cover design by Peter Lang Group AG

The writing of this book was supported by a grant from the *Austrian Agency for International Cooperation in Education & Research* (OeAD-GmbH) via the *Aktion Österreich-Tschechien, AÖCZ-Habilitationsstipendium*.

ISBN 9783034351669 (paperback)
ISBN 9781636674605 (hardback)
ISBN 9781636674612 (ebook)
ISBN 9781636674629 (epub)
DOI 10.3726/b22154

© 2025 Peter Lang Group AG, Lausanne
Published by Peter Lang Publishing Inc., New York, USA
info@peterlang.com - www.peterlang.com

All rights reserved.
All parts of this publication are protected by copyright.
Any utilization outside the strict limits of the copyright law, without the permission of the publisher, is forbidden and liable to prosecution.
This applies in particular to reproductions, translations, microfilming, and storage and processing in electronic retrieval systems.

This publication has been peer reviewed.

> "I would like people to know that even such small newspapers are really useful, that they have an irreplaceable role and that even a small newspaper like ours can discover something really big."
> —journalist-entrepreneur Pavel

Contents

List of figures and tables ix
Preface xi
Acknowledgements xiii

Chapter 1. The margins of journalism 1
Chapter 2. Individuals on the margins 15
Chapter 3. Habitus, capitals, and practices of an individual on the margins 37
Chapter 4. Newspapers on the margins 105
Chapter 5. Disposition and position of a newspaper on the margins 121
Chapter 6. The margins of journalism revisited: Alongside journalism 191

Appendix 217
Index 219

List of figures and tables

Figure 1: Number of local newspapers in the Czech Republic — 107
Figure 2: Distribution area — 108
Figure 3: Frequency of publication — 109
Figure 4: Copies sold per issue — 109
Figure 5: Type of ownership — 110
Figure 6: Longevity of publication — 110
Figure 7: The sub-field of journalism on the margins — 209

Table 1: Capitals on the individual level — 24
Table 2: Comparison of local newspapers in the Czech Republic — 107
Table 3: Capitals on the organisational level — 112
Table 4: Habitus, forms of capital, and practices of the class fractions of individual agents — 194
Table 5: Forms of capital and practices of classes of organisations — 202

Preface

When as a 16-year-old high school student I saw my first published article in a newspaper, I knew that I was a journalist. I had no doubt that I was already "part of the circus" and would probably have been startled had anyone questioned it. I assumed that if I did everything right – followed the editor's rules about genre, made use of various sources, behaved, and wrote ethically – I would meet the requirements of the job and meet them well: the job of journalist.

Two years later, I began my career with a similarly straightforward and naïve perception of what being a journalist involved. I assumed that the local newspaper that employed me marked the beginning of a homogeneous career. Five years later, after working in larger newsrooms and in different forms of media, I had already learned that the smallest newsrooms on the margins of journalism are in many ways unique. What drew me to them most of all was the "voicelessness" of the local press, despite the fact that these newspapers gave a voice to so many. The boundaries of its relevance were very strictly drawn. While newspapers could have an unassailable position within the localities they served, they were largely invisible at national level. It was as if wider society could not appreciate their position within the media system. It became my goal to emancipate these peripheral newsrooms, to transcend arbitrary boundaries to give them a greater voice, and to highlight the wider impact they have.

In my attempt to emancipate the unseen and the underestimated in journalism, I have focused my study on the framework of a media system in the Czech Republic, which is both post-socialist and, after more than thirty years of transition to democracy, also post-transitive. Writing about these things in the context of non-American and non-British media can sometimes be frustrating: the de-westernisation of journalism studies is devoutly desired, loudly discussed – and seldom achieved.

When I exchanged my career as a journalist for that of academic, I was in some respects disappointed by who the researchers considered to be a journalist. From their point of view, I would certainly not have merited the description when I was sixteen. I was thus aware of a kind of blindness in those who look at journalism from the outside.

For me, stepping into this area of research meant closing a gap. At first, and without realising it, I unconsciously returned to the terminology and style of my journalistic days. It was like putting on an old coat. My knowledge of the environment of the small newsroom was both an advantage and, it would turn out, a disadvantage. It gave me an opportunity to observe and evaluate developments and differences from what I had experienced and what I now witnessed, and often, did so at opportune moments. It helped me to break through the reserve of my communication partners – the journalists. At the same time, from both my journalistic experience and my position as a scholar, it was sometimes difficult to find anything positive and optimistic in their remarks, especially since they were ready to express blunt, emotional views about their job, title, colleagues and sometimes the locality in which they worked.

All of this has shaped my attention to researching the local newspapers of the Czech Republic, a snapshot of a larger concern facing journalism studies that is timely – these journalists on the outskirts of the news industry need to find their voice – and urgent, as if they do not, they will "die". One of the local editors-in-chief describes his mingled frustration and resignation in these terms: "I'm already so calm that I'm almost clinically dead." Within a global media environment where the local and peripheral are at once necessary, and overlooked, and simultaneously unique, and ubiquitous, understanding the ways in which these local newspapers have experienced the recent years of digital transition give us insights into journalism writ large. And they give us reason to pause and reflect on the conditions in which these newspapers and local media are struggling.

Despite the wary prognosis summarised above, local journalists are still breathing, and their strength seems to draw upon common roots. It is time to give these peripheral actors a voice and by reflecting on their difficulties enable them to find their salvation.

Acknowledgements

This book is the result of sabbatical leave throughout the academic year 2019–2020. The long period gave me the opportunity to focus primarily on research, and at last to carry out my long-delayed plan of conducting a deep investigation into the gradual disappearance of local newspapers and local journalists in the Czech Republic. The year enabled me not only to travel and visit the newsrooms of local newspapers, meet the journalists there, discuss with them and observe them, but to complete data analysis, write this book, start writing several articles[1] and finally to bring the subject of local newspapers and local journalists to wider attention. In addition, the creative part of this period was supported by a grant from the *Austrian Agency for International Cooperation in Education & Research* (OeAD-GmbH) via the *Aktion Österreich-Tschechien, AÖCZ-Habilitationsstipendium*, so I was able to spend half a year in Vienna and analyse, write, and discuss my work with colleagues from the Universität Wien.

I am immensely grateful for the whole year. When for the first time in my sixteen-year academic career I was relieved of teaching and everyday duties, I once again found simple pleasure in reading scholarly articles and books, in being creative, and above all in my ability to "hear" my own thoughts and ideas again. For all this, many thanks are in order.

First of all, I would like to thank the many journalists, entrepreneurs and other local newspaper workers who made it all possible, both those who repeatedly filled in survey questionnaires, and the many who talked to me, discussed with me, argued with me and helped me.

Many thanks also go to colleagues from Masaryk University who made this year-long adventure possible, from the then dean of the Faculty of Social Studies, Břetislav Dančák, through the then head of my home Department of Media Studies and Journalism, Jakub Macek, to Rudolf Burgr, who took over my duties in the teaching and administration. Similarly heartfelt thanks must go to two colleagues from the Universität Wien, Folker Hanusch and Phoebe Maares.

I offer special thanks to the friendly colleagues who readily and helpfully discussed my thoughts and ideas – Barbora Vacková, Johana Kotišová and Benjamin Ferron. The completion of the project would have been unthinkable without the help of my student assistant, Anna Svobodová, who organised a collection of questionnaires and transcribed interviews. For this, much thanks.

As the writing of the book progressed, my copy editor Andrew Crisell became my most loyal supporter. He ensured that the English text was fluent, with the aim of making it as stylish and beautiful "as a polka dot dress". Moreover, he gave me confidence in the moments that I was losing faith, and for that I am infinitely grateful.

However, the greatest influence on the final shape of the text had Scott Eldridge, editor of the series Frontiers in Journalism Studies for Peter Lang. I especially appreciate his collegial editorial approach – professionally rigorous, respectful, and friendly in discussions.

I would also like to thank the Peter Lang publishing house for the support, and all their employees who did not hesitate to help and support me, namely Elizabeth Howard, Acquisitions Editor for Media and Communication, for her accommodating attitude.

My largest thank-you goes to my friends Martina Fojtů and Monika Metyková, and especially to my family. They always reminded me that somewhere behind the laptop screen there is real life.

Brno, December 2023
Lenka Waschková Císařová

Note

1 I have published two open-access articles with a particular analytical perspective not used in this book, but based on the same data: Waschková Císařová (2023a, 2023b).

CHAPTER 1

The margins of journalism

My intention in the chapters ahead is to define the *margins of journalism,* not in order to simplify the opposition between periphery and core or to draw an imaginary boundary between them, but rather to emancipate those actors and practices that are less visible and more difficult to pigeonhole. By pointing a spotlight at the non-mainstream, I will illuminate in greater specificity how the margins of journalism can be imaginative, diverse, complex, hybridised, messy, creative, intimate, and emotional spaces.

From the very core of journalism studies comes an ever-stronger call for a shift – a change of perspective from core to periphery, from the centre to the margins. This has been an effort to give a voice to *all* actors and practices in the field. Scholars mention particular "journalistic tribes" (Wahl-Jorgensen, 2009, p. 28) who are almost completely ignored or marginalised. Among them are local groups, community, grassroots and minority groups, women, people of colour, what may be termed precarious workers, and holders of unorthodox political views (Deuze & Witschge, 2020; Mathisen, 2023; Wahl-Jorgensen, 2009; Zelizer, 2017).

Moving from studying the core towards understanding the periphery is not the promotion of a binary opposition (Deuze, 2019; Zelizer, 2017), or distinction (Eldridge, 2018), rather, it argues that such divisions limit the perspectives we allow ourselves when making sense of journalism. Such a dominant discourse also tries to universalise the understanding of what is journalism and who is a journalist. When the focus is too narrow, things may look neat and easily definable, something Mark Deuze and Tamara Witschge (2020, p. 4) strictly refuse to adopt: such a "dream of coherence and consensus is a fallacy". According to Scott Eldridge (2018, p. 68), this is because "narrowness privileges a dominant 'centre' of journalism when viewing traditional actors" against "a peripheral set of 'other' (…) actors whose work may match similar ideals of journalism if explored more fully". These calls for a shift in our attention highlight how boundaries of the journalistic field, when reductively drawn by those who adopt the dominant discourse, give a distorted impression because they exclude alternative views "which one seldom gets to hear, in particular [those of] journalists working in publications with low legitimacy in the field" (Hovden, 2008, p. 33).

In line with this research agenda, and instead of trying to achieve consensual definitions about journalism and journalists, scholars now turn to discerning a wider and less restrictive framework which reveals the unruly character of both. Deuze and Witschge propose we "move *beyond* journalism, allowing for a broader definition and understanding of the field", to widen the conceptualisations "*beyond* the false core–periphery dichotomy, understanding that the core is no more homogeneous than the so-called periphery, while neither necessarily represents the other's antithesis" (2018, pp. 166, 168, emphasis mine). Aljosha Karim Schapals (2022, pp. 6, 7) suggests having "an open-minded approach when conceptualising journalism nowadays"; "as journalism's boundaries not only become more porous but also are seemingly dissolving" to focus on "what journalism is *becoming* in relation to established, normative definitions we have held close for many years". Schapals (2022, p. 9) also stresses that "we need an all-encompassing definition of journalism that embraces a plethora of forms, styles and outlets", so he suggests that journalism "*coexists* alongside a range of new forms, styles, and outlets" and "what emerges is an assemblage of *journalisms*". Eldridge (2019, p. 15) suggests doing so by focussing on similarities among actors, while at the same time remaining aware of limits, and "consider where to maintain a certain degree of 'differentiatedness' in order to continue seeing journalism as a field, just a more diverse and dynamic one".

Nevertheless, my focus is not so much on moving *beyond* journalism as it is on understanding what exists *alongside* it, for these unorthodox practices and actors are not new – they have always existed in the journalistic field. Indeed, contrary, peripheral, and exceptional practices "make up the essence of the profession" (Deuze & Witschge, 2020, p. 3). Or, as Barbie Zelizer has argued, "since journalism's beginnings, it has been shaped by outliers" (2017, p. 193).

However, and not to beat around the bush, the challenge that emerges is one of trying to understand the *margins of journalism*, while acknowledging both the dichotomy of centre and periphery and avoiding an overly reductive view. It is about getting to the very boundaries of journalism, where there are actors for whom it is more difficult to determine whether they still belong to the field of journalism. The margins of journalism refer to a place where these boundaries of journalism are negotiated more concretely, more tangibly, and more frequently. The actors who appear on the margins are at the same time those who are often less visible, less audible, and less privileged within the field of journalism. In various senses of the word, the *border of the periphery* is where the dispute over inclusivity begins for journalists, whether individual actors are rightly called journalists, or able to call themselves journalists. To be able to map a bit of the territory of the periphery of journalism, we can assume that the following conditions for the journalists on the margins prevail. First, they are less visible to those at the centre of national journalism, but also less visible from the perspective of readers. Second, they have little power when it comes to raising issues and influencing the social agenda. Third, they are not considered as important within professional organisations, dominated by journalists in traditional (and) national media. However, these conditions may not correspond with how so-called peripheral journalists see and understand themselves. For example, these categories do not account for whether such journalists feel peripheral themselves, whether in geographic, social, or political terms, but also in relation to their own media organisations.

To avoid the simplistic approach of core/periphery criticised above and the pitfalls of any narrowing of definitions that would be overly restrictive, I have approached what I term the margins of journalism from below and from the inside out. In this respect I follow the injunction of Deuze and Witschge (2020, p. 6), to "invent journalism from the ground up". In doing so, I allow different voices to be heard and only then do I try to systematise them. This is aligned with a prioritisation Zelizer (2017, pp. 113–114) establishes, in arguing "different voices offer more – and more complete – ways to understand what journalism is, each having evolved in conjunction with its own set of premises about what matters and in which ways". My approach to understanding these actors in this book builds from their individual stories. Focusing on their life histories, memories, experiences, lessons learned and emotions in order to illuminate the "messy reality" (Deuze & Witschge, 2020, p. 5), I am able to contribute to a wider understanding of what it means to be a journalist on the margins, doing journalism from the periphery.

Nevertheless, while resisting unhelpful limitations, and in order to focus this discussion, I build my understanding of the margins of journalism by studying one specific group of journalists: a semi-autonomous group of journalists on the fringe of the profession, working in the Czech local newspaper industry. As Pierre Bourdieu notes, "the deepest logic of the social world can be grasped only if one plunges into the particularity of an empirical reality, historically located and dated, but with the objective of constructing it as a special case of what is possible" (1998a, p. 2). Thus, in order to consider journalism in all its dynamism, and as a field, the Czech local newspaper industry offers "an exemplary case in a finite world of possible configurations [where] the aim is to try to grasp the invariant, the structure in each variable observed" (ibid.).

For many reasons, this group of journalists can be viewed as "peripheral". From the broad perspective of international journalism scholarship, case studies of local media such as these are often considered to be minor, worthy of attention only at critical moments, such as when news gaps and news deserts emerge in their absence (Abernathy, 2018; Currah, 2009; Lindgren et al., 2019). In other instances, they are simply shoehorned into the universal frameworks, sidestepping, or ignoring the unique nature of their journalism. When they are addressed in research, the emphasis is placed on the tradition and authenticity of local journalism. Jock Lauterer (2006, p. 2), for instance, defines local journalism as journalism in its natural state, where we can explore its particularities, and how they are configured.[1]

From a narrower, systemic point of view, Czech local newspapers are, as a group and atypically, almost invisible at the national level. In their view of local journalists, the national media show both prejudice and condescension. At a systems level, Czech local newspapers are understood as part of a post-socialist, post-transitive media system,[2] itself treated as peripheral in the homogenising perspective of a predominantly Westernised academic study of journalism.[3]

Looking from the bottom-up, journalistic insider's perspective, I focus on actors, who are not "newcomers" to the journalistic field, but rather gradually drifted to the periphery of the profession. I focus on individuals who are working under increasingly precarious conditions, in small teams or alone, and some of whom have been entrepreneurial journalists for as long as thirty years. To make sense of these journalists, working on the margins in Czech local newspapers as this area of journalism continues to struggle, there is also an urgent need to re-consider the professional existence of those individuals who are on the broader "floor plan" of the newsrooms (Waschková Císařová & Metyková, 2020) where these still exist. Therefore, to consider their professional existence within a broader media setting (Usher, 2019), including expanding beyond the traditional newsroom and newsroom-centric studies (Wahl-Jorgensen, 2009), and by working from where these journalists "are" to understand, where they are going. As John Pauly and Melissa Eckert (2002, p. 312) put it, let's not "whistle in the dark" or talk through our hats, but try to explore the margins of journalism from the ground up.

However, it is worth noting that 'the local' is not the key point of complexity here,[4] it is merely an example of a specific, homogeneous group operating on what are assumed to be the edges of the journalistic profession. It is both a unique group, in the nature of their work, and also emblematic of the various challenges faced by those on journalism's periphery. Nevertheless, being in more senses than one "in the lee" has conferred unique characteristics on these media. In so far as the premise applies that in order to understand the larger societal macrocosm we must first understand the microcosm, as Bourdieu (2005) has argued, we can treat peripheral journalism and journalists as a locus for understanding key characteristics and active changes in the field – for what they can offer as an unexpected recipe for the future, whether in providing best practices, or identifying what aspects of change cause problems, or leads to dead ends, the knowledge of their practices and their place in journalism is crucial to the survival of news media in general.

The margins of the journalistic field

The second way in which I have circumscribed my topic is through the choice of analytical framework. I considered what would be the most suitable to assess the relational disposition of the margins to the other parts of the system. Thinking about the margins of journalism is relational thinking, which best facilitates Bourdieu's *theory of action* and is based on his understanding of *journalism as a field:*

> a field is a field of forces within which the agents occupy positions that statistically determine the positions they take with respect to the field, these position-takings being aimed either at conserving or transforming the structure of relations of forces that is constitutive of the field. (Bourdieu, 2005, p. 30)

Crucially, the emphasis here is on the nature of agents, and the way they relate to the field, keeping in mind that the journalistic field cannot be reduced to a physical space, it is rather a space for social action and interaction by various agents. Adopting this approach enables me to (1) focus on the interplay of various kinds of actors at various levels, from different types of journalist-individuals to different kinds of media organisations within the framework of the margins of the national media system. A field approach encompasses "the entire universe of journalists and media organizations acting and reacting in relation to one another" (Benson & Neveu, 2005, p. 11), allowing one "to investigate both 'internal' and 'external' laws of the journalistic field" (Willig, 2012, p. 376).

This viewpoint also (2) works with an idea of distinctions (Bourdieu, 1984), one which accounts for borders and peripheries in the field and its sub-fields. This does not perceive distinction as an instrument of exclusion but as an enrichment of the whole. It highlights where there is a struggle to set the boundaries of the field, to enter the field, and to become part of it (Bourdieu, 1995). Therefore, the researcher must think inclusively, from the ground up, rather than "draw a dividing line between the agents involved in it by imposing a so-called operational definition", and rather work account for "these struggles (…) by the competing agents" (Carlson & Lewis, 2015, p. 5).

In addition, field theory (3) allows me to move beyond seeing a binary opposition, where at the centre there is a rigid understanding of journalism as professional and on the periphery a problematic understanding of it. On the contrary, it (4) takes into account deeper and less visible contexts such as the passage of time, weighing this as *path dependency*, or: "the likelihood that the outcomes of past historical struggles will tend to have constraining effects on the future to the extent that these outcomes are transformed into implicit rules" (Benson & Neveu, 2005, p. 11). Finally, (5) it considers the *tacit* dispositions of belonging to the field (Bourdieu, 2005). As Amanda Brouwers points out, tacit knowledge is rooted in lived experiences: "applicative knowledge, which is often referred to as experience, common sense, or wisdom, closely connected to personal emotions and interests" (2017, p. 222). These are five specific reasons why the theory of action is suitable for analysing the margins of journalism: sensitivity to different levels of actors, considering various distinctions, rethinking inclusivity, not simplifying, taking into account development in time and tacit dispositions.

For all these aspects Bourdieu's approach is appropriate, therefore, I will now focus on the essence of his understanding of journalism as a field. The *field* can be seen as an autonomous social world, within which there is a struggle to enforce the principles of public interpretation of reality. In the field there are power relations and interests, struggles for hierarchy and relevance. But the field is also unique, distinguishable, a world of its kind, with specific characteristics and its own processes (Bourdieu, 1998a). As Jan Fredrik Hovden explains, the *journalistic field* is "a relatively autonomous microcosm with its own specific logic and schemes of perception" (2008, p. 53). As such, fields are living environments, which are emerging, becoming autonomous, evolving over time through mutual struggles between actors, changing and reversing, separating, and merging, and ceasing to exist. In the journalistic field, the agents can be seen as "editors, freelancers, journalism teachers, video editors, news anchors, small local newspapers, large tabloids, television companies, magazines, journalist unions", which engage in journalistic struggles, "where one of the basic struggles uniting the field's members is the question of good and bad journalism", a "symbolic struggle fought in daily discussions in newsrooms and hiring of staff, by juries awarding journalistic prizes, by teachers and active journalists lecturing journalism students" (Hovden, 2008, p. 32).

Thinking about the field's characteristics, the journalistic field appears as *heterogeneous*.[5] Philippe Marlière (2000, p. 202) describes it as having "a variety of the brilliant and the dull, the hard-working and the ineffective, and the self-serving and the simplistic among its members". Therefore, we can think about the existence of the specific, distinguishable *peripheral journalistic sub-field of the local newspapers*, with specific actors, their capitals (cf. Maares & Hanusch, 2022), and particular trajectories (Bourdieu, 1998a). Nevertheless, Bourdieu characterised the journalistic field as a *heteronomous* field in comparison to other, more autonomous intellectual fields – this reflects its dependence on and permeability with other fields, particularly with other fields of power such as the economic field and political field (Bourdieu, 2005).

Fields are constructed according to underlying *nomos*, "the fundamental law of the field, the principle of vision and division" (Bourdieu, 1995, p. 223). As Hovden explains, for Bourdieu,

> nomos refers not only to "the law of the field", its "functioning according to its own rules" (the meaning of which is etymologically implied in the very concept of autonomy). He also stresses the contestional nature of nomos and its role in domination, it being "a principle of vision of division", a fundamental classificatory struggle to define who are the "worthy" and the "unworthy" participants in the social field. (Hovden, 2008, p. 169)

The nomos, the routinised and naturalised rules of the game, is defined by the agents with the more powerful positions in the field. The rules are often understood as traditional journalistic norms, but "it might also be reflected in meta-journalistic discourse on what is deemed 'good' journalism and 'good' journalistic practice; thus, it is an ideal" (Maares & Hanusch, 2020, p. 746); regarding "who are 'not really journalists' and 'not really doing journalism'" (Hovden, 2008, p. 171). The nomos, the characteristic of the heteronomous field, can be influenced by the powerful actors from different fields.

For journalism, there remains an important role for *doxa*, or the practical schemes, which Ida Schultz explains as "set of implicit, tacit presuppositions in the journalistic field, not least the practical schemes that editors and reporters take for granted" (2007, p. 194). Bourdieu considers it "the universe of the tacit presuppositions that we accept as the natives of a certain society", which can have a specific form as "a system of presuppositions inherent in membership in a field" (Bourdieu, 2005, p. 37). It can be understood as "the conventions we do not question, the deeply rooted tacit understandings of the world which are difficult to express in words, or the everyday circumstances that are so naturalised that we do not see them" (Willig, 2012, p. 378).

The role of the doxa is intertwined with *illusio*, a concept which describes "the necessary belief in the game" (Willig, 2016, p. 54); "the emotional and cognitive investments which secure the commitment of professionals within a specific field" (Lamour, 2019, p. 1168); "[a] strong feeling for the journalistic mission" (Maares & Hanusch, 2020, p. 748); "[the] attraction of a field" and "a fundamental belief in the interest in the game and the value of the stakes" (Hovden, 2008, p. 72). Agents subscribe to a particular field by their acknowledgement of the stakes, implicit in the very "playing of the game": it implies the degree of actor's identification with the field, belief in the value of what is being played in the field, and in the importance of fighting for it, aspiration, motivation, commitment, believing that the game is worth the effort (Hovden, 2008).

Ida Willig (2012, p. 374) retells the key concepts with reference to Bourdieu's analogy with a game: *the journalistic doxa* is "the unspoken, unquestioned, taken-for granted, understanding of the news game and the basic beliefs guiding journalistic practice"; *the journalistic illusio* is "the necessary belief in the game, the unquestionable conviction that the journalistic game is worth playing"; *the journalistic habitus* is "a specific way of playing the news game, the certain dispositions which the player (agent) has for positioning himself in the game, or, more simply, the embodied 'feel for the game'"; *journalistic capitals*[6] are "the resources the agent (media or journalist) can put into the game, resources that are recognised in the field and by the other agents in the field"; *the journalistic field* is the journalistic game:

> looking at journalism as a *field* means understanding journalism as a semi-autonomous field with its own logics of practice as an ongoing game or struggle over defining what journalism is, what good journalism is [*nomos*, note mine], and so forth. (Willig, 2012, p. 374)

The margins of journalism from the ground up

The overall purpose of this book is: (1) to demonstrate the feasibility of a field theory approach for studying the margins of the journalistic field; (2) to develop my arguments from the ground up, working from the individual actors to the journalistic field, in order to lend an openness to the concept of *the margins* and ensure that certain actors and processes do not suffer from a lack of visibility; and (3) to set out the sub-field of local newspapers by investigating the journalists according to their habitus(es) and practices, the positions of local newspapers as media organisations within the sub-field, and the situation of these peripheral players within the journalistic field. As Bourdieu puts it, the researcher should focus on distinctions and curiosities but not become a collector of curiosities. Better that she[7]

> seeks to apprehend the structures and mechanisms that are overlooked – although for different reasons – by the native and the foreigner alike, such as the principles of construction of social space or the mechanisms of reproduction of that space, and that the researcher seeks to represent in a model aspiring to a universal validity. (1998, p. 3)

In a similar vein, Thomas Gieryn (1999, p. 21) suggests paying attention to "the contingencies of each local and episodic" set of conditions and locating them on the map with a context, rather than focusing on the broadest framework. Local newspapers may be considered appropriate for this purpose, because they are at the same time considered a key part of informing people about what is happening in their proximity, yet they are relegated to the periphery because of their small reach, the fragility of their existence, or simply underestimated as being of insufficient quality (Hess & Waller, 2017). Separately, Brouwers considers empirical knowledge as a form of knowledge,

> which depends on experience – gained through the senses or through introspection – for justification (...). This is a very concrete form of knowledge, constructed bottom-up through e.g. observations or experiments, focussing on what actors are doing, saying, thinking, and feeling. (2017, p. 221)

Towards this end, the empirical findings I present in the chapters ahead are the result of focused, half-year study of the local newspaper journalists and organisations of the Czech Republic, building upon the concentrated scholarly attention given to Czech local media since 2001. The mixed-method study consisted of two parts, each with its own focus and research methodology. Using a *survey* of all the owners of the local newspapers, first in 2009 and then repeated in 2014 and 2019, the first, and quantitative, part of my research captured the sub-field and histories of the media organisations, their trajectories of development and current state. In addition, a *thematic map* (Soukup, 2014, p. 116) was created based on survey findings and depicting the sub-field of local newspapers from a geographical point of view (lokalnik.cz/localmedia.cz).

The second and key part of my study, was ethnographic. My approach follows Christopher William Anderson's argument that "a central aspect of ethnography is that it is interested in participants' perspectives" when the researcher takes "a detailed look at what is going on in the social setting" (2013, p. 168). As David Wolfgang and Joy Jenkins add, an ethnographic approach "allows the researcher to travel up and down the ladder of abstraction through iterative observation and interpretation – and provides an opportunity to continually refocus on the important aspects of the group and the areas that need closer observation" (2018, p. 6).

This chimes with my view of journalists as the bearer of a field memory. Through qualitative methods, including *in-depth interviews* (Legard et al., 2003) and *participant observations* (Brennen, 2013), I focus primarily on how the local journalists and local newspaper organisations function, and what their trajectory of development is. This offers insight into what happens "behind the scenes", since it allows the researcher to capture the invisible part of journalistic and organisational work. As Simon Cottle puts it:

> Participant observation goes behind the scenes of media output to help reveal the complex of forces, constraints and conventions that shape the selections and silences of media output. (2007, p. 5)

Using all these methods allows both a comprehensive and a profound insight into the sub-field thanks to the mixed-method approach and the triangulation of findings.

Specifically, (1) 30 questionnaires were distributed between January and August 2019, and their completion gave a picture of every local newspaper organisation in the Czech Republic at the time. From there, (2) in-depth interviews[8] were carried out with 33 workers in local newspapers, representing a variety of positions and expertise. These were conducted between November 2019 and February 2020; alongside (3) 17 days of participant observation in three different newspapers in December 2019 and in January and February 2020.[9]

The overall structure of the book reflects my thinking around the concept of marginal journalism. Chapters 2 and 3 reflect my inductive method, focusing on journalists as individuals and discussing them as the peripheral actors and unique agents of Bourdieu's journalistic field. Specifically, and following from my interviews and participant observations, I identify and contextualise distinctive characteristics within the habituses of my interviewees, particularly the journalists and entrepreneurs. Chapters 4 and 5 turn attention to media organisations as actors in the journalistic field (next to individuals), exploring their priorities, interactions, and struggles. Based on the interviews, observations, and survey data, I emphasise the individualistic tendencies of organisations within the peripheral sub-field of local newspapers. At the last and most general level, the specifics of local newspapers as an autonomous peripheral sub-field of the wider journalistic field are analysed in Chapter 6. This chapter summarises the field theory approach and includes all actors and levels of the analysis. The final chapter offers concluding remarks on the revisited *margins of journalism* approach and proposes the application of a developed analytical framework to a similar analysis focused on journalistic peripheries.

So, let us "dive, head first, into the chaos" (Deuze & Witschge, 2018, p. 166) – the chaos of the individual and organisational histories of peripheral actors in the journalistic field. This inductive approach may look like building an inverted pyramid, nevertheless, I believe that telling the stories by the actors themselves may end up contributing to a more general formulation of theoretical and research frameworks.

Notes

1. For an assessment of the local media as the "backbone of journalism", see Pauly and Eckert (2002).
2. For more on the Czech post-transitive journalistic field, see Chapter 4.
3. For critiques of this homogenisation, see Usher (2019), Deuze and Witschge (2018), and Maares and Hanusch (2020).
4. However, Nikki Usher (2019, p. 12) considers local media to be "a productive starting point for thinking about the boundaries between professional journalists and amateurs".
5. For a criticism of Bourdieu's "stigmatization of 'the journalists' as an undifferentiated category" see Marlière (2000, p. 202); or Hovden (2008, p. 74), who adds, that "journalists are very often presented in a monolithic fashion".
6. For more on capitals, see Tables 1 and 3.
7. When generally referring to individual persons, I use only she/her. Nevertheless, where one gender is used, the other is also implied.
8. The face-to-face interviews, which ranged from 40 minutes to 3 hours 30 minutes (median: 1 hour 40 minutes), were recorded and transcribed verbatim. Three of the interviews were conducted at the same time with two interviewees who were newsroom colleagues. I interviewed local newspaper workers at several levels of the hierarchy: owners, managers, journalist-entrepreneurs, editors, editors-in-chief, reporters, and freelancers, all of varying ages, experiences, education and gender (cf. Waldenström et al., 2019).
9. I analysed the data (from the interviews and observations) with two cycles of coding. The primary-cycle coding focused on structural, descriptive, and thematic matters (Ritchie & Lewis, 2003); followed by the secondary-cycle of focused coding (Saldaña, 2009). The data are presented here as continuous texts which were translated by me to English and slightly adjusted only to be grammatically and stylistically correct.

References

Abernathy, P. M. (2018). *The expanding news desert*. www.usnewsdeserts.com

Anderson, C. W. (2013). *Rebuilding the news. Metropolitan journalism in the Digital Age*. Temple University Press.

Benson, R., & Neveu, E. (Eds.). (2005). *Bourdieu and the Journalistic Field*. Polity Press.

Bourdieu, P. (1984). *Distinction. A social critique of the judgement of taste*. Harvard University Press.

Bourdieu, P. (1995). *The rules of art. Genesis and structure of the literary field*. Stanford University Press.

Bourdieu, P. (1998). *Practical reason. On the theory of action*. Stanford University Press.

Bourdieu, P. (2005). The political field, the social science field, and the journalistic field. In R. Benson & E. Neveu (Eds.), *Bourdieu and the journalistic field* (pp. 29–47). Polity Press.

Brennen, B. S. (2013). *Qualitative research methods for media studies*. Routledge.

Brouwers, A. D. (2017). Failure and *understanding-with* in entrepreneurial journalism. *Journal of Media Business Studies, 14*(3), 217–233.

Carlson, M., & Lewis, S. C. (Eds.). (2015). *Boundaries of journalism. Professionalism, practices and participation*. Routledge.

Cottle, S. (2007). Ethnography and news production: New(s) developments in the field. *Sociology Compass, 1*(1), 1–16.

Currah, A. (2009). *Navigating the crisis in local and regional news: A critical review of solutions*. Reuters Institute for the Study of Journalism.

Deuze, M. (2019). What journalism is (not). *Social Media + Society, 5*(3), 1–4.

Deuze, M., & Witschge, T. (2018). Beyond journalism: Theorizing the transformation of journalism. *Journalism, 19*(2), 165–181.

Deuze, M., & Witschge, T. (2020). *Beyond journalism*. Polity Press.

Eldridge II, S. A. (2018). *Online journalism from the periphery. Interloper media and the journalistic field*. Routledge.

Eldridge II, S. A. (2019). Where do we draw the line? Interlopers, (ant)agonists, and an unbounded journalistic field. *Media and Communication, 7*(4), 8–18.

Gieryn, T. F. (1999). *Cultural boundaries of science. Credibility on the line*. The University of Chicago Press.

Hess, K., & Waller, L. (2017). *Local journalism in a digital world*. Palgrave.

Hovden, J. F. (2008). *Profane and sacred. A study of the Norwegian journalistic field* [Unpublished doctoral dissertation]. University of Bergen. https://bora.uib.no/bora-xmlui/bitstream/handle/1956/2724/Jan%20Fredrik%20Hovden.pdf?sequence=1

Lamour, C. (2019). The legitimate peripheral position of a central medium. Revealing the margins of popular journalism. *Journalism Studies, 20*(8), 1167–1183.

Lauterer, J. (2006). *Community journalism. Relentlessly local*. The University of North Carolina Press.

Legard, R., Keegan, J., & Ward, K. (2003). In-depth interviews. In J. Ritchie & J. Lewis (Eds.), *Qualitative research practice. A guide for social science students and researchers* (pp. 138–169). Sage.

Lindgren, A., Jolly, B., Sabatini, C., & Wong, C. (2019). *Good news, bad news. A snapshot of conditions at small-market newspapers in Canada*. Local News Research Project, National NewsMedia Council. https://portal.journalism.ryerson.ca/goodnewsbadnews/wp-content/uploads/sites/17/2019/04/GoodNewsBadNews.pdf

Lokálník – Local media. Database of local newspapers in the Czech Republic. lokalnik.cz / localmedia.cz.

Maares, P., & Hanusch, F. (2020). Interpretations of the journalistic field: A systematic analysis of how journalism scholarship appropriates Bourdieusian thought. *Journalism, 23*(4), 736–754.

Maares, P., & Hanusch, F. (2022). Understanding peripheral journalism from the boundary: A conceptual framework. *Digital Journalism, 11*(7), 1270–1291.

Marlière, P. (2000). The impact of market journalism: Pierre Bourdieu on the media. In B. Fowler (Ed.), *Reading Bourdieu on society and culture* (pp. 199–211). Blackwell Publishers.

Mathisen, B. R. (2023). *Journalism between disruption and resilience: Reflections on the Norwegian experience.* Routledge.

Pauly, J. J., & Eckert, M. (2002). The myth of "The Local" in American journalism. *Journalism and Mass Communication Quarterly, 79*(2), 310–326.

Ritchie, J., & Lewis, J. (Eds.). (2003). *Qualitative research practice. A guide for social science students and researchers.* Sage.

Saldaña, J. (2009). *The coding manual for qualitative researchers.* Sage.

Schapals, A. K. (2022). *Peripheral actors in journalism. Deviating from the norm?* Routledge.

Schultz, I. (2007). The Journalistic Gut Feeling. Journalistic doxa, news habitus and orthodox news values. *Journalism Practice, 1*(2), 190–207.

Soukup, M. (2014). *Terénní výzkum v sociální a kulturní antropologii* [Field research in social and cultural anthropology]. Karolinum.

Usher, N. (2019). Putting "place" in the center of journalism research: A way forward to understand challenges to trust and knowledge in news. *Journalism & Communication Monographs, 21*(2), 84–146.

Wahl-Jorgensen, K. (2009). News production, ethnography, and power: On the challenges of newsroom-centricity. In E. S. Bird (Ed.), *The anthropology of news and journalism: Global perspectives* (pp. 21–35). Indiana University Press.

Wahl-Jorgensen, K. (2019). Challenging presentism in journalism studies: An emotional life history approach to understanding the lived experience of journalists. *Journalism, 20*(5), 670–678.

Waldenström, A., Wiik, J., & Andersson, U. (2019). Conditional autonomy. Journalistic practice in the tension field between professionalism and managerialism. *Journalism Practice, 13*(4), 493–508.

Waschková Císařová, L., & Metyková, M. (2020). Peripheral news workers expelled to the periphery: The case of camera reporters. *Journalism, 21*(6), 838–854.

Willig, I. (2012). Newsroom ethnography in a field perspective. *Journalism, 14*(3), 372–387.

Willig, I. (2016). Field theory and media production: A bridge-building strategy. In C. Paterson, D. Lee, A. Saha, & A. Zoellner (Eds.), *Advancing media production research. Shifting sites, methods, and politics* (pp. 53–67). Palgrave Macmillan.

Wolfgang, D. J., & Jenkins, J. (2018). Crafting a community: Staff members' conceptions of audience at a city magazine. *Community Journalism, 6*(1), 1–20.

Zelizer, B. (2017). *What journalism could be*. Polity.

CHAPTER 2

Individuals on the margins

The media are a product of people, not systems, and this is even truer of media on the margins where it is often the case that one individual embodies an entire newspaper. Systems set only the broadest boundaries and the range of their achievement varies according to individual actors. The further we shift our attention from the national press at the field's "core", the more vibrant a picture of the actors and their practices we can form at the "periphery". My aim is therefore to proceed from the bottom up: to place these peripheral actors under a spotlight and illuminate their self-understanding, life and career histories, and everyday practices. It is also to do so with clarity as to the pros and cons of the ways in which they are changing. Since people are the cornerstone of the system, it is only by focusing on those individuals who provide coherent definitions of journalism, whether it takes place at the centre of the field or on the margins, where we can build understanding. I therefore focus on the self-understanding of these individuals, taking a bottom-up approach to the types and categories into which they fall (Brouwers, 2017). My aim is to focus on their perception of boundaries, their discursive articulation of identities (Hanitzsch & Vos, 2017) and their positions within the journalistic field (Hovden, 2008).

The bottom-up approach I adopt is twofold. First, I conceive of those peripheral journalists who work for local newspapers as members of an *interpretive community*, that is, a "frame that might explain journalism by focusing on how journalists shape meaning about themselves" and which "addresses elements of journalistic practice that are central to journalists themselves" (Zelizer, 1993, pp. 222, 223). Second, I attempt not only to reappraise the conventional understandings and expectations about journalists and journalism but consider the historical reasons that led to these in order to address further changes and developments. In this context, I consider the *life histories* of peripheral actors (Wahl-Jorgensen, 2019c; Waschková Císařová, 2021). Zelizer (1993) stresses the importance of these sorts of stories about journalists' pasts, including their autobiographies, memoirs, and retrospectives, while Wahl-Jorgensen favours a longitudinal approach and a focus on the course of the journalists' professional life spans. Life histories are

> an approach that tells us much about the nitty-gritty of everyday lived experience, which may often be unglamorous and unworthy of note, but is intrinsically tied to broader social, political, economical, and technological transformations. Through the use of in-depth interviews, it sheds light on how individuals negotiate their identities over a lifetime, placing their accounts in broader contexts and highlighting how they experience major changes. (2019, p. 672)

Rodney Benson summarises these approaches, connecting them with field theory,[1] in outlining how "society consists of 'objective histories' embodied in systems, organizations, codes, and hierarchies," and "histories incorporated in habitus," which are "personal dispositions toward sensing, perceiving, thinking, acting, according to models interiorized in the course of different processes of socialization" (1999, p. 467).

Journalists who are on the margins, who are working for local newspapers, very often working alone in the newsroom (Wiik, 2009). Economic and technological changes have shrunk these newsrooms; teams consist of fewer and fewer individuals, and in many cases only one individual. This introduces a complexity for situating these actors within the field, as it blurs the boundaries between the responsibilities of the workers in the newsroom and thus blurs the line that can affect who is perceived a journalist. The smaller the newsroom, the more interconnected and (simultaneously) the less specialised its occupants become (Hess & Waller, 2017).

Yet there is a lack of research about these peripheral, marginal, "second-class journalistic citizens" as the producers of news content (Zelizer, 2004, p. 40). The conventional approach to journalists and their work lumps all types together and misrepresents their image, "privileging (…) some actors and [excluding] others" (Wahl-Jorgensen, 2009, p. 25), who nevertheless help to "make up the essence of the profession" (Deuze & Witschge, 2020, p. 3). This includes addressing their unique susceptibility to failure, deprived of the legacy and resources of more established news media; as Eldridge (2018, p. 184) adds, "'failing' at the field's core is treated as the work of a few bad apples, whereas failures on the periphery spoil the bunch".

Peripheral actors

The journalistic field is not homogeneous, it may only appear so from the outside, when we define journalism according to the apparently similar forms of journalism at its core; those Benson (1999, p. 470) describes as having greater weight in defining the field, due to factors like prominence or legacy. This apparent homogeneity also reflects how those who work on its margins and should be considered integral to it, are mostly unheard from. However, to consider the margins of journalism means considering the *boundaries* of the journalistic field, how they look, whom they contain, and what is happening at the boundaries. Matt Carlson and Seth Lewis argue that journalism "is not a solid, stable thing to point to, but a constantly shifting denotation applied differently depending on context", and disputes about who is a journalist, "who counts", are struggles over boundaries. This raises the important questions about "how boundaries are constructed, challenged, reinforced, or erased; about who should rightfully gather and disseminate the news – and who should not" (Carlson & Lewis, 2015, p. 2).

Nevertheless, the boundaries are not carved in stone, they are actively shaped by the negotiation of the social actors: they are the result of the *boundary work* of all agents in the journalistic field. Scholars stress the boundaries "not as divisive, but as meeting points for distinct groups", as a "means of communication, as opposed to division" (Carlson & Lewis, 2015, p. 6). In addition, the boundaries are not static; on the contrary, "different participants, norms, or practices move across the cells over time" and they are at the same time social and material (Carlson & Lewis, 2015, p. 12). As part of the boundary work, actors can experience "expansion of authority into domains claimed by other professions, monopolization of professional authority by excluding rivals with labels such as 'pseudo' or 'amateur', and protection of autonomy over professional activities" (Mathisen, 2023, p. 29).

Naturally, the uncertain, blurry boundaries of the journalistic field create a whole range of ambiguous positions. Laura Ahva, for example, depicts "citizens who are *not professional journalists* yet play a greater role in the journalistic process than mere receivers" as *in-betweeners* (2017, p. 142, author's emphasis). Eldridge (2018, p. 2) considers new actors in the journalistic field, which are seen as "claiming a journalistic authority they have no right to claim, and marginalized accordingly", as *interlopers*. Avery Holton and Valerie Belair-Gagnon add more types and terms for those who are on the journalistic periphery: journalistic strangers; interlopers or intralopers, who are "distinct from explicit and implicit interlopers because they work from the inside out, bringing non-traditional journalistic expertise and perspectives to news organizations and disrupting news production through advancements in digital and social media" (2018, p. 75).

There is a further boundary which has traditionally separated two roles in journalism, the editorial and the commercial (Vos & Singer, 2016). While normative expectations draw a strict distinction (or *wall*, cf. Deuze & Witschge, 2018) between the editorial and commercial teams of the newsroom, there also exists a whole set of interconnected in-betweeners. These roles largely determine the journalists' identity, which provides individuals with a "fixed sense of self" (Ferrucci & Vos, 2017, p. 868), taking into account the "meanings, symbols, ideologies, rituals, and conventions by which journalists maintain their cultural authority" (Zelizer, 2004, p. 101), their attitudes toward their jobs, their everyday practices (Anderson, 2011), and the "attributes, beliefs, values, motives, and experiences through which individuals define themselves in professional roles" (Jenkins, 2019, p. 1070).

Examining journalistic identity within the context of journalism on the margins can yield insights into how the groups of actors there make decisions and define journalistic roles. Zelizer quotes reporter Daniel Schorr, who "once offered the view that reporting is not only a livelihood, but a frame of mind". This discussion similarly tries to address "how that frame of mind is set and kept in place" (Zelizer, 1993, p. 234), sharing the attitude that

> we need to theorize contemporary journalism as a complex and evolving ensemble of attitudes, activities, emotions, perceptions, and values of (organizations, groups or teams of) individuals: it is not a stable object, but continuously comes into being through each enactment of these elements. (Deuze & Witschge, 2020, p. 29)

In other words, to understand "how transformations in journalism have shaped journalists as individuals and journalism as a professional identity over the longer term", we have to focus on the rational as well as the *emotional* element of the journalists' life histories (Wahl-Jorgensen, 2019c, p. 671). While the rational element of journalistic identity consists of more homogenised, coherent, and more frequently depicted activities or practices, the emotional part brings to the definition "clutter" and inconsistency (Deuze & Witschge, 2018), focusing on the journalists' *emotional labour* (Hochschild, 1983; Wahl-Jorgensen, 2019; Waschková Císařová, 2021), their attachment to the job, their passion for and loyalty to the profession (Deuze & Witschge, 2020, p. 6).

Karin Wahl-Jorgensen stresses that journalists "view their work as a 'calling'. (…) they are motivated to enter the profession by abstract ideals, frequently bordering on the spiritual: they view journalism as a public service" (2019, pp. 674–675). The emotional relationship to the job is also one of the common findings of other international and comparative research on peripheral actors. This relationship is manifested by understanding work as a passion project or higher calling (Deuze & Witschge, 2020, p. 62). Schapals (2022, p. 27) describes this in arguing that for these peripheral journalists, "their work is personal – something that they are invested in emotionally". Nevertheless, there is a clear contradiction between the passion for the job and (mostly) economic conditions for its functioning. For Deuze and Witschge (2020, p. 104), journalism at the margins is both a passion project and a precarious project: "Passion can be a beautiful thing – and it also can get you into trouble. Doing what you love makes everything you do very personal, making it hard to maintain boundaries (between work and life, for example)." They elaborate:

> As these journalists dive head over heels into their work, they subject themselves, their careers, and their loved ones to intense periods of activity that more often than not come with a range of stressors: working overtime, meeting deadlines, securing financing, trying out new things without any assurances it will work, working without well-established structures for feedback and support. (2020, p. 104)

With this in mind, I aim to understand the identities of these peripheral journalists in the way that they understand their occupational boundaries, their attitude to the job and the reflection of their everyday practices in the timespan of their life histories. The aim is to dig deep enough into the everyday reality of peripheral journalists, and local newspaper journalists as a group, and to offer a broad spectrum of life histories that take place on the journalistic margins.

During my fieldwork[2] I met about 60 workers[3] working for Czech local newspapers, interviewing 33 of them in greater depth. They represent the entire population of local newspapers in the Czech Republic. This approach in a qualitative study might be considered unnecessarily broad, but it was motivated by the ability to capture the whole sub-field of local newspapers. Sufficient insight into the character and activities of this group on the margins of journalism was made possible by the length and focus of the interviews and the intensity of my observations. Topics defined in the interviews were also used in the observations, so comparisons could be made between what the interviewees said and what was observed in the field. I focused on the life histories of the interviewees and the positions they held in the journalistic field; the hierarchy of the journalistic field; changing journalistic practices and the functioning of media organisations; relations with other actors in the journalistic field, including interlocutors; and the structure and specifics of the journalistic sub-field of local newspapers.

The three newsrooms selected for observation were experiencing three different situations, which as the interviews show, are typical for local newspapers. One newspaper was observed during the publication of its very last issue, before closing down after more than 20 years of existence. Another was observed as an example of a seemingly successful and problem-free operation, despite the struggle of most local newspapers to stay afloat. And a third was observed as a "survivor" within a highly competitive locality and in the context of preparation of the issue and planning the next issue. Since I was interested in the interplay between individuals, I chose newspapers which still maintained functioning newsrooms, nevertheless the observation took place both in the newsroom and in the field (Anderson, 2013).

In this book, I refer to my interviewees as *communication partners*. This reflects both the complexity of the interviewer-interviewee relationship and how the research approaches the interviewees as partners in an ethical, respectful, and courteous way (Rubin & Rubin, 2005). Similarly to other scholars (see e.g. Kotišová, 2017), this acknowledges a specific approach to qualitative, ethnographic research in which the interviewer and interviewee are in a closer relationship than an interviewer-interviewee dynamic would suggest. It also indicates a shift from thinking of participants as research subjects to thinking of them as partners or collaborators in knowledge production (Angrosino, 2007). Nevertheless, the researcher still maintains an inherent power position and authority over who asks the questions and sets the structure of exchanges. This is in line with Bourdieu's (1984, p. 318) understanding of the position of researcher, describing the research interview as a professional conversation. However, interviewees also often bring their own relevant themes and patterns to the interviews that add to the overall picture; this contribution is especially relevant in the bottom-up approach that is adopted in this book. More pointedly, the decision to approach interviewees as communication partners affords the researcher an ability to be quiet so as to allow the interviewee to speak, affords the ability to listen, and fosters empathy, in order to respect the expertise of the interviewee while maintaining the expertise and power of the interviewer. The term communication partner is used alongside the term interviewee; the latter refers to the specific interactive method used, where the former is used to reflect on the relationship between the actors. In their use, I am able to highlight and affirm my position as a researcher who is both aware of the relationship of researcher and interviewee, and interested in working within this relationship to foster a knowledge-exchange partnership based on mutual understanding, self-reflection, recognition of research roles and social boundaries, openness, all criteria that Herbert Rubin and Irene Rubin (2012) define in their framing of a *conversational partnership*.

My group of communication partners[4] consisted of 11 women and 22 men. They were mostly older (median age 55 years) and more experienced (median 26 years of work as a journalist), but there was also a younger group.[5] The interviewees could certainly be described as loyal employees: 15 had spent their entire careers with a single newspaper, mainly because more than half of the group (18) are (or were) journalist-entrepreneurs or owners of the newspapers they worked for. While 14 of the interviewees were university-educated, none had received an education in the field of journalism.

Habitus, capitals, and practices of the peripheral actors

In the following chapter, I develop a field theory approach to what I have termed *the margins of journalism*, starting inductively with the individual agents, local newspaper workers. My aim is to demonstrate that a field study of these actors can be done, to show the different types of habitus, practice and forms of capital distributed among them, and to analyse the structure of the peripheral journalistic field. Scholars consider Bourdieu's theory to be a "research program" (Hovden, 2008, p. 60), an "open concept", or an "analytical toolbox" (Rosenlund, 2009, pp. 3, 50), through which the least visible and most profound features of journalism can be accessed. In that light, it "will assist the researcher to break with the illusions bound up in every-day and professional ideas of journalistic practice, and gradually help with the construction of a relational scientific object" (Hovden, 2008, pp. 59–60).

According to Bourdieu, to speak about the individual, personal or subjective is to speak about the social and collective at the same time. *Habitus* reflects this. It "is this kind of practical sense for what is to be done in a given situation – what is called in sport a "feel" for the game, that is, the art of anticipating the future of the gamer which is inscribed in the present state of play" (Bourdieu, 1998a, p. 25). This practical sense of subjects includes preferences, taste, types of actions and perceptions, and related responses. Habitus is a socialised subjectivity:

> The notion of habitus expresses a reasonable hypothesis: that individuals' predispositions, assumptions, judgments, and behaviors are the result of a long-term process of socialization, most importantly in the family, and secondarily, via primary, secondary, and professional education. (Benson & Neveu, 2005, p. 3)

Therefore, habitus is not unchangeable, and similarly to how we understand life histories, it is constantly changing over time. Its analysis must be based on consideration of the structural position of an agent within the field, and her trajectory, the life history, which brings her to that position.

As Hovden points out, habitus is social history transformed into "generalised and relatively stable tendencies to think and act in certain ways, a practical sense which we use to orient ourselves in the world, a kind of practical awareness with a margin for improvisation, error, and deviation. Our habitus is by its nature intentional/directional and intrinsically bound up with social struggles" (2008, p. 64). In short, it is the set of agents' dispositions, inclinations, and habits in childhood as an initial position, and later trajectory influenced by life conditions and experiences.

Jenny Wiik argues that the concept of habitus is in many respects similar to the identity concept "inasmuch as it represents the accumulation of experience, capital, and struggles shaping a person" (2015, p. 120). Schultz describes the journalistic habitus as a feel for the journalistic game, played from different positions and dispositions, which indicate different forms of mastery of the game.

> It is thus possible to imagine that there will be more specific forms of journalistic habitus within journalistic fields, such as "editorial habitus" (...) but also forms of journalistic habitus differentiated according to journalistic genres such as a (...) "newspaper habitus". (2007, pp. 193–194)

Nevertheless, habitus itself does not embrace all social or journalistic practices. Bourdieu suggests an equation which includes other variables, the range of effects that are their basis, and their relationships:

[(habitus) (capital)] + field = practice. (1984, p. 101)

For journalists, their *practices* – "where they work, how they work, what positions they take on important questions in the field, what kind of journalism they prefer to work in (...) their perceptions of what events are 'journalistically interesting', their journalistic ideals" – depend on the specific structure of their habitus, the volume and composition of capital and dynamics of the specific field in which the social practice takes place (Hovden, 2008, pp. 32, 64). More specifically, "why a certain story is chosen and written in a certain way, is a process of detailing the convergence of 'disposition' (habitus) and 'position' (structural location within a field)" (Benson, 1999, p. 467).

In completing the overall picture, it is important to reflect on how a journalist's position in the journalistic field is not fixed or static. On the contrary, we have to think about *field trajectories*, "the movement in time through positions in social spaces by an individual" (Hovden, 2008, pp. 157–158).

Understanding habitus as a generalisable principle, "a structured structure", allows us to generate "clusters" of agents with similar habitus as a *class* or *class fraction* in the social space and in particular fields. Bourdieu (1984, p. 260) sets out the logic of class origins: (1) the dominant class constitutes an autonomous space "whose structure is defined by the distribution of economic and cultural capital among its members" and "each class fraction being characterized by a certain configuration of this distribution to which there corresponds a certain life-style, through the mediation of the habitus"; (2) "the distribution of these two types of capital among the fractions is symmetrically and inversely structured"; (3) "the different inherited asset structures, together with social trajectory, command the habitus and the systematic choices it produces in all areas of practice".

Therefore, the similar habitus of the various agents, the shared "practical knowledge, attuned to the positions in the social space", changes individual practices to the social practices of classes and class fractions (Rosenlund, 2009, pp. 45–46). A similar structural homology can be assumed between the habitus of journalists and that of their audiences, for instance, in the choices of journalistic products that they make (Hovden, 2008). Nevertheless, Bourdieu (1984) adds, that the analysis of the class can be complicated, because some members of a class fraction may take individual trajectories in the opposite direction, which he argues does not mean that individual practices are not influenced by the class direction.

To fulfil the whole equation, I describe the spectrum of *capital* defined by Bourdieu. There are four types of capital: social, cultural, economic, and symbolic. *Social capital* reflects "a durable network of more or less institutionalized relationships of mutual acquaintances and recognition". With respect to media, this is the strength of networks of the journalists with their colleagues, competitors, audiences, and sources (Benson & Neveu, 2005, p. 21). *Cultural capital* – knowledge, skills, education, and the ethical framework of journalists – can be converted into *economic capital*: income, often based on economic capital of an organisation: circulation, and advertising revenue. Moreover, "any of these forms of capital might be converted to *symbolic capital* when it is deemed legitimate and/or prestigious in a certain field" (Erzikova & Lowrey, 2017, pp. 922–923, italics mine); manifested "through the recognition, institutionalized or not, that [one] receive[s] from a group", which transforms into power (Benson & Neveu, 2005, p. 21). However, Hovden (2008, p. 177) points out that symbolic capital is not, according to Bourdieu, "a distinct species of capital (a common misunderstanding of Bourdieu's work) in the way cultural or economic capital is: it is a form that capital takes when it is misrecognized as capital." Scholars add the fifth type of capital, the *journalistic capital*, which they understand as the specific form of cultural or symbolic capital of the journalistic field (Schultz, 2007; Willig, 2012). Nevertheless, Phoebe Maares and Folker Hanusch (2020) consider the definition of journalistic capital to be still very much in flux.

Table 1: Capitals on the individual level

Capital	Definition
Social capital	Strength of networks of a journalist, relationships with colleagues, competitors, audiences, sources
Cultural capital	Knowledge, skills, education, and ethical framework of a journalist
Economic capital	Income, often based on economic capital of an organisation
Symbolic capital	Peer and group recognition which transforms into power

Credit: The Author, based on definitions above.

To sum up, my aim is to explore the way in which the habitus and capital of peripheral actors in the journalistic field are constructed, and through it their practices, and vice versa. I focus on the *doxa* and *illusio*, on the structure of journalists' dispositions, tastes, experiences, practical know-how, second sense, struggles with their own personalities, and their specific social conditions and capital. I am further interested in the answers to several questions: What was your career trajectory like before you reached here? In light of your upbringing and the people and situations that have influenced you, who are you as a journalist? Based on your life experiences, what are the deeply ingrained habits, skills, and predispositions that you possess? I take into account the specifics of the local social space and the habitus of the local journalists to examine a particular example of the more general features of the journalistic habitus, shared by all who work on the margins of journalism.

Journalists

There are often problems of definition with such a seemingly ordinary term as *journalist*. For example, Hovden claims, that "journalists do not exist", preferring to speak of "participants in the journalistic field" (2008, p. 33). I assume that on the margins of journalism the actors see their identities as more diverse than the professional normative theories presuppose. However, the point is not to reject current approaches to the definition. On the contrary, these afford an opportunity to take a step in a different direction, to move *alongside*. It is the opportunity to step out of charted territory to the unknown, the region marked *Hic sunt leones*. Through extensive fieldwork that deploys a bottom-up approach, first, draw it on the map and, second, do not treat it as falsely static but focus instead on the process of its formation and redefinition.

It is the extremes in the definition of a journalist that cause problems. Too narrow a definition excludes peripheral actors;[6] too broad a definition brings a confusion about whether the "orbital" newsroom's positions, including managers or administrators, should still be regarded as journalists. A narrow definition which excludes peripheral actors would be an impoverishment of the journalistic field. As Zelizer notes, the differences between central and peripheral roles in creative activity can be "simultaneously vast and minute" (2004, p. 23). There is also a full spectrum of more technical journalistic workers and contractual workers,[7] who are mostly labelled "support staff", for example, print setters, proofreaders, and copyeditors. A "blindness" to the range of definitions can help researchers discover through their interviews with journalistic workers how the latter view the boundaries of the journalistic field (Smethers et al., 2017). Moreover, if the marginal workers gain recognition, they can expand its boundaries (Zelizer, 2017).

A more balanced approach can be achieved through Hovden's definition of *participants in the journalistic field* and by distinguishing the individual positions and dispositions (habituses) of various actors in the journalistic field. In my view, journalists are, to paraphrase Zelizer (2017), individuals who engage in a broad range of activities associated with journalistic content-making. And as you will see in the chapters ahead, my communication partners see themselves as such.

My communication partners – journalists[8] – have no problem in setting a boundary, defining who is and who isn't a journalist and therefore show the classificatory struggle to define nomos in terms of the "worthy" and the "unworthy" (Hovden, 2008, p. 169). Although they themselves work under what are the "typical conditions" for journalists on the margins, in the local newspapers of the Czech Republic, at least, they are still capable of impugning someone's journalistic credentials or excluding her from the journalistic field. They occupy part of the spectrum of peripheral actors: entrepreneurs, freelancers, journalists under short-term contract, journalists without a newsroom who work from home, and a minority of full-time journalists. Nevertheless, there is still a clear boundary between journalists and non-journalists: more precisely, the latter are those, whom the ones who consider themselves journalists, do not consider to be part of the field.

Among journalists working on the margins, the flexibility in defining the boundaries of their profession that we see is also the result of a wide range of organisational models found in small newsrooms. This points to one trend which I want to identify, emerging both from my literature review and from my fieldwork: That is, the growing number of *freelancers* in newsrooms and the related emancipation of freelance journalists as professionals (Gollmitzer, 2014). This is found both in freelancers perceiving themselves as professional journalists, and in the way "editors have begun changing their views of freelancers, seeing them less as professional outsiders and more as exemplars of journalistic innovation" (Holton, 2016, p. 918).

At the same time, journalists on the margins work in difficult or even precarious conditions, struggling economically just as a more traditional local journalism might. Shrinking newsrooms mean, on the one hand, full-time journalists have to work longer, harder and more efficiently (Reinardy, 2011), losing "hours previously designated as 'time off'" (Ekdale et al., 2015, p. 384). Increased workloads and cost-cutting pressures mean, as well, that freelancers are hired more frequently and that employees are transformed into contractual or freelance workers. This is in part because freelancers usually work for lower wages with limited social benefits (Cohen et al., 2019), and therefore experience stress, uncertainty, and anxiety about the future. The shift from full-time or permanent staff towards "freelancers, part-time workers, contractual workers, temporary workers or atypical workers" is a move which is considered to be *precarious*.

Moreover, and as Deuze and Witschge (2018, p. 175) argue, "the real or perceived freedom of working as an 'independent' comes at a cost to many", not only because of the precarious working conditions but because of freelancers' "low level of identification with the journalistic profession, low journalistic capital, and a low degree of faith in journalistic institutions" (Mathisen, 2017, p. 913). The relative freedom that the freelancers experience could work as an independence from decision-making processes within the newsroom, putting them in the position of *intrapreneurials*, with their own agenda and autonomy within a particular journalistic team (Holton, 2016). Moreover, an owner's decision to convert from employing full-time journalists towards hiring freelancers could lead to a loss of managerial control over their actions. Further complications can cause ethical conflicts – for instance, when freelance journalists accept second jobs as journalists in a competitive medium, public relations workers or as spokespersons (Mathisen, 2017).

It seems that the nomos of the journalistic field on the margins is characterised by two dividing lines. The first runs between what we might term the core journalists and the "externs", those collaborators outside the newsroom (even, somewhat surprisingly, in those newspapers which no longer have newsrooms). Although most of my interviewees, including reporters and their colleagues, work as contractual workers, they do not think of themselves as externs.

This reflects how there is a full range of freelancers we need to consider when contemplating the field's margins, from reporters and proofreaders to graphic designers and advertising workers. What determines their inclusion or exclusion from the journalistic field is, for the most part, tradition, and financial savings. There has been a tradition in the Czech Republic that local newspapers make use of the contributions of freelance reporters. These were typically local historians, chroniclers, teachers, and locals who were informed about cultural or sporting matters, and who could report from that foundation of expertise. They were not accidental "citizen journalists". On the contrary, they regularly supplied specialised content to the newsroom, such as essays about local history, reports of sporting events, or theatre reviews, and they were on a list of regularly paid externs.

While traditionally part of the local news ecosystem, my interviewees regard these colleagues as "non-journalists", because journalism wasn't the main thing they did for a living. Hence as a result of financial savings an interesting situation arises: as the core staff in the newsroom become more and more precarious, the peripheral and supporting staff – cultural journalists; lifestyle journalists; sports journalists; graphic designers – get beyond the "event horizon" first and become externs, yet they should not be considered journalists any more. At the same time, in some newsrooms' economies have caused a significant cut in the numbers of *both* internal reporters *and* externs. Therefore, if we define a journalist as a person who is involved in the content production, all these external collaborators should be considered journalists. We can see this in the comments of journalists, here:

> We have six to nine externs and basically you can only count on six to write regularly. [They come from] a wide range of ages, thirty to eighty years old, which also brings the advantage that the opinions are different. (entrepreneur-journalist Dan)

> Until last year, we used to have four externs in the lifestyle section. We are without them now, we have only one extern [so] we regularly call around twenty sportsmen who give us results to make our sport section colourful. (journalist Radim)

On the one hand, the drive to create economic security means that some newspapers rely more and more on external contributors and, irrespective of traditional attitudes, that owners more often regard them as journalists. On the other hand, when faced with financial hardship, some owners cut the external contributors first, meaning the journalists in the newsroom are obliged to work harder, and in less specialised ways:

> The change is that we as reporters now have to do layout. We used to have an external graphic designer but now there is no money for that any more. (journalist Emil)

> We have few [externs], because if the internal reporters want to make money, they have to write. Each newspaper has [only] one or two externs. (journalist-entrepreneur Marie)

> We have [externs], but we use our reporters more. There are fewer externs than in the 1990s. Hard to say, the money is a big problem, but they probably don't even want to write for us anymore. (manager Anna)

The second dividing line also runs between journalists and "non-journalists", but according to the journalists I have met with, it separates the editorial and commercial parts of the newsroom. Whilst editors-in-chief are considered to be journalists, often because in small newsrooms they are the only internal reporters, there is greater uncertainty about journalist-entrepreneurs and other workers such as managers, secretaries, distribution and advertising workers. These are regarded as actors in the commercial part of the newsroom and therefore as "interfering" with those who see themselves as "inside" the journalistic field. However, the small size of the peripheral newsroom means that even this distinction, and any "wall" between the two, is porous (Harlow & Chadha, 2019; Vos & Singer, 2016). One interviewee, a journalist-entrepreneur, describes the "patchwork structure" of her newsroom this way:

> We have a workload for two sports journalists, but one of them is also a part-time news reporter. We have a girl who works half-time as a secretary and half-time as a reporter, because we have limited opening hours for readers, who don't come that much to the newsroom any more. (journalist-entrepreneur Marie)

Entrepreneurs

There are individual actors on the margins of journalism who are clearly different from journalists but who, just like them, operate in the journalistic field: *journalist-entrepreneurs*. Broadly speaking, they could be understood as journalists who, either as individuals or in small groups, start their own media businesses.[9] I am not going to narrow this broad definition, as it allows me to adopt my bottom-up approach and allow journalist-entrepreneurs to define themselves (Ahva, 2017; Brouwers, 2017). Some attempts at self-identification of journalist-entrepreneurs have proved problematic: Summer Harlow and Monica Chadha (2019, p. 905) found that they considered themselves entrepreneurs and no longer as journalists, "because they had started something new or were trying strategies that, while not necessarily universally new, were new to them," adding "founders hesitated to wear the hats of both entrepreneur and journalist; most identified either as journalists or as entrepreneurs". As they outline,

> in cases when subjects saw themselves as entrepreneurs and journalists (...) it seemed to be out of necessity as lack of resources meant they were responsible for everything. At the same time, their passion for journalism made them unwilling to forsake their journalistic identity. (2019, p. 905)

The journalist-entrepreneurs' position in the journalistic field has been heatedly discussed. Because it seems to be on the very edge of the journalistic field and is complicated by economic factors, it raises related doubts of a commercial and ethical nature and concern about the crumbling wall which separates the editorial and business sides of the newsroom (Vos & Singer, 2016). This situation can be described as a clash between the journalist, who is relationally rich in cultural capital and poor in economic capital, and the businessman whose position is categorised by an inverse relationship (Bourdieu, 1998b).

Initial criticism of scholars towards this dynamic was replaced by a conciliatory tone which reflected an understanding that the emergence of the entrepreneurial journalist was a direct response to the media crisis that has accompanied the digital age, and the economic crises that have pocked the media field in recent years. In other words, it is a means of ensuring their survival (Scott et al., 2019). Entrepreneurial journalists are sometimes depicted as *pioneer journalists* in order to stress that they "incorporate new organizational forms and experimental practice in pursuit of redefining the field and its structural foundations" (Hepp & Loosen, 2021). In fact, the rise of journalist-entrepreneurs is nothing new. Although Deuze and Witschge depict it as a relatively recent phenomenon, "coinciding with a gradual breakdown of the wall between the commercial and editorial sides of the news organization" and as "generally small-scale and online-only journalism companies" (Deuze & Witschge, 2018, pp. 174–175), they have been in existence for some time.

Beyond serving as a form of salvation for the media industries, entrepreneurial journalism is also a form of empowerment for the journalists themselves and can be seen in specific and repeated reactions to different types of crises in the journalistic field. This has been an instrument for journalists to emancipate themselves from such situations as ownership change, market monopolisation, economic pressures, and just plain confusion. Entrepreneurial journalism is a response to a lack of clarity about how the journalistic field should function and where its boundaries lie, and has been a way out from difficult situations, including by former editors-in-chief of certain major Czech newspaper dailies after their publishing company was purchased by a businessman and politician (Waschková Císařová & Metyková, 2015). Peripheral journalists, embracing entrepreneurial opportunities, also emerged in the messy newspaper industry right after the Velvet Revolution of 1989.[10]

Nevertheless, entrepreneurialism has its drawbacks. Being a solo businessperson at the same time as being a journalist means that the individual has sole responsibility for the success, failure, and sustainability of her endeavours (Brouwers, 2017). It is a highly individualised position, "which tends to reinforce a 'you are on your own' credo of individualized patchwork career trajectories" (Deuze & Witschge, 2018, p. 176). Moreover, juggling economic, organisational, and operational tasks "requires a business acumen and training many journalists lack" (Harlow & Chadha, 2019, p. 893).

Based on how they manage their business operation, Emanuelle Fauchart and Marc Gruber (2011) divide journalist-entrepreneurs into three types of "founder identities": *Darwinians*, *Communitarians*, and *Missionaries*, according to the amount of different capital – social, economic, cultural, or symbolic – that each brings to their ventures (Harlow & Chadha, 2019 added a fourth category – the *Guardian*). Therefore, we can consider four types of founder identities: Darwinians, Communitarians, Missionaries, and Guardians.

Among journalists in the Czech local newspaper ecosystem, the position of journalist-entrepreneur[11] typifies those working at the margins of the field. The role was established thirty years ago and corresponds to current definitions of pioneer journalism and entrepreneurial journalism (Deuze & Witschge, 2020; Hepp & Loosen, 2021). Whereas conventional newsroom workers have a diverse workload which is somewhat like a patchwork, entrepreneurs often integrate their duties. Without exception among the interviewees, all worked in the newsroom either alone or with a partner: "I am an owner, editor-in-chief, reporter, newsroom manager and responsible for advertising. My colleague is a reporter and at the same time responsible for distribution" (journalist-entrepreneur Filip).

I distinguish my communication partners-entrepreneurs in the following ways. A *journalist-entrepreneur* (10 interviewees) began as a journalist and then started a publishing business on her own. An *entrepreneur-journalist* (5 interviewees) began as an entrepreneur and then started to regularly write journalistic pieces for her own newspaper. An *owner* (3 interviewees) is an entrepreneur who owns a newspaper but without personal journalistic ambitions. And a *manager* (2 interviewees) works in the commercial part of the newsroom and is responsible for the economic and organisational functioning of the newspaper.

At the same time, entrepreneurs in the Czech local press have ambivalent roles: some are former journalists who (mostly in the 1990s) saw entrepreneurship as the only way to keep local newspapers alive; others started newspapers as a business but then fell in love with journalism and began to see their job as a calling or a passion and became entrepreneurs and reporters at one and the same time. The final type of entrepreneur on the margins have remained the owners with no ambition to write anything for the newspaper. Some of the interviewees believe that the more entrepreneurs there are who have an emotional attachment to journalism, the better. As manager Anna states: "Newspapers whose owners are at the same time journalists are more stable and better."

Yet, curiously and paradoxically, owners who are former journalists or entrepreneurs who write factual content for their newspapers do not regard themselves as journalists at all. They try to convey that in becoming entrepreneurs they have crossed some kind of journalistic Rubicon:

> I am not a journalist any more. (journalist-entrepreneur Ivo)
> I am an entrepreneur: I am no longer a journalist. (journalist-entrepreneur Barbora)
> I am not a journalist. I just produce a newspaper. (entrepreneur-journalist Dan)

Notes

1. For more about habitus and understanding individuals through field theory see below.
2. Interviews (31 with 33 communication partners) and observations (17 days) took place over a four-month period (November 2019 to February 2020) (cf. Bowd, 2004; Cottle, 2007; Zelizer, 2004). Interviews were conducted with representatives of all local newspapers in the Czech Republic. The participant observations took place in three newsrooms and in the various localities, extensive and systematic fieldnotes were made and analysed together with the interviews (cf. Hermans et al., 2014; Lamour, 2019).
3. As follows from the survey, in 2019 there were 88 local newspaper workers in the Czech Republic who are considered to be journalists.
4. The sample was constructed according to the knowledge of local newspapers' media organisations gained from the survey. I did my fieldwork in every local newspaper's newsroom in the Czech Republic existing at the time plus with communication partners who experienced the newspapers' closures. My access to the newsrooms was mainly provided by the editors-in-chief, who helped me to select communication partners according to my criteria which ensured sensitivity on all topics. They covered: (1) experiences and memories (communication partners with experience from the beginnings of the journalistic field which included a variety of situations and crises); (2) hierarchy (communication partners from various levels of the newsroom and field hierarchies); (3) diversity of habitus (variety of age, gender, education, roles – from freelance reporter to newspaper owner).
5. There were 3 interviewees in their twenties; 2 interviewees in their thirties; and 4 interviewees in their forties.
6. For a critique of definitions which are too narrow see, for example, Zelizer (2017), Usher (2019b), Deuze and Witschge (2018, 2020).
7. By *contractual worker*, I mean someone who works for a newspaper as self-employed. She is thus distinguishable from a full-time employee, a part-time employee, or a freelancer, who has no contract but receives money as an honorarium.
8. I have labelled my interviewees simply as *journalists* whether they are full-time, part-time, contractual, or freelance. Nevertheless, where the distinction becomes essential to the analysis, I give a more specific description of the journalist's position. There were 13 journalists in my sample.
9. E.g. in contrast to media owners with little or no journalistic experiences or ambitions.

10 The so-called Velvet Revolution in November 1989 (also referred to later in the text as November events) marks the beginning of the transformation from socialist Czechoslovakia to a democratic state. For more on 1989 and the transformation of society and the media, see Chapter 4 (cf. Možný, 1991; Paletz & Jakubowicz, 2003).

11 See the list of interviewees in the Appendix.

References

Ahva, L. (2017). How is participation practiced by "in-betweeners" of journalism? *Journalism Practice, 11*(2–3), 142–159.

Anderson, C. W. (2013). *Rebuilding the news: Metropolitan journalism in the digital age.* Temple University Press.

Anderson, C. W. (2011). Blowing up the newsroom: Ethnography in an age of distributed journalism. In D. Domingo & C. Paterson (Eds.), *Making online news – Volume 2: Newsroom ethnographies in the second decade of internet journalism* (Vol. 2, pp. 151–160). Peter Lang Publishing.

Angrosino, M. (2007). *Doing ethnographic and observational research.* Sage.

Benson, R. (1999). Field theory in comparative context: A new paradigm for media studies. *Theory and Society, 28*(3), 463–498.

Benson, R., & Neveu, E. (Eds.). (2005). *Bourdieu and the journalistic field.* Polity Press.

Bourdieu, P. (1984). *Distinction: A social critique of the judgement of taste.* Harvard University Press.

Bourdieu, P. (1998a). *Practical reason: On the theory of action.* Stanford University Press.

Bourdieu, P. (1998b). *Teorie jednání* [*Theory of action*]. Karolinum.

Bowd, K. (2004). Interviewing the interviewers: Methodological considerations in gathering data from journalists. *Australian Journalism Review, 26*(2), 115–123.

Brouwers, A. D. (2017). Failure and *understanding-with* in entrepreneurial journalism. *Journal of Media Business Studies, 14*(3), 217–233.

Carlson, M., & Lewis, S. C. (Eds.). (2015). *Boundaries of journalism. Professionalism, practices and participation.* Routledge.

Cohen, N. S., Hunter, A., & O'Donnell, P. (2019). Bearing the burden of corporate restructuring: job loss and precarious employment in Canadian journalism. *Journalism Practice, 13*(7), 817–833.

Cottle, S. (2007). Ethnography and news production: New(s) developments in the field. *Sociology Compass, 1*(1), 1–16.

Deuze, M., & Witschge, T. (2018). Beyond journalism: Theorizing the transformation of journalism. *Journalism, 19*(2), 165–181.

Deuze, M., & Witschge, T. (2020). *Beyond journalism.* Polity Press.

Ekdale, B., Tully, M., Harmsen, S., & Singer, J. B. (2015). Newswork within a culture of job insecurity: Producing news amidst organizational and industry uncertainty. *Journalism Practice, 9*(3), 383–398.

Eldridge II, S. A. (2018). *Online journalism from the periphery. Interloper media and the journalistic field*. Routledge.

Erzikova, E., & Lowrey, W. (2017). Russian regional media: Fragmented community, fragmented online practices. *Digital Journalism, 5*(7), 919–937.

Fauchart, E., & Gruber, M. (2011). Darwinians, communitarians, and missionaries: The role of founder identity in entrepreneurship. *The Academy of Management Journal, 54*(5), 935–957.

Ferrucci, P., & Vos, T. (2017). Who's in, who's out?: Constructing the identity of digital journalists. *Digital Journalism, 5*(7), 868–883.

Gollmitzer, M. (2014). Precariously employed watchdogs?: Perceptions of working conditions among freelancers and interns. *Journalism Practice, 8*(6), 826–841.

Hanitzsch, T., & Vos T. P. (2017). Journalistic roles and the struggle over institutional identity: The discursive constitution of journalism. *Communication Theory, 27*(2), 115–135.

Harlow, S., & Chadha, M. (2019). Indian entrepreneurial journalism: Building a typology of how founders' social identity shapes innovation and sustainability. *Journalism Studies, 20*(6), 891–910.

Hepp, A., & Loosen, W. (2021). Pioneer journalism: Conceptualizing the role of pioneer journalists and pioneer communities in the organizational re-figuration of journalism. *Journalism, 22*(3), 577–595.

Hermans, L., Schaap, G., & Bardoel, J. (2014). Re-establishing the relationship with the public: Regional journalism and citizens' involvement in the news. *Journalism Studies, 15*(5), 642–654.

Hess, K., & Waller, L. (2017). *Local journalism in a digital world*. Palgrave.

Hochschild, A. R. (1983). *The managed heart*. University of California Press.

Holton, A. E. (2016). Intrapreneurial informants: An emergent role of freelance journalists. *Journalism Practice, 10*(7), 917–927.

Holton, A. E., & Belair-Gagnon, V. (2018). Strangers to the game? Interlopers, intralopers, and shifting news production. *Media and Communication, 6*(4), 70–78.

Hovden, J. F. (2008). *Profane and sacred. A study of the Norwegian journalistic field* [Unpublished doctoral dissertation]. University of Bergen. https://bora.uib.no/bora-xmlui/bitstream/handle/1956/2724/Jan%20Fredrik%20Hovden.pdf?sequence=1

Jenkins, J. (2019). Elevated influences: The construction of journalistic identities at a city magazine. *Journalism Studies, 20*(8), 1069–1087.

Kotišová, J. (2017). Cynicism ex machina: The emotionality of reporting the 'refugee crisis' and Paris terrorist attacks in Czech television. *European Journal of Communication, 32*(3), 242–256.

Lamour, C. (2019). The legitimate peripheral position of a central medium: Revealing the margins of popular journalism. *Journalism Studies, 20*(8), 1167–1183.

Maares, P., & Hanusch, F. (2020). Interpretations of the journalistic field: A systematic analysis of how journalism scholarship appropriates Bourdieusian thought. *Journalism, 23*(4), 736–754.

Mathisen, B. R. (2023). *Journalism between disruption and resilience: Reflections on the Norwegian experience.* Routledge.

Mathisen, B. R. (2017). Entrepreneurs and idealists – freelance journalists at the intersection of autonomy and constraints. *Journalism Practice, 11*(7), 909–924.

Možný, I. (1991). *Proč tak snadno ...: Některé rodinné důvody sametové revoluce: sociologický esej.* [*Why so easily ...: some family reasons for the Velvet Revolution: A sociological essay*]. Sociologické nakladatelství.

Paletz, D. L., & Jakubowicz, K. (2003). *Business as usual: Continuity and change in central and eastern Europe media.* Hampton Press.

Reinardy, S. (2011). Journalism's layoff survivors tap resources to remain satisfied. *Atlantic Journal of Communication, 19*(5), 285–298.

Rosenlund, L. (2009). *Exploring the city with Bourdieu.* VDM Verlag Dr. Müller.

Rubin, H. J., & Rubin, I. S. (2005). *Qualitative interviewing (2nd ed.): The art of hearing data.* SAGE.

Schapals, A. K. (2022). *Peripheral actors in journalism: Deviating from the norm?* Routledge.

Schultz, I. (2007). The journalistic gut feeling: Journalistic doxa, news habitus and orthodox news values. *Journalism Practice, 1*(2), 190–207.

Scott, M., Bunce, M., & Wright, K. (2019). Foundation funding and the boundaries of journalism. *Journalism Studies, 20*(14), 2034–2052.

Smethers, S. J., Bressers, B., & Mwangi, S. C. (2017). Friendships sustain volunteer newspaper for 21 years. *Newspaper Research Journal, 38*(3), 379–391.

Usher, N. (2019). Putting "place" in the center of journalism research: A way forward to understand challenges to trust and knowledge in news. *Journalism & Communication Monographs, 21*(2), 84–146.

Vos, T. P., & Singer, J. B. (2016). Media discourse about entrepreneurial journalism: Implications for journalistic capital. *Journalism Practice, 10*(2), 143–159.

Wahl-Jorgensen, K. (2009). News production, ethnography, and power: On the challenges of newsroom-centricity. In E. S. Bird (Ed.), *The anthropology of news and journalism: Global perspectives* (pp. 21–35). Indiana University Press.

Wahl-Jorgensen, K. (2019). Challenging presentism in journalism studies: An emotional life history approach to understanding the lived experience of journalists. *Journalism, 20*(5), 670–678.

Waschková Císařová, L. (2021). The aftertaste you cannot erase: Career histories, emotions and emotional management in local newsrooms. *Journalism Studies, 22*(12), 1665–1681.

Waschková Císařová, L., & Metyková, M. (2015). Better the devil you don't know: Postrevolutionary journalism and media ownership in the Czech Republic. *Medijske Studije, 6*(11), 6–17.

Wiik, J. (2009). Identities under construction: Professional journalism in a phase of destabilization. *International Review of Sociology, 19*(2), 351–365.

Wiik, J. (2015). Internal boundaries: The stratification of the journalistic collective. In M. Carlson, & S. C. Lewis (Eds.), *Boundaries of journalism: Professionalism, practices and participation* (pp. 118–133). Routledge.

Willig, I. (2012). Newsroom ethnography in a field perspective. *Journalism, 14*(3), 372–387.

Zelizer, B. (1993). Journalists as interpretive communities. *Critical Studies in Media Communication, 10*(3), 219–237.

Zelizer, B. (2004). *Taking journalism seriously: News and the academy*. Sage.

Zelizer, B. (2017). *What journalism could be*. Polity Press.

CHAPTER 3

Habitus, capitals, and practices of an individual on the margins

Based on the self-understanding and self-definition of my communication partners, this chapter analyses the habituses, capitals and practices of individual actors on the margins of the journalistic field. Their stories, which describe the peripheries of the journalistic field, can expand the perception of who is a journalist and, employing the bottom-up approach, what are journalistic practices. I focus particularly on the quotidian character of journalistic work and, in a bigger picture, on the journalists' life histories. I locate the habitus of these peripheral actors in the intersection of their attitudes, perceptions, discourses, behaviour, emotions, ideals, values, skills, and the historical trajectory of their careers (Benson & Neveu, 2005). As certain scholars observe, "journalism is understood as a contested and dynamic social practice, embedded in specific contexts, whose characteristics are continually negotiated" (Scott et al., 2019, p. 2037). And, to paraphrase Deuze and Witschge (2020, p. 29), individuals continuously create journalism through the exercise of the attributes listed above.

As part of my bottom-up approach, I will begin by telling the stories of four of my communication partners. These stories represent the different forms of habitus, capitals and practice that occur on the margins of journalism as embodied by Czech local newspapers. These will be followed by a thematic analysis.

Habitus, capitals, and practices of a journalist on the margins

Story of journalist Milan

Becoming a journalist wasn't so much my decision as the decision of a friend who knew I had a close relationship, with writing texts of all kinds, mostly essays. My friend knew they were looking for a reporter for a local newsroom, he put me in touch with them, arranged a meeting, but it didn't work the first time, they chose someone else. But after half a year, the newsroom asked me if I was still interested, and I said yes. I probably wouldn't have thought of applying to be a journalist, it was more of a combination of circumstances that I was in the right place at the right time and met the right people. It was a challenge for me then. I took it as a challenge, maybe a bit like a game – why not try it?

I had a lot of distorted ideas about journalism because I didn't study it. I knew the film All the President's Men, I think I was watching the movie at the time I got the offer. This was perhaps such an interesting impulse. I thought I'd be somebody like Woodward and play an investigative reporter who could depose a president. At that time, I was making a living as a worker and I worked for a small private company, so I was specialised in something completely different.

My ideals about journalism disappeared very quickly because I soon understood the difference in working for a small local newspaper, writing about lost dogs and car accidents. The first sections I wrote for were obituaries and invitations to cultural events. So I was acquainted with newsroom practices, with daily operations. Nevertheless, it was sobering for me, I was expecting "big" journalism, big investigative topics, and they didn't come to the locality right away and there aren't many of them here.

Despite that, I stayed because the work was interesting, it was colourful. I had the opportunity to get acquainted with environmental topics, meet interesting people I wouldn't otherwise have met. Later, there was the opportunity to hold debates on political topics. It was my daily adrenaline rush, to get the newspaper published, have it well-sourced, not get surprised the next day when someone called and filed a criminal complaint against me. It was the adrenaline, the variety of topics and an interesting circle of people you meet, so you're so overwhelmed and sucked in that you enjoy the work, after all, even if it's no big deal.

At that time, I got a short internship in a big national daily newsroom, and it seemed to me very similar to the work of a local journalist. I also took a journalism course organised by an NGO. It gave me another qualification and was offered by my employer. I must say that none of the journalists I knew in the local newspaper had a journalistic education; they all had completely different educations or were professionally in a completely different field. I think that everyone needed to learn at least the basics of journalism. I appreciated that and I still take it as a great benefit, as an experience.

Then I left, after four years. Unfortunately, my relationship with my boss, the local editor-in-chief, became soured. She was a member of a political party, and I didn't like it. When the offer of another journalistic position came up, I decided to up sticks and try it on another local newspaper.

In the new newsroom, I found the atmosphere and enthusiasm very similar, I might say even more intense, if you thought about the more modest equipment. The job was the same, but the relationships were friendlier. The newsroom was one big family. Maybe it sounds like a cliché, but that's how it really was, and I still see it that way to this day. We can really rely on each other, otherwise the newspaper might not get published, a lot of it is personal. I think that's how all small newsrooms work.

I'm the only full-time journalist in the newsroom now, there's a colleague who works as a part-time reporter, we used to have three journalists here. I write most of the articles, I edit them, and I participate in the distribution. I basically work from the newsroom, using phone and emails, there's no time to get out. It's very rarely that I get out into the region and meet people.

We've never had any code in the newsroom, but we've basically followed the same principles as any other newsroom: defending our independence; following the basic rules of journalism – well-sourced and corroborated articles, freedom from pressures, whether political or economic. I think we've done well, although the publisher was at one time involved in local politics and a member of the town council. That lasted about eight years, but I have to say that I've never felt any pressure from the publisher. Nevertheless, it wasn't pleasant, the owner of a paper shouldn't get involved in politics.

The most common debates were about how to fill the newspaper. Times have changed radically. While in the past public administration made good copy, it's become very difficult in the last few years, especially for local journalists, to obtain relevant information. According to the publisher, there had to be a main article in every issue from the biggest town in the district, and it was really hard to manage this. But the audience is too local, readers are happiest when they can read what's happening in their street, not in a town ten kilometres away.

The priority from the beginning was of course the print, due to advertising. The online version of the weekly paper was always rather secondary, but traffic to the site was very decent for the region. I think people liked the online version, but we always treated it like a step-child, mainly in order to keep the print version alive.

After more than twenty years spent in one newsroom, I began to feel burnt-out. I felt it mentally for sure, but I think it also had an impact on my body. I sometimes had migraine attacks, abdominal pain, so I think the burn-out started to be quite devastating for me. I thought about leaving several times and I always put on the scales all the negative things I was aware of, but also the positive ones that the work of a journalist brings. And once you "smell" journalism, I don't think you want to leave so readily. After so many years, one has a feeling of a kind of certainty. The comfort zone always kept me from leaving, so when the company decided to close the newspaper, I was suddenly faced with finishing. I took it as a sign, as an impulse, and perhaps to some extent as a deliverance, because I knew that staying in that newsroom for a long time would affect my health more and more. The annual losses were almost astronomical, so under those conditions it was very clear that there was no way to keep the newspaper alive. It was only the enthusiasm that had kept it going for so long.

I had to start looking for a new job. I tried to meet the wishes of the publishers and basically worked on the paper out of a sense of moral obligation. But everyone knew it had a lifespan of only a few more months, so it wasn't easy. It was clear to me that I would probably not work as a journalist anymore, at least in the foreseeable future. There are currently no journalists' jobs in our region. I could climb over the barricade and do PR, but even in this field there aren't many openings. So, in the end I'm actually leaving the field completely.

For about ten days I've been trying to come to terms with the idea that I won't write again, and I believe I've probably come to terms with it. I thought I could try some literary activity, but this is probably a crazy idea. For a while I've been thinking about establishing my own newspaper. But I'm not thinking about doing it yet, at least not in the foreseeable future, I lack the energy to do it. I often dream of the best possible universe where someone decides to come up with a working model of the medium. Because somewhere in my subconscious, I have a hunch that I'm simply going to miss this work.

If we look at the life history of a particular journalist we can see the entire trajectory chronologically, watching the development – the path dependency – of habitus, capitals, and practices (Benson & Neveu, 2005). Running through it are both rational and emotional threads, with emotions playing an inevitable part in journalists' self-understanding (for more on the "emotional turn", see Wahl-Jorgensen, 2019). Antje Glück argues that the self-understanding of journalists "requires empathetic understanding alongside ethical and pragmatic considerations" (2016, p. 894); Schultz writes similarly about a journalistic "gut feeling" as a remarkable part of the journalists' professional self-understanding (2007, p. 190). In other words, it is through these feelings, including emotional aspects of journalistic understanding, that we can identify a journalistic *doxa* and *illusio* (Bourdieu, 2005; Hovden, 2008).

Drawing from the narratives in my interviewees' life histories, we can locate constitutive elements of the habitus, capitals and practice of those journalists who work on the margins. Three subjects emerged from my interviews with the journalists, which can be understood as part of the journalistic doxa and illusio, all of them reflected in the introductory story: the motivation to become and continue as a journalist; the meaning of the job; and the working practices of a journalist.

The motivation to become and continue as a journalist

In terms of the initial cultural capital (Hovden, 2008) of my communication partners, none of those who were reporters had a journalistic education. Before they worked as journalists, they were teachers, engineers, workers, artists, or lawyers, among other professions. However, this does not mean that they have no affinity with the profession as part of the illusio (Lamour, 2019): on the contrary, their motivation to become a journalist was mostly a strong, emotional pull[1] and it identified them as belonging to one of two groups.[2]

The first group were the interviewees who understand the work as a *calling*. These individuals represented themselves either as having shown talent since childhood, so that journalism was their "destiny"; or as having had strong dreams about the job and subsequently the good fortune to be able to enter the profession. These naïve-sounding statements should be considered within a set of considerations. On the margins, the entry requirements are less demanding and the competition less daunting. Importantly, these are journalists who are mostly at a late stage of their career, so when recalling their early essay-writing abilities, the memories of those initial motivation may no longer include the passion they originally felt or the emotional pull of what seemed to be a vocation. We see this in the ways they talk about their own histories:

> I was so keen to be a journalist from elementary school, I really enjoyed writing essays. (journalist Tom)

> I've always loved to write, and I always did excellent essays at school. I think I have a natural talent for writing, so journalism was easy for me. (journalist Robert)

> I wanted to write for a newspaper. So I went to the local newspaper and asked, can I write something for you? And they said, no problem. (journalist Radim)

Apart from the emotional pull, itself a strong factor in these journalists' initial motivation, there is a sense of a cultural capital found in some of the journalists' families and in particular we can see the influence and example of those who were close to them shaping their habitus, while the habitus represents the accumulation of experiences, capital, and struggles forming a person (Wiik, 2015). It is mostly a parental example that motivates the interviewees to become journalists or work for a newspaper. As journalist-entrepreneur Pavel recalls, "I used to see how my mum wrote at home and my dad took pictures, so I enjoyed taking pictures and writing";

while manager Anna admits: "I always had a positive attitude towards journalism because my dad was a journalist and even in later life, he reads newspapers a lot, so it was always like that with us at home."

At the same time, the job's calling is so strong that some have overcome significant obstacles in order to pursue it. One of my communication partners' topics was their inability to be journalists during the communist regime (before 1989), and the dissident past of some of these interviewees[3] contributes to their social and cultural capital and shapes their habitus (Dopita, 2007; Možný, 1991).[4]

> My relative was excluded from the Communist Party so I could forget about it, I was never going to get to university to study journalism. And even to work as a journalist I had to wait until the late 80's. (journalist-entrepreneur Marie)

> I was excluded from university as an anti-socialist. Nevertheless, I published several samizdat magazines. (…) Although I wasn't a dissident, (…) I gained a local reputation. (journalist Robert)

The second group are communication partners who recall their motivation to become journalists as an *accident*. There are, however, patterns suggesting that this was less accidental than they acknowledge. The ostensible accident relates to their cultural and social capital, reflected in their knowledge, skills, experiences, talent(s) and network of relationships. It is found in an often-repeated expression: "I was in the right place at the right time" (as with journalist Milan). The cultural and social capital took different forms: "I always wrote peculiar essays, I always played around with the language, and I wrote different sketches for my classmates" (journalist-entrepreneur Ota); "It just fell into my lap. The mayor of our village supported me" (journalist Jana).

> That was at a time when I was still working as an IT specialist, and a friend who worked in the local newspaper as the editor-in-chief offered me a job. They were looking for someone, so he asked, did I want to try it. (journalist David)

> It's like in a life you have to come across the right people. (…) It was a brand-new newspaper and the editor-in-chief, who knew my parents, came to me and said: come and work as a reporter. I'd worked as a maid so I replied: I can't be a reporter. And he asked: Can you write a letter to your auntie? If so, you can definitely be a reporter. (journalist-entrepreneur Lucie)

To avoid painting too rosy a picture, there was also a group of interviewees for whom journalism was not a dream job: they do not regard "the accident" as something that was necessarily positive. Some of them aimed for higher positions, including in related professions, but ended up being journalists. These experiences still inform their relationship with the profession: their attitude to it is more matter-of-fact, even "dis-*illusio*-ned" or cynical (MacDonald et al., 2016).

> I never wanted to be a journalist. I wrote short stories, which of course couldn't be published before the November [1989] events. So I came into journalism through writing. (journalist-entrepreneur Cyril)

> For me, this job was a last resort. I wanted to study photography. (journalist-entrepreneur Karel)

An emotional relationship with the work, a passion and strong motivation for it, the journalistic illusio, seems to be a constitutive part of the journalistic habitus, and similar findings are found in wider studies among journalists on the margins, who understand their work as a passion project or higher calling (Reinardy, 2011). The interviewees expressed their commitment to it not only historically, as part of the memory of their beginnings, but as an integral part of their current working life, creativity, and loyalty to the profession: "It's about having a relationship to it, about wanting to do it, and enjoying it" (journalist-entrepreneur Barbora); "Wherever I go, the first thing I do is walk past the newsagent and buy a local newspaper straightaway" (journalist Radim); "I've been a journalist just two years and I still enjoy the job. It still hugely attracts me" (journalist Ben). Moreover, my communication partners were able to identify the reason that they could stay motivated: freedom.

> I am very pleased with this job because I have a completely free hand, I can decide where I want to go, what I'm going to do, and what I'm going to publish. I don't think I abuse it, it's terribly liberating. I do everything myself and it's amazing. I think only a few journalists can enjoy this, because I know that colleagues from other newsrooms are really tied by a shortage of time and lots of instructions. (journalist Alena)

Nevertheless, asking a journalist who has stayed in the newsroom (some of them for decades) whether she still has the motivation to do the job often fails to elicit a clear answer. Their ambivalence reflects both sides of the coin – a passion for the job, or adrenaline as Milan highlighted, and the precariousness of it. This contradiction between the passion for the job and precarious nature of it is also one of the main findings in international research. Schapals (2022, p. 32) identifies it as a "recurring theme throughout the research, constantly appearing and re-appearing as a guiding red line". As journalist Emil admits, "sometimes it seems pretty overwhelming to me and at other times I say to myself, damn, that topic or person is so interesting it recharges me". On the one hand, as the entrepreneur-journalist Dan sums up: "You need to know when somebody is (not) doing it with joy. And you will discover this not only by looking at the journalist, but at what she creates." On the other hand, precariousness and emotional exhaustion can have consequences, eroding a journalist's motivation (Anderson, 2013). It is the ambivalence of the relationship to the job, the constant shifting "from love to hate", reflecting the illusio, that is specific to the journalistic habitus.

> Well, I was in a crisis last year. Last year, my motivation didn't increase, in fact it fell from a peak. My energy drained away and I finally rested for fourteen days at Christmas. Now I'm motivated again, but I'm afraid that when spring comes it'll be the same. (journalist Jana)

Some interviewees more precisely compare their relationship to the newspaper with a relationship to a child because it involves the same ambivalence, for example, journalist Eva laughed, while saying: "It's my baby, one hundred per cent my baby"; journalist Marta sighed when she admitted: "Look, it's such a baby for me, so it would be hard to say goodbye to it"; similarly to journalist Tom, who said, "because I was at the birth of the newspaper, I'd be sorry if it disappeared".

Meaning of the job

The second cluster of topics relating to the journalistic habitus is the meaning of the job for journalists, the search for it, the acquisition of it, and sometimes the loss of it. The most straightforward expectation in terms of a job's meaning is the economic capital acquired from it (Benson & Neveu, 2005). Nevertheless, and perhaps because it is still widely felt that the topics of money or income are not suitable for public discussion, my interviewees hardly talked about the financial rewards of their work. Some offered this simple observation related to the journalistic illusio: dedicated journalists do not care about money. As journalist Alena remarked with respect to her colleague while at the same time actually referring to herself: "She doesn't care about money, she just wanted the newspaper to be good, so she helped me out."

Journalist David claimed that he and his colleagues were for the most part devotees of journalism: "We got some equipment at the beginning, essentially a camera, and that's all we needed. (…) But we're real enthusiasts, we take our own equipment." At the same time, David reveals another important topic affecting the journalists' economic capital – the economic capital of the organisation for which they work and the extent to which their superiors do, or do not, pass it on to them. The reactions of the journalists (as part of their illusio) range from a gradual loss of motivation to resignation and from enthusiasm to pragmatism (which is often connected with their tacit presuppositions, the doxa). David perceives economic problems as "the sword of Damocles hanging over the newsroom": however, he adds that "in fact, it has conditioned us so much over the years that we are fairly resilient to the economic uncertainty".

This resonates with Deuze's finding, that "understanding of contemporary workstyles by definition includes structural uncertainty and risk, thus framing every aspect of our lives within that context" (2007, p. 20). The economic capital of other journalists is similarly "shaped", as journalist Milan explained: "the owners always made sure that they could pay the newsroom staff", "but we knew about the economic problems".

> I work on a contract and get a monthly fee. But I still get the same fee, it hasn't increased for the last four years. We didn't even get our usual Christmas bonus, so that was another demotivation. (journalist Jana)

Journalists are not typically very open about their feelings, but they do tend to form an emotional relationship with their newspapers (Russo, 1998) and these relationships are crucial to understanding these journalists' habituses. To explore these relationships, and as an attention-getting start to our interview, I asked them a specific question: if your newspaper were a human being, what it would look like? "It would look like me", said journalist Robert. They often projected their tacit understanding of journalistic values, roles, and culture (doxa) onto their answers – "the paper is a man who is grounded in ... truthfulness, trying to throw light on everything so that people understand everything" remarked journalist Ben. But, even more often, and significantly, they admitted that they identified the paper with themselves or with someone or something they like (illusio): "He would be some favourite with a rather scattered following or a local patriot" (journalist David); "Sympathetic? Yes, probably because she knows a lot" (journalist Jana); "He'd be, let's say, a middle-aged man, a kind-hearted chap willing to help others" (journalist Emil). Gender roles and associated stereotypes also featured in the responses, when assigning certain characteristics and at the same time specific gender to newspapers, and it was often the opposite gender to the interviewee (Steiner, 2012):

> He would probably be a smart ... educational, informative, educated person, he might be quite a conservative (laughs), he'd be nicely dressed to look nice, he would be probably liked by people in the street (laughs). (journalist Eva)

> (Exhaling) Personalising a newspaper, I'd never have thought of that in my life. (...) One has to have a relationship with a newspaper, so when mine is already so intense, I should have it with a woman. (journalist Milan)

> I picture him as a warrior, he would probably be a Renaissance man and a warrior at the same time. (laughs) (journalist Marta)

If the significance of the job exceeds certain limits, it upsets the work-life balance of the journalists, and the interviewees were willing to comment on this topic more openly than on financial matters. It is connected to both doxa and illusio, an understanding of their job as a calling and their role as heartfelt: it informs the passion/precariousness ambivalence of the job[5] (Curtin & Sanson, 2016; Örnebring & Möller, 2018). Nevertheless, the imbalance this often entails can have more serious consequences. As a result of too much time spent at work, interviewees spoke of their experiences with divorce (sometimes more than one divorce), a lack of time devoted to their children, a lack of time for themselves and their pastimes, burn-out, mental problems, and illnesses.

> When my kid was small, I took him to his grandma's for the weekends and then went to work. At the time I didn't realise it was a problem. (journalist Tom)

> There are professions where only a person who does the same thing can understand you. My first wife could never understand, so it just didn't work. (journalist Radim)

Burn-out[6] was a particular condition stressed by my interviewees. For example, journalist Alena said: "When I was left alone in the newsroom I couldn't catch up, so I vented my anger on my husband and had no time for my grandchildren."

Moreover, a set of principles and values which build a meaning for the job is part of the journalists' cultural capital (Vos et al., 2019) and is involved in the gain or loss of symbolic capital (Erzikova & Lowrey, 2017). These principles and values inform the way in which journalists understand their work: as a public service; as immediate in impact; as objective; as an effect of a perceived journalistic autonomy and a sense of ethics (Scott et al., 2019).

Considering cultural capital, my findings resonate with other studies which have shown that, even though most peripheral journalists who have been studied don't have specific journalistic training or any formal qualifications, and that they perceive their role as deviant, at the same time "they demonstrate a surprising degree of ideological continuity in the face of industrial disruption" (Schapals, 2022, pp. 27, 28). Deuze and Witschge (2020, pp. 95–96) depict peripheral journalists as those, who "frame their work and career in mythical terms, such as the need to be autonomous, the significance of the craft, and their belief in the power of the profession to matter and make a difference in society".

Interestingly enough, my communicative partners did not speak unprompted about these things. Two possible reasons are either that they take them for granted as a doxic part of the tacit, self-evident norms (Bourdieu, 2005), or their environment has shaped them not to perceive them as important. The second possibility is supported by what in terms of orthodox journalistic principles and values is an unconventional approach to the journalists' active participation in local politics.[7] On top of that, and perhaps due to years of experience, a related erosion of the illusio, particularly their values, and sometimes even to cynicism (Kotišová, 2017), the journalists' views of their professional principles are coloured by a certain relativism.

> I still think journalism is about to change the world. I'm naïve in this, I'm probably still a bit young for it. (journalist Ben)

> My rules are that I write what I feel is the objective truth. You'll never get to "the truth", that's clear. (journalist Marta)

My interviewees prefer to mention their principles and values when they hit a breaking point at which they have to decide whether or not they should quit the job. As journalist Tom narrated, "I left twice. The first time it started to bother me that the owner was meddling in my work too much and that I had to write things I didn't really want to write … The second time was more for financial reasons." This borderline situation gives them the space to more clearly define what is acceptable to them and what is not (Pihl-Thingvad, 2015), therefore build their journalistic autonomy (Örnebring, 2013). "My limit is tabloid journalism. We've always been a serious newspaper because I said that people here are intelligent, they are serious and always believe what's written is true," the journalist Radim said.

The interviewees also believe that marginal journalism imposes a particular limit on their doxa, principles and values. As Ota, a journalist-entrepreneur, described in distinguishing between their work and that of the journalistic "core": "A journalist from the national press can just fly in here to cover a story, make a mess, and never return again. But we have to keep coming back to the 'crime scene'." The proximity to their audience and sources also prompts[8] a reassessment of what they do (Bowd, 2005). This can be the source of significant tension, as journalist Robert describes in his town, where "almost every topic is controversial, if you insult someone, the person is always able to come to you in the newsroom and want to fight with you and it was actually one of the reasons why I quit the job, because I'd had enough". Ota describes this in terms of adjusting their approach to practice.

> Sometimes we have to be more of a diplomat than an intrepid journalist. We have to tread our patch without leaving footprints that are too dirty. We're more answerable for what we do. Luckily, with the passage of time, we're no longer the wild ones we used to be. (laughs) (journalist-entrepreneur Ota)

The meaning of the job also reflects the social capital of the local journalist, which she accumulates through relationships with other actors, including interlocutors from the neighbouring fields: colleagues, audiences, and sources. To begin by shattering a few myths: most of my interviewees do not refer to their colleagues as "family", neither do they have a close relationship with their readers. Indeed, they do not seem to even know who their audience is and often underestimate or "hold a condescending view of their audiences" (Gaziano & McGrath, 1987, p. 318). The assumed strength of their social capital is therefore much more complicated.

There is a visible difference among various actors – while those interviewees who are entrepreneurs and owners speak about the newsroom and their colleagues as "a family", those who identify as journalists are rather more sceptical. This may be because they are far more rooted in the newsroom environment than their bosses and have witnessed its gradual depopulation over the years; or because growing competition or economies have modified their relationships with colleagues. They thus have no reason to wear rose-tinted spectacles. The journalist Radim is an interesting example. He describes the members of his newsroom as "family", yet later on expresses disappointment with his colleagues' behaviour in very strong terms, in relation to their lack of responsibility to the job and to him as a colleague. In answer to my question whether he still enjoyed the job, he even began with doubts about whether he could tell me:

> If you don't record it, I'll tell you[9] ... Eighteen years ago, I took the job as a mission and I really loved it. But this year I can't go on holiday because none of my colleagues was willing to do me a favour, and my superior said, arrange it somehow. I lost the holiday, so it was bad. I've always had a family in the first place and this work in the second. It has to be done by someone who likes the job. The others are mere workers, they come, they do their own thing and go away, and when you want something extra from them, they say, I'm off today. I always try to accommodate everyone in everything, so I expected them to do the same, but unfortunately, they didn't. (journalist Radim)

These comments resonate with the findings of some scholars, who stress the importance of local journalists' understanding of people and communities they work with and cover (Bowd, 2005; Rivas-Rodriguez, 2011), but differ in how they are perceived as the close, even intimate, relations between local journalists and their readers (Le Cam & Domingo, 2015). None of my interviewees had any detailed information about who their general audience is. "I don't know anything about readers and readership, that's the editor-in-chief's business", remarked one journalist, Alena. And Jana, another journalist, remarked similarly, adding "our editor-in-chief doesn't give us any information about readers or the size of the readership".

Instead, journalists' relationships with audiences are limited to individuals, and based on these relationships they construct an understanding of the overall readership. "I see them as a projection of myself", commented Radim, which resonates with the *imagined audience member Lucy* described by David Wolfgang and Joy

Jenkins (2018). Journalist Jana tells the story of a blind reader to whom she sends every issue of the newspaper in a word document so that he can read it using a special programme, as an individualised, anecdotal example of the readership: "He always brings us a bottle of eggnog. He used to bring a becherovka, but we told him we don't drink it" (laughs).

Mostly, journalists have old, faded, and mute images of their readership (Zelizer, 2017), if they have one at all. And they don't see this as a problem, as the journalist Robert remarked "I make newspapers irrespective of who the readers are. Now I have complete freedom to do the newspaper. I do what I enjoy, and when there's something I don't enjoy, I give it up." Moreover, journalists forfeit the opportunities they do have to meet and get to know their readership. While engaging readers has been tried – "In the beginning we did some competitions for readers and asked them questions. We learned that older people are mostly interested in local history and what's going on around us, so I think we've got an overview," said journalist Tom of his newspaper – those described as entrepreneurs mostly relied on surveys to determine the composition and wishes of the readers, though the extent to which these were helpful varied. "Truth be told, we tried a survey years ago. It just didn't show anything to improve the newspaper enough to make more people buy it", said journalist Emil. In addition to their own ambivalence about their audiences, readers also seldom go to the newsroom. And here, this depends on a second consideration, whether a newsroom still exists (Usher, 2019). "People come into the newsroom less and less. At first, they came a lot, but over time, just like fences spring up between houses, people came less," Radim lamented.

The lack of knowledge about their readers also affects the practices of the journalists, especially with respect to the different platforms and the different audiences these might attract. Many of the interviewees' answers showed that they had not even given it a thought. For example, when asked: "When you say that the readers of your print version are mainly seniors, do the print version and the online version attract different audiences?", journalist-entrepreneur Lucie replied, "No, certainly not". Similarly, journalist Monika (in her twenties) admitted that she couldn't predict what sort of online news her readers would be interested in: "I would be interested in something different. I don't get it. When I did an interview with a food blogger, I thought it was great, but I don't know if our readers understood it."

As well as a two-way relationship with their readers, a two-way relationship with their sources is crucial for journalists since it forms part of their social and symbolic capital. As Deirdre O'Neill and Catherine O'Connor add, there is a symbiotic and mutually beneficial relationship between sources and reporters: "[reporters] despite believing themselves to be freely acting agents, finding and investigating their own stories, rarely behave independently of their sources" (2008, p. 488). Although interviewees hardly ever raise "obvious" topics without being prompted (cf. doxa), the reporters' skill in communicating with their sources is still traceable in their reflections of the latter. Unsurprisingly, journalists mainly appreciate "ordinary talk with ordinary people" and professional communication with official sources (e.g. the municipality, the police) (Splendore, 2020). Journalist Eva, for example, admires a colleague, "Mister Journalist", who "visited pubs, spoke to people there and brought the subjects of their conversation to the newspaper, but he is retired now". Journalist Radim likes spontaneous conversations with people on the street: "If we talk to each other, then a person will enrich me, and I'll enrich her. It's never as if I'm interrogating her. I think that when you chat, you learn something as an inspiration or a topic for the newspaper."

However, journalists' opinions differ about the professional communication which comes from official sources. Some (e.g. journalist Milan) believe that it might be just as professional if someone from the municipality were willing to talk to them freely without the need of a spokesperson. But others (e.g. journalists Jana, Emil) also appreciate it when a spokesperson sends them adequate press releases and always and promptly answers their questions. Entrepreneur-journalist Jan observes: "At the moment every street sweeper has his own spokesperson, you won't know anything anymore."

Another view of official sources deplores the routinisation of journalists' job which they have created and the degree of passivity which exists among journalists. As public watchdogs, they are not expected to receive information without applying some critical evaluation to it (Pihl-Thingvad, 2015). Failure to do so is considered by entrepreneur-journalist Dan to be a dereliction of their public service duty: "Our competitors absorb information from the press releases, whereas we absorb it from people so they can't provide the service that we provide." But the *journalists' passivity* has wider consequences, as O'Neill and O'Connor (2008, pp. 497–498) sum up: "Journalists are becoming more passive, often merely passing on information to the public that they have been given. The local journalist's role as the gatekeeper in the news selection and production process (…) is diminishing and shifting towards the source, often a public relations professional."

The limited space in which journalists on the margins and their sources meet is seen by my interviewees as a double-edged sword (Bowd, 2005): As journalist-entrepreneur Ivo summed it up: "You're definitely skating on thin ice." The knowledge of their space, their locality, is crucial for these journalists, and the fact that almost everyone knows everyone is an advantage; on the other hand, the closeness of the sources and the obstructions they can throw up are a handicap. Ivo added: "If you want certain information and you have to fill the newspaper every week, you just have to be fine with these people. If you're in conflict with everyone, they'll just mess with you and then where will you get the information?" On the contrary, journalist Eva experienced situation, when "an organisation has a bad spokesperson, we have poor cooperation with its press department. He'll punish us by not giving us the material we want. All he wants is for us to publish his press releases and then he'll be our 'friend'." Journalist-entrepreneur Ota admitted "a few people don't greet me, that's true, the former city leadership and a few people whose feet we've stepped on, as they say". Nevertheless, this ambivalent relationship with other actors is an important part of the habitus and practices of journalists on the margins.

> You go to someone you know very well in private, so you get more information than you would normally get officially, that's an advantage. And you won't publish anything you haven't verified because they'd make you eat it. (journalist Alena)

> I'm on first-name terms with a mayor because we've known each other since I was a kid in a completely different relationship. Sometimes it helps me when I need something. (journalist Monika)

> When I write local topics, I will certainly approach it differently from a colleague who comes here from a national daily and simply doesn't have to be so sensitive. (journalist-entrepreneur Filip)

Focusing on the local journalists' social capital, it is important to consider journalists' ambivalent relationship with sources and readers, which caused my interviewees a degree of fatigue and disappointment. The close quotidian contact made all participants feel alienated and emotionally exhausted – and over time their audience became distrustful. "People don't want to be in newspapers – they say: don't take pictures of me. They won't tell you anything," said journalist Eva. In response, the journalists became more passive and looked for easier ways to do their job. This development can break their confidence in the "game", the illusio, which may in turn change their latent expectations about the professional rules, the doxa. Journalist Ben points out, that "everyone is scared to say something in a newspaper". Journalist Radim ties this to the more visible:

> When you went out with a camera fifteen years ago and did a vox pop, people responded and let you take pictures of them. Five years later, they'd respond to you but add: don't write that. Within another two years, they told you not to take pictures. By then they didn't want to be identified, they wanted to be hidden. (journalist Radim)

> I don't like vox pops and I've always avoided them because I don't like walking down the street and asking people. (…) The thing is that when people know me as a

journalist, they want to solve their problems through the newspaper. They think I'll find out, arrange things, and let them know. (journalist Jana)

Still, some of the interviewees enjoy their symbolic capital in the specific locality, believing their position to be important and seeing themselves as "faces" of the newspaper (cf. *the authority of local journalism*, Anderson, 2013). Laura Ruusunoksa refers to a paper which "wanted to have a reporter who would become a familiar face among the public and would also create more natural interaction between the newsroom and the readers" (2006, p. 91).

What annoys me about the job? People probably. (…) They tell me how I should write stuff according to them. I enjoy everything else. I do it mainly because I enjoy it: I enjoy writing, I enjoy getting to know people, I enjoy writing about them. And I enjoy being the face of the newspaper, being THE journalist. When I arrive somewhere, they already know me and when I enter some place with a camera, I feel special, it's so important, it's a mission. (journalist Monika)

It's stupid here in a small town, where you are visible, with a by-line every week under something in the newspaper. Everyone knows you. I'm always very happy when I go somewhere where nobody knows me. (journalist-entrepreneur Ota)

Other journalists regard the decline of their local status, significance, and relevance as part of the decline of their symbolic capital, although only to a limited extent in comparison with the journalist-entrepreneurs and entrepreneur-journalists. My interviewees felt squeezed between the different forces and actors present in, or interfering with, the field; their own understanding of the profession; the preferences of their readers; and competition from other media. They prefer to point to the general decline in the social status of journalists. As Stephen Cushion notes, "journalists, in short, are fast becoming devalued" (2007, p. 127). But perhaps more important is the strong connection between journalistic status and the journalists' social capital – their relations with other actors in the field (Vos et al., 2019). Scholars point out that "a key aspect of diminished newspaper credibility was the distance people felt between themselves and their newspapers" (Gaziano & McGrath, 1987, p. 317); and "insofar as local journalism's image of the public is grounded in a vision that sees the public as a unitary, structural, or even interlocking entity that journalists can either confidently speak to or call into being, the authority of journalism has become deeply problematic" (Anderson, 2013, pp. 165–166). My interviewees' sense of their declining status, combined with the gradual decline of their economic capital, weakens their illusio with the belief that they are disregarded by everybody, alone in their respective localities with a role that is outdated and irrelevant: they are on the margins of journalism.

Sometimes I am ashamed to be a journalist, I always say I'm a writer AND a journalist. (journalist-entrepreneur Cyril)

I don't like the fact that journalists exaggerate so much. Just because of that journalism is being taken less seriously. (journalist Ben)

At one time I was convinced that I was doing well and that I was doing it better than my competitors. Today I don't know if I would. (journalist Tom)

Working practices of a journalist

The last topic treated as significant by my interviewees concerns the working practices of a journalist. In order to convey the journalists' unique point of view,[10] I focus here on journalism as a set of specific practices carried out under specific conditions but outside the context of the newsroom hierarchy (Ahva, 2017). Nevertheless, during my fieldwork I witnessed the variable character of journalistic practices, and this prompts a perception of journalism "as a moving object, as a process, as something that is continuously constituted as it is practiced" (Deuze & Witschge, 2020, p. 17). However, Anderson (2013, p. 57) notes: "On first glance as I watched journalists work, little about their daily routines seemed to have changed. This apparent stasis, however, was an illusion."

At the same time, the seemingly coherent set of practices is in fact performed differently and under variable conditions. The biggest debate focuses on the relevance of a *newsroom-centric approach* in the research into journalistic practices. Some scholars criticise what they see as a limited approach which could exclude those journalists and their practices "at the margins of this spatially delimited news production universe" and lead "to an emphasis on routinized and controlled forms and aspects of newswork" (Wahl-Jorgensen, 2009, pp. 23, 25). Provided that researchers take into equal account non-newsroom, atypical practices, others are not so strict in considering the newsroom as a space[11] for journalistic practices. As Anderson adds, "the newsroom's role remains central. However, we can no longer take its primacy for granted; the status of the traditional institutional newsroom must be continually problematized" (2011, p. 152).

My interviewees do not regard the newsroom as a restrictive framework, they understand their job has no temporal or spatial limitations: "I work everywhere and at all times, the job has no fixed working hours or place" (journalist Radim); "It's hard to explain that you don't have to go to work every day, but you have to think about it every day, and that is like being at work" (journalist David); "My work and life cannot be separated. I can't just come home and say I'm not a journalist for the time being" (journalist Emil).

Based on the above-mentioned variables, which affect the journalists' habitus, journalistic practices reflect all the forms of capital. As a consequence of their dispositions and the forms of capital they possess, the main theme of my interviewees' discussion of their practices was their passivity, which can be understood as a manifestation of a fading illusio and changing doxa. As Deuze recalls, the journalists' activities are a key to fulfilling the normative idea of journalists as watchdogs, "active collectors and disseminators of information" (2005, p. 447). Nevertheless, the relation between activity and passivity in a journalists' work is not a simple, contrastive one: it forms something of a vicious circle which includes the above-mentioned components of doxa, illusio, habitus and various kinds of capital. My interviewees are schooled in understanding their work as "waiting for what is about to happen". Rather than being pushed to produce dozens of stories a day, they were content to publish topics which people brought to the newsroom (Kleinsteuber, 1992). Now they are overwhelmed by the volume of information which bombards them every day and is easily accessible online: as journalist Marta puts it, "now you can download everything".

When this is combined with declining economic capital (being paid less for fieldwork), declining social capital (growing alienation between journalists-sources-readers) and declining symbolic capital (the decreasing social relevance of local newspapers and journalists), it pulls journalists into a vicious circle of confirming (but not necessarily reflecting) passivity as a new and latent norm of journalistic practice. As journalist-entrepreneur Lucie sees it, "today the topics fly to you by themselves".

> I do less fieldwork and use social networks more. First it saves money, and often when I arrived somewhere to take a photo, they'd later upload two hundred pictures to Facebook which we could then download. So I was asking myself why I should go there instead of spending the weekend with my kids. (journalist Jana)

> A journalist can now process thirty per cent of her work without picking up the phone, she can find all the facts on the internet. (…) But the journalism is the same, the days are the same and the stereotyping is just awful, it's boring. I've already learned over twenty-seven years what these people are going to tell me, no one will say anything to surprise me. People change, personnel change, but it's still the same. (journalist Eva)

Paradoxically, passivity brings not less but more work to journalists and a related inability to control their workflow. As journalist-entrepreneur Pavel points out, there is so much information that one can drown in it and "no one is catching up, everyone is completely destroyed". Passive journalism looks less demanding and so the management, eager to save money, often expects that the newspaper can be filled by fewer journalists and/or that the latter can simultaneously do several jobs. Sasu Siegelbaum and Ryan Thomas use the term *subbing* to describe journalists "substituting in another role in order to get the necessary tasks completed – as a routine part of the workday, with a resultant effect on personal health and wellbeing" (2016, p. 397). Deuze and Witschge (2020, p. 102) understand it as precarious, when peripheral journalists studied in their research described how they are forced to "combine the responsibilities of newsgathering, writing, editing, and producing stories with publicizing and promoting the work". These precarious working conditions contribute to journalists' further passivity and burn-out (Reinardy, 2011). One of the youngest interviewees, journalist Monika in her 20s, is already "not sure, if anyone can do journalism all her life. I'm afraid of a burn-out, now I have a passion, but I am not sure how long I can do this". This is in line with the view of Brian Ekdale et al. that "younger journalists, in particular, are highly susceptible to burn-out and are uncertain about their intentions to work in the industry long term" (2015, p. 384). Other interviewees note:

> I do in fact three and a half full-time jobs here as I've gained work from the colleagues who left. But we're losing substitutability. (…) Colleagues always told me at the beginning of my career that in order not to burn out, I would always need to take a break. But nowadays if you were to take a break from this profession, you'd never come back, no one would take you back. (journalist Radim)

> In our family conversations we think that I should quit the job. I'm the editor-in-chief, I basically write a third of the content of the newspaper, I do layout. And on top of that we have a family business, so I basically do three fully-fledged jobs and I'm not getting any younger. (journalist Robert)

> We substitute for each other in the summer so that we have at least some time off, even though we have to work while we're off, so we take turns and one is here while the other is almost free. When my colleague quit, we did two weeklies at once and I ended up in an ambulance going to the hospital (laughs). (journalist Jana)

Habitus, capitals, and practices of a freelancer on the margins

Story of freelancer Leo

I was still very young when I was grabbed by the "citizens' journalism" section of a local newspaper – it gave me an opportunity to write an article and get some money for it. I've always had a mindset which alerted me to all the things that are wrong in towns, so I decided to write about one such small thing in my home town. And the journalists liked it, so I got the money and the thing I criticised was put right.

I liked the fact that I saw my name in the newspaper, that I had my article there, but more importantly that I could point out a fault and someone would rectify it, so I carried on writing. Moreover, it led me to the fact that the things I actually see in everyday life when I walk in the town have a political background. Some politicians had to initiate it, so I went to council meetings, read a lot of newspapers. I enjoyed writing. I started going to events and the range of topics I wrote about expanded.

They didn't pay a penny because I wrote as a citizen journalist. All I was offered was a free weekly copy of the newspaper. But I was glad to be getting an article published somewhere and in addition I set up my own website. Nevertheless, I gradually established myself as a critic of the municipality, where local politicians own the local media or have their own interests in them. But if I started writing up stories on a daily basis, the problem was that as a single person I was starting a train that wouldn't stop. People started calling me, I had several meetings a week with my sources, and I still wrote, wrote, wrote and got onto a merry-go-round from which it was very difficult to get off. But I had other work to do. I enjoyed everything about journalism more than writing, I preferred finding the information. However, I received awards for my articles.

I tried to convince local journalists to write about the cases I discovered, but they refused. These topics were interesting only for the local correspondents of national media. So I wrote up these topics myself either for online publication or for local media that were not in the pockets of the local politicians. Sometimes I received an honorarium for my articles, sometimes the local newsrooms couldn't afford to give me anything. I did it because I enjoyed it and because I saw the value of shedding light on stories about the municipality.

The problem was that at the same time I publicly criticised the failings of local journalists, especially their close relationships with the local politicians. This and constant writing about problems at the town hall caused me and my family some problems of our own. I didn't even get much support from the organisation that represents professional journalists.

I was increasingly perceived as an activist. On the one hand, I decided that I didn't want to get involved in community politics because that would close a door for me in journalism. On the other hand, people kept contacting me on social sites and asking me for advice or help, so I help them without writing the case and understand it more as my activist role.

Now I'm focusing on something other than journalism, and in a different town. I'm not sure if I can get back into journalism or if it's a closed chapter – it's just terribly exhausting. Nevertheless, I still read online about the council decisions of my home town or the news from its official outlet. Will I return to journalism and my home town? A year ago, I would have said definitely not!

In order to keep my promise not to confine myself to a conventional understanding of journalists or to a newsroom-centred approach, I focus on the habitus, capitals and practices of freelancers[12] (Benson & Neveu, 2005). To complete the picture of the peripheral journalistic sub-field, I will analyse the situation of the freelancers – their differences from and similarities to the other journalistic workers (Rosenlund, 2009).

Generally speaking, freelancers' "feel for the game" (habitus) is similar to that of their colleagues (Bourdieu, 1998b). Nevertheless, having looked at this in more detail, I find that it evokes a similar picture, but, as in a jigsaw puzzle, is composed of different parts. While the freelancers' disposition, their habitus, can seem similar, their position in the field is different. This difference emerges from a bottom-up approach as well as from forming an external view. When I focus on the self-definition of freelancers (Holton, 2016), I find that they don't question being journalists in any way: yet when I consider their position in the field from outside, I learn that their journalist-colleagues place them in a separate position from themselves, albeit within the boundaries of journalism; they still follow its nomos, or principles of vision and division that shape these boundaries. Nevertheless, freelancers commonly speak about themselves as a different group from the journalists (cf. story of freelancer Leo).

Moreover, it is not only a question of power, as authors suggest with respect to peripheral actors: "we can recognize that those who have traditionally been at the core of the field, embedded in its institutions and traditional outlets, have little interest and much at stake in acknowledging interlopers as peers" (Eldridge, 2019, p. 12). The location inside or outside boundaries of journalism has not just a spatial, but also a temporal nature, because being outside journalistic field can change in time (Tandoc, 2019). And similarly, most of my communication partners, journalists, were external contributors and freelancers at the beginning of their careers, so they are more open to those so-called "newcomers" (Eldridge, 2019, p. 10).

I will therefore address the same topics, analysing the journalist-freelancers' habitus, capitals, and practices: the motivation to become and remain a freelancer; the meaning of the job; and the working practices and working conditions of freelancers. The analysis will be structured in such a way as to reflect the similarities and differences between journalists and journalist-freelancers as they are perceived both by the freelancers themselves and by other journalists.

The motivation to become and continue as a freelancer

When it comes to becoming and remaining a journalist-freelancer, the interviewees show a similar level of motivation to their full-time colleagues. They also see the job as a calling, with additional financial motivations. Echoing Leo's experiences above, journalist Monika remembers this from her days as an extern: "I wrote articles in high school and sent them to newspapers, and I also wrote for a website. As a student at the time, I also got paid for it quite decently, so I enjoyed writing."

Both journalist-freelancers and full-time journalists possess similar cultural capital based not on education in the field but on the newsroom socialisation, where older journalists teach the newcomers journalistic skills, crafts, and rules, irrespective of whether they are internal or externs. On top of this, freelancers are often recruited from the ranks of former journalists (e.g. the experiences of journalist Robert). Nevertheless, sometimes the editor-in-chief had to mould people into being cooperative because they underestimated themselves. This is something Holton also found in his study of freelancers as "intrapreneurs", showing "editors have begun changing their views of freelancers, seeing them less as professional outsiders and more as exemplars of journalistic innovation" (2016, p. 918). We see the same thing in Dan's reflections, here:

> They turned out to be skilled people. I corrected their articles at the beginning, I told them: this is a mistake, that's wrong, that it's not news, you have to realise news is one thing, opinion is another, and you can't put both into the same article. They learnt it quickly, it's not complicated. Who, what, where, why and how is news, and as for the rest … write what you want. (entrepreneur-journalist Dan)

The meaning of the job

An investigation of the freelancers' attitudes to what their job means – the search for it, the acquisition, and sometimes the loss of it – brings slightly different findings. As the accumulation of economic capital loses its primary significance, especially as freelancers usually have more than one job, the meaning of the job as a way of raising social and symbolic capital increases. Freelancers are recognised as journalists by the readership and gain a notable position in a respective locality. Freelancer Leo points out that he considered himself a journalist even when he wasn't being paid for his work. Moreover, he was recognised nationally as a valuable local journalist when he received several awards for his articles.

This apparently simple inclusion of freelancers in the journalistic profession is complicated, however, by the freelancers' practical application of their cultural capital, normative and ethical expectations, as part of the doxa. Their approach to the job is much more relaxed: some of the externs and contractual workers are at the same time print journalists and journalists in a competing medium; PR workers; spokespersons; secretaries; managers or advertising workers (e.g. as reflected by entrepreneur Mirek)[13] – and they thus break down several normative and ethical "walls". While they gain economic capital, they lose symbolic capital.

In terms of social capital – their relationships with colleagues, audiences, and sources – a whole range of differences between freelancers and other journalists appears which justifies the freelancers' different position in the journalistic field and their different habitus. This difference is based on two, seemingly contradictory but related grounds – *distance* and *proximity* – which are connected to other elements of the freelancers' habitus. A distance exists because the freelancers have become estranged from their colleagues in the newsroom. Whether or not the newspaper still has a newsroom, they see each other less often. This results in their and their colleagues' sense of belonging to the field of journalism fading. No wonder internal journalists often see freelancer-externs as readers rather than journalists and therefore regard the attenuation of their relationship as part of their own weakening rapport with the audience. Henrik Örnebring comes to the same conclusion when he notes

> an increased individualisation of labour and insecure forms of employment must have a weakening impact on occupational professionalisation, as this form of professionalisation relies on strong occupational socialisation and a strong collective sense of belonging (both more difficult to achieve in an environment of individualised career management). (2009, pp. 9–10)

He adds that it can "have a strengthening effect on organisational professionalism, as research notes that freelancers normally are in a position of weakness vis-à-vis their employers and employers can dictate the conditions of labour" (2009, p. 10). As entrepreneur Mirek adds, "I saved up in order to hire externs, but it is no longer journalism as it should be." Mirjam Gollmitzer similarly found out, that

> a regular physical presence in one or several news organizations turns out to be of crucial importance for journalists (…) Those who are able to cultivate relationships with editors and colleagues on site are less anxious about continuing to receive assignments and have access to valuable knowledge about their employer(s). (2014, pp. 836–837)

The alienation between freelancers and internal journalists is caused on the one hand by the perennial efforts of most media organisations on the periphery to cut costs, and on the other by the impact of technology, and it confirms the importance of the newsroom or any other physical space, in which all the reporters can gather and meet each other (Usher, 2018). As Wahl-Jorgensen points out, "freelance journalists are, by definition, structurally excluded from the "field" of the newsroom", and their "tenuous connection with the centralized and routinized forms of news production means that they are often invisible as members of the journalistic tribes" (2009, p. 30).

> We all meet twice a year, for example, and that's because it's so hard to meet. Everyone's got a job and they're from different parts of the region, so the meetings are getting fewer and fewer, and modern communication is used more instead. (journalist-entrepreneur Karel)

> We have editorial meetings once a month, probably no more often, we often call each other and the vast majority of communication happens on email, but most of the time everything's so routinised that everyone knows what to do. (journalist-entrepreneur Filip)

The distance brings frustration and disrupts the illusio on both sides. Freelancers feel abandoned, bereft of leadership and support, sometimes in a precarious position (cf. Örnebring, 2009), while their full-time colleagues and bosses feel unsure whether they can rely on them (cf. *intrapreneurs*, Holton, 2016). Entrepreneur-journalist Dan summed it up: "One advantage is that you pay lower fees; and a disadvantage is that you can't order these people to do anything because if they don't write the piece, you have to write it yourself." These emotions often feed off one another and further disrupt the freelancers' social capital.

> I was a freelancer, and the editor-in-chief was a freelancer as well, he had his job and he had no time to really manage the newspaper. He was so busy that over time he threw everything at me. Within a couple of months, I was doing everything by myself and organising all the externs. It was killing me mentally. It all failed because he didn't have time. And I had no support either. When I sent the owner an invoice for the first published issue which was priced at the standard price for lines and pictures, he shouted at me as if I was some silly little bitch that it was too high. Then they paid me almost ten times less than the going rate. (journalist Alena)

The relationships between the different kinds of journalists are further complicated by the worsening of a newspaper's economic condition. To speak about freelancers is to speak about a different class of workers with a different disposition and position in the journalistic field. Such workers are differently viewed from the specific positions of entrepreneurs, editors-in-chief and internal journalists. An entrepreneur will see freelancers as both cost-savers and potential risks; a journalist will see them as potential competitors. The competition, the expected rivalry of power (Eldridge, 2018), is especially felt in newsrooms, where freelancers are paid for the exact amount of work – the number of articles or lines – that they produce (e.g. manager Anna; journalist-entrepreneur Marie). Cushion points out that "more casual and freelance journalists are being employed at the expense of more experienced journalists in long-term positions" (2007, pp. 121–122).

The second element of the freelancers' social capital which contributes to their habitus is, paradoxically, their proximity.[14] In addition to the economic advantages, proximity is a good reason for an editor-in-chief to hire a freelancer instead of a full-time journalist. Editors-in-chief are reluctant to ponder the problematic relationships which their full-time journalists have with their audience and sources: they prefer to remember that freelancers lack such problems, pretending that just their proximity only brings benefits.

> We absorb information directly from the people, thanks to the externs we have in all the small villages in the area. They're of different ages, so our weekly is relatively colourful. (entrepreneur-journalist Dan)

> These newspapers are actually about freelancers, we have a lot of them in all sorts of villages, far and wide, so that's why the newspapers are so colourful. (journalist-entrepreneur Dana)

Nevertheless, similar to internal journalists, freelancers also tire of close proximity to their topics, sources, and readers, but do so without the collegial and/or organisational support the full-timers have. Some freelancers become weary (e.g. Leo), and others are frightened to pursue more investigative topics in their respective localities (e.g. the entrepreneur-journalist Dan). This is in line with Gollmitzer's (2014) findings that investigative journalism may be on decline, because internal journalists are overworked from day-to-day reporting and administration, while external journalists face uncertainty, for example, in potential lawsuits.

> I respect them, I really appreciate the freelancers, because I know that they are rooted even deeper in an environment where they can't be anonymous. These people when they write articles from the villages, are probing some really sore wounds. They live in a hell of self-censorship and have to be pretty damn careful whose feet they step on. (journalist-entrepreneur Dana)

Working practices of a freelancer

The working practices of a freelancer are not very different from those of an internal: there is a similar vicious circle of passivity and precariousness (e.g. the story of freelancer Leo). Birgit Røe Mathisen (2023, p. 63) adds, that freelancers' practices are influenced by the fact, that they "find themselves caught between autonomy and professional freedom on the one hand and precarity, constraints, and uncertainty on the other". Freelancers are passive on a more general level, as we can expect their belief in the game, illusio, is not as strong as internals: fewer and fewer of them are willing to contribute to a newspaper's content,[15] partially due to deteriorating financial conditions (Ekdale et al., 2015).

> Unfortunately, over twenty years all these externs left, with a few exceptions. A few new ones appeared, but they no longer had the character of those interesting, relatively regular contributions. (journalist Milan)

> My idea was that part of the content would be supplied by externs, and that I would simply offer the work to ex-journalists. That very quickly turned out to be basically impossible because for the fees you can offer no one is interested and the capable people who might do it are usually busy with something else. (journalist Robert)

Like the full-time journalists, freelancers are trapped in a cycle of increasing workloads, in their case complicated by the fact that most will have more than one job, as was the case for freelancer Leo. Their subbing (Siegelbaum & Thomas, 2016) is spread across different jobs. Contractual journalist David is a good example:

> I write sixteen articles a week for newspapers. Plus, I have other jobs – I write press releases for state authorities and regional municipalities, speeches for politicians. And I work as a journalist for another local online medium, for a town which is about a hundred kilometres away from here. My friend there needed subbing, but that's OK, topics are seventy per cent similar across different localities. (journalist David)

Nevertheless, in the discourse about working practices there is one particular topic repeatedly raised only by freelancers: that of *journalistic activism*. It is encapsulated in the story of freelancer Leo and connects different aspects of the freelancers' doxa, illusio, habitus and capitals. The social capital of the freelancers/externs is structured differently, they have a greater distance from both the positive and problematic settings of the newsroom and in their relationships with the various other actors. This means that they are freer to maintain their own integrity, autonomy, rules, and values (doxa). Freelancers navigate a balance between autonomy and precariousness that depends on their motivation (illusio), where "even the most precariously employed newsworker tends to love journalism, seeing it as the noblest of media professions, going well beyond the call of duty to make it work as a journalist" (Deuze, 2019, p. 1). Nevertheless, this motivation, which mirrors the public service ideal of journalism, is often reductively labelled as "activism". It should be noted that this label comes from the interviewees – internal journalists, who are not themselves willing to share this expectation of journalistic work, which can be considered a manifestation of a power struggle (Eldridge, 2019).

To conclude, the habitus of a journalist on the margins – the attitudes, perceptions, discourses, behaviour, emotion, ideals, values, skills, and the historical trajectory of their career – is clearly identifiable. As the interviewees asserted, the key element in the habitus of a journalist on the margins is an emotion (Benson & Neveu, 2005).[16] Emotion manifests differently: as motivation to become and remain a journalist; as part of an attitude to the job; as part of the perceptions of media in general and the journalist's newspaper in particular; as part of professional relationships with other individual agents in the journalistic field – colleagues, competitors, sources and audiences. The illusio, the "affective dimension" (Deuze & Witschge, 2020), is equally part of the different kinds of capital which journalists on the margins possess, for both good and bad, passion and precariousness (Schapals, 2022). They contain a whole range of expected features: a declining economic capital and a related and declining symbolic capital; a cultural capital which consists of newsroom socialisation rather than educational attainment. But there are some new insights into the composition of the journalist's habitus – a non-reflexive, doxic attitude to journalistic values as part of cultural and social capital; a deterioration of social capital, mainly in terms of the journalist's relationships with the readers.

To complete Bourdieu's (1984) equation: habitus + forms of capital + position in the field = the practice of the journalist on the margins. Journalists' practices encompass such expected routines as corroborating and writing stories, and practices in which their habitus and capitals are more clearly recognisable; understanding sources as people rather than press releases; working from a newsroom; substituting in other journalistic roles and resigning from investigative journalism. Nevertheless, to characterise the practice more deeply, we need to look deeper into the structural location of the individual actors in the media organisations (Benson, 1999).

At first glance, the habitus of a freelancer does not differ greatly from that of an internal journalist: the set of dispositions is similar. However, there are key differences, including the remote position of freelancers in the journalistic field, and their greater proximity to other societal actors, as well as the sources and the readers, leads to differences in their habitus. This enables freelancers to reflect critically on some of the specifics of the journalist's habitus (e.g. the adaptation to a situation in which the owner is politically active; the disintegration of traditional values and rules; the deteriorating relationships with the readership; the precariousness of the job). Conversely, the freelancer may possess much more social capital in the respective locality, thus making her a valuable member of the newsroom even though some of her internal colleagues don't consider her to be a journalist. Nevertheless, these differences also reflect the specific affective dimension of the freelancer's habitus, the illusio. Among interesting aspects of freelancers' practices that emerged from my interviews and observations are their withdrawal from investigative journalism because of a lack of organisational backing; working from home; and substituting for internal journalists in the newsroom.

A comparison of the habituses and practices of two journalistic class fractions, the journalists, and the freelancers, affords interesting insights into the different dispositions and positions of individual actors in the journalistic field. If we look at the differences and similarities through the life histories of the individual actors and their classes, it is clear that the positions of the respective actors and the roles they fill are converging. The growing weariness of the journalists and the growing reflectiveness of the freelancers, as well as changes in the types of working contracts and settings, are bringing them closer together.

Habitus, capitals, and practices of a journalist-entrepreneur on the margins

Story of journalist-entrepreneur Marie

I always wanted to be a journalist. I think I wanted to do it even when I was in elementary school. I've been writing for various newspapers as a freelancer ever since I was a young girl. But because my relative was barred from the Communist Party, I could forget about studying journalism or becoming a journalist. Nevertheless, later on the Communists said they would authorise even non-partisan journalists, so I got on the radio. I had a speech defect at that time, so when I went to the audition, they told me that if I got rid of it within a fortnight, they would take me. I went to speech therapy, they showed me how, and I eradicated it within the fourteen days.

Paradoxically, I encountered interference in my work only after 1989, so I got angry and left. And I said to myself that I was going to make it in the medium in my own way. I started publishing a local weekly with my husband, and its demands destroyed our marriage. But I knew the newspaper was successful, so I kept going as a self-employed person. I was expanding my business, even though it meant I had less time for journalism and had to relocate several times with my family. Even though I went through some really hard times with the business, I always knew it was what I had to do and that I wanted to do it.

From the beginning I insisted that we would be completely impartial. We've never been attached to any local interest groups, whether political or economic. And as long as the weeklies sold well, we could afford the impartiality.

The way my business expanded was that sometimes I chose a new publishing project, and sometimes my colleagues persuaded me to start one. Some were successful, some not, but I didn't have time to check all of them, so I trusted the editors-in-chief a lot, which sometimes brought problems. No one can make their own policy using my money. I still edit most of the content of my weeklies, write articles, run a publishing company. I'm a workaholic and I even think that maybe some colleagues are put off by that. Of course, after almost thirty years I can go fast, I know who to call, I know where to go for information and how to get it, and so on. But I think I'm really a workaholic because I get up at 5 in the morning, reply to readers' emails, and work until ten in the evening. In the meantime, I go and see my grandchildren. But I work all the time, Saturdays, Sundays, and I enjoy it. When my marriages broke up, my husbands blamed me. They said it wasn't a job, it was my bit of fun because I enjoy it so much. It's weird that younger colleagues are coming in today, and I work harder than any of them.

However, I do have experience of journalistic burn-out. I had a friend/colleague who was an excellent worker, but it ended badly. In the end, due to burn-out, she didn't even deliver the newspaper contents. I was faced with the utterly brutal decision to either fire my friend or axe the newspaper. So I just had to fire her, and she took it badly. It felt like Sophie's choice.

The business expanded, so I decided to convert it from an operation run by me as a self-employed person to a legal entity, a limited liability company. And surprisingly, it brought problems with my colleagues. They thought I would establish a joint stock company and give them shares, but I kept it in the family. So there was an unpleasant atmosphere in the newsroom. Later on, they tried to destroy me by moving en masse to a rival newspaper. On the other hand, when I had problems getting enough money and they had to wait for their salaries, they were rock-solid. It's interesting. During the hard times we all pulled together, and when times got easier, relationships crumbled. But I would say that the team is now relatively stable and that these people have their hearts in it. I'm lucky to have a colleague, a business manager, who has helped me a lot with the financial and administrative side. I'm too soft, but he brought a measure of toughness and a rational business head.

I think we're currently experiencing the best of times: we've recovered from all the crises and we're much more experienced. My biggest wish now is not to have to edit so much and be able to write more. And currently I'm also devising a handover strategy. The handover is a big preoccupation for me now. I thought I'd retire within five years and spend my time with my grandchildren. I'm hoping someone else will lead the company and free me from calculating salaries, tracking money in the account, and solving the problems of distribution. So I've started to negotiate with my family members with the aim of them taking over the publishing company. At first it seemed like no one among my relatives wanted to do it, maybe because they saw how much it had cost me. But one of the family, who had already worked in the newsroom, suddenly surprised me by saying: I've tied my life up in this and I won't let it fall. I've been negotiating the handover since then, and I think it will take a few years, I assume five, to finish it. But it looks like my newspapers have a future.

To be able to show similarities and differences among classes of actors, I will focus again on their motivation to become and continue as an entrepreneur; the meaning of the job; the working practices of an entrepreneur. Nevertheless, to show the full spectrum of actors and their positions and dispositions in the journalistic field, I focus on two classes,[17] distinguishing between journalist-entrepreneurs and entrepreneur-journalists. I will briefly sketch the similarities and differences between them using the opinions of the different kinds of actor: entrepreneurs, owners, and managers.

The motivation to become and continue as a journalist-entrepreneur

For my interviewees, the main part of their illusio, their motivation to become a journalist-entrepreneur, is a need to do things their way, and to do them better and without the intervention of anybody else: to be the master of their own house. As Harlow and Chadha note, the founders of publishing businesses "considered themselves entrepreneurs because they had started something new or were trying strategies that, while not necessarily universally new, were new to them" (2019, p. 905). In a separate study, Tim Vos and Jane Singer describe,

> the impetus for entrepreneurialism is shifting from the publisher to the editor. Most entrepreneurial journalists have newsroom backgrounds or journalistic training at the university level; few spent any time sitting in the publisher's leather chair before venturing out on their own. (2016, p. 155)

But the idea of becoming an entrepreneur does not normally occur to them *ex nihilo*: rather, it is often a reaction to a certain type of crisis or uncertainty (cf. the story of journalist-entrepreneur Marie). The need to preserve their profession or the desire to rescue a newspaper title often helps them overcome the uncertainty associated with a total lack of business experience (Harlow & Chadha, 2019). In most cases, crisis, and uncertainty, as interviewees perceived them, were the result of historical factors, namely the social and media transition after November 1989.[18] During this period, there was uncertainty about the continued existence of the media, whether the media associated with the former Communist regime would disappear or metamorphose, and the legal governance of private businesses (journalist-entrepreneur Karel). In this sense, the journalist-entrepreneurs could be regarded as *pioneers* who, following Andreas Hepp and Wiebke Loosen (2021, p. 581), engage in a "multi-layered process of restructuring" how journalism is practiced, by people,

> who, in a self-reflexive process, develop 'new' practices and techniques that may never flourish in their more extreme manifestations but which, as models or imaginaries of

new possibilities, influence transformation as a whole (...) embedded in specific sociocultural environments. (Hepp & Loosen, 2021, p. 581)

To respond to uncertainty, some journalists founded, bought, or privatised their own newspapers. They saw this as an attempt to save the work and/or the title that they loved, without giving a thought to economic viability. For example, journalist Emil recalled: "[T]he publisher, which was the district municipality, was legally bound to stop publishing a newspaper, so we journalists just took it over." On the contrary, journalist-entrepreneur Cyril remembered, that before November 1989, he "had a plan to escape from the newsroom. Then came November and I decided to privatise it, so I did, and offered membership to two colleagues." Others described their experiences similarly:

> I wrote to a newspaper, but all the newspapers were slowly disappearing. All the journalists knew each other, and so when they took the newspaper from us, we thought, why don't we buy the district newspaper? But we didn't have enough money, and they preferred to sell it to foreigners. So we started a new newspaper, but it was difficult. If we'd preserved the newspaper that was already here it would have been easier, it had a huge base here. We had to start from scratch – when I tell you that we went round pubs every night to sell newspapers ... they knew me in every pub. (laughs) (journalist-entrepreneur Barbora)

> The individual patrons began to back away from the newspaper and started selling their shares. The last one told me: look, I want to get out of it too, you're on your own. And I basically stayed because I just came to love the job over the years, so it made me happy [to be the entrepreneur]. (journalist-entrepreneur Lucie)

Interestingly enough, the more cultural capital (journalistic experience or/and skills, creativity), social capital (relationships in their locality) and symbolic capital (renown in their locality) these journalists on the margins possessed, the likelier it was they would become entrepreneurs.

> I was sent by the Civic Forum to the Communist newspaper[19] and later I became its editor-in-chief, but in the few months I was there I created such a revolution that the district municipality, who owned the paper, decided to close it. So I founded a private newspaper. (journalist Robert)

> I decided on the future of the newspaper while I was a city councillor. Then I joined the newspaper as a reporter. (journalist-entrepreneur Pavel)

On the other hand, the journalist-entrepreneurs show a great sense of responsibility in their relationship to the job (Vos & Singer, 2016). In contrast to their journalist-colleagues, they responded to the question, "If your newspaper were a human being, what it would look like?" with a sensitivity to other actors in the journalistic field. They imagined the newspaper as a person with qualities related to responsibility or care: "a person who is interested in everything" (journalist-entrepreneur Marie); "this is the subject of twelve thick books, which I will reveal in one word (laughs) – a caring, tired, young man" (journalist-entrepreneur Cyril); "a nice person, not underhand" (journalist-entrepreneur Lucie); "a man (…) who makes an effort not only to keep informed but to solve things and entertain people" (journalist-entrepreneur Ota). Or they include other actors in their idea, such as the audience, as journalist-entrepreneur Filip: "I'd probably associate it with whoever reads it, so it would probably be an older person, fifty-five plus, who has ties to the locality. Overall, he is likeable, but not everyone's cup of tea, that's the way it is with everything." Others saw this responsibility and care comprehensively, albeit in a figurative sense:

> The newspaper would be very bushy, with big roots, a crown, and many branches, so I would probably give it a name associated with bushyness and sprawl. I saw it as a tree from the first moment. (journalist-entrepreneur Pavel)

The more highly motivated the journalists were to become entrepreneurs, the more tired and disillusioned they are now, and this contributes to the way their illusio has developed. They are trapped in the middle of conflicting feelings: on the one hand, passion for the journalistic job, a sense of responsibility as an entrepreneur to the title and the workforce, respect for the tradition of publishing and responsibility to the readership; on the other hand, weariness from the multi-tasking and the subbing that are part of the journalist-entrepreneur's role (Siegelbaum & Thomas, 2016); tiredness from the burden of responsibility (Brouwers, 2017); frustration at doing something different from what they love. This led to a loss of motivation among my interviewees, a growing passivity and gradual loss of passion. For some, it is clear how the journalistic and entrepreneurial elements of their habitus militate against each other. These findings are in line with what scholars observe: "news management is no longer focused solely on editorial content; it equally involves responsibility for strategic, financial and technical decisions"; "from a journalistic perspective this development tends to be problematic. Concerns have been expressed within academia that leadership characterised by a management culture contributes to the eradication of journalistic work" (Waldenström et al., 2019, p. 504). For example, as journalist-entrepreneur Cyril saw it, "I suddenly found that I was in charge of a lot of things, and it was serious" and he sought "the freedom" in fiction books writing. Others tried to manage all their responsibilities:

> I wish I could just concentrate on writing and get some relief from this [entrepreneurial responsibility]. In the end you can't write something because you have to teach

the youngsters. (...) On top of that, I don't belong to the journalists' "circle" in the newsroom any more. They behave more like a family. They meet but they don't invite me. (journalist-entrepreneur Pavel)

[*Do you still enjoy the work?*] You know what it's like, you can't get out of it now. Of course I'm glad we're still in business but I have twelve people around my neck. You have a load of responsibility. I just try to make it work and I'm happy when it does. When someone calls to say that she wants a subscription it makes me happy, or when I see someone coming out of the newsagent with our newspaper, or when someone opens a newsagent's shop and tells us that she wants to sell our newspaper. (journalist-entrepreneur Ivo)

In so many words, the core identity of a journalist-entrepreneur is journalistic. Their entry into a business is motivated by saving newspapers and journalistic jobs. As journalist-entrepreneur Filip sums up: "I definitely don't consider myself an administrator, or even an entrepreneur. But it was either me as an entrepreneur or the end of the newspaper, so I had to deal with it in some way and I've dealt with it gradually, I wouldn't say that it was definitely done and dusted." Nevertheless, as Harlow and Chadha (2019) point out, the entrepreneurial identity does not depend on whether a person prefers the label *entrepreneur* or *journalist*.

At the same time, some of the journalist-entrepreneurs believe that it is not appropriate to combine their journalistic and their entrepreneurial roles, though this is described more in terms of a vague, doxic feeling than a clearly articulated problem. As journalist-entrepreneur Pavel puts it: "[to be a journalist and entrepreneur at the same time] could be a problem, I think. It would be illogical not to admit it, but now I can't remember anything. (...:) It has to be a problem, because it's not normal ... so surely a clash must be there, but I don't know what." The interviewees reflect on an awareness that their cultural capital should include "the ethical admonition for news organizations to maintain a wall of separation between (...) 'church and state', their news and business functions", following Vos and Singer (2016, p. 144).

Only one of the interviewees – journalist-entrepreneur Ivo – no longer regards himself as a journalist. This is not because he realised, he had crossed a wall between the editorial and commercial part of the newsroom but because he no longer has time to do a journalist's job – namely, writing and editing articles. Now he is just a proprietor and editor-in-chief. Nevertheless, if we analyse the motivation of journalist-entrepreneurs, which gradually arises from their journalistic and then entrepreneurial identity, it is important to consider both elements of their habitus and the way in which they interweave.

Meaning of the job

Answers to the question about what meaning the job holds in terms of work-life balance and its consequences, brought an interesting insight into the variable significance of the two roles that the journalist-entrepreneurs possess – the role of the *journalist* (with a passion for the job) and the role of *entrepreneur* (with its burden of responsibility, financial problems, and organisational work). Paradoxically, instead of seeing the need to sit on two chairs as a problem, my communication partners perceive the journalistic job in this situation as a relaxation from entrepreneurial responsibilities, but never vice versa. Consequently, for them it is even harder to balance their two roles *and* a private life. As Jasmine MacDonald et al. sum up, one of the "factors associated with emotional exhaustion (…) [is a] work-family conflict" (2016, p. 39).

> I go on vacation and publish the newspaper when I'm on vacation. I don't remember taking a holiday when I didn't bring work with me or declined to do work. I really enjoy it, mainly because every day the job is different. I don't know – look, probably [I'm] not [burned out], probably not. (journalist-entrepreneur Lucie)

> I'm fine so far, it's true that when it fully passed on to me, I had to deal with a lot, because I'd started another job and I had to cut it and this job prevailed. So that's one thing I regret. Now, there's a lot of operational stuff to deal with. I'm happy when I can write something for my newspaper, but I still have to do other things. (journalist-entrepreneur Filip)

> I went to find another job, but then I came back (laughs). I feel as if we're always living a week in advance because I know what's going to be published in the newspaper next week. (…) I live by deadlines, always some deadlines, and life seems a whole lot faster. (…) But it's an interesting job, you get to know a lot of interesting people. (journalist-entrepreneur Ota)

The clearest example of an imbalance between a journalist-entrepreneur's roles and his private life is the story of journalist-entrepreneur Pavel, who describes its development through his career history. He has maintained a real passion for the job of journalist for the past thirty years. Socio-historical circumstances after November 1989 forced him into becoming a journalist-entrepreneur to save a local newspaper – "I put a lot into it, a whole lot – I got divorced … I really enjoyed the job, but it's an addiction, not just workaholism." The growing workload and responsibility brought Pavel to the brink of collapse: "It was every Saturday, every Sunday and it lasted 'x' years and it was a lot. And then I felt that it wasn't burnout, it was that I was going crazy. I just couldn't cope any more. Now I'm doing a lot less than I did, I'm trying to handle everything during working hours, which is unfortunately still not possible." What bothers him most is that as a journalist-entrepreneur he doesn't have time for the "real" journalism, and this adds to his dissatisfaction and worsens his feeling of burn-out, no matter how he describes his situation. As Scott Reinardy points out, "journalists with depleted trust, morale and job satisfaction are experiencing significant degrees of burnout" (2013, p. 6).

> I went to cover a dance competition and I was short of time. I took a picture, but then I started to think about it – that I could do a better picture from this angle, and that it would be nice to do an interview with these people. Finally, I covered it with a single picture and a few lines, but I couldn't get rid of the idea of an extended piece and how nice it would be. (…) Nevertheless, I won't do it any more, once I devoted that time to things and I came home late. Then I was alone, so it didn't matter, I could come in when I wanted to. I don't want to live like that now and I know that I don't have it in me anymore. (journalist-entrepreneur Pavel)

Nevertheless, while he solved his dilemma, as a publisher he values in his subordinates the very same qualities that led him to a breakdown. He acknowledges that it is a problem and that it causes issues in the journalistic team in the newsroom, but he still values a passion for the job for two reasons: first, he identifies himself with those colleagues who possess it; second, it brings to his newspaper a quality that he is no longer able to provide. But it is hard for him to admit it. It can be understood as a duel between the two habituses, which further influences the illusio. The entrepreneur's position can lead to a discrepancy between his ideals for the job and actual organisational practices which can result in reduced job commitment and burn-out (MacDonald et al., 2016).

> We have a colleague here who is very hardworking, he works Saturdays and Sundays. Often, I don't even need his work, but he still does it because he has also got this addiction in him. It's terrible, it's hard for me to say it. (…) At first, I thought it was wrong, and then after a while I came to the conclusion, as a publisher, that such subordinates are the best. I don't force him to do it. Should I stop him? It would be against my own nature. I feel that it's actually wrong, but I'm not telling him, I'll keep it to myself. So now, now maybe, I'm the wicked capitalist. (journalist-entrepreneur Pavel)

There are some journalist-entrepreneurs whose habitus is balanced and attitude to the work-life balance can be understood as an exception that proves the rule. They either fight for a balance between work and life or continue to understand journalism as "not a poison but a cure". For example, journalist-entrepreneur Ota thinks that him and his colleagues do their best "to prevent work from beating us. We play sport and we have a band, which is an amazing relaxation." In fact, however, it looks as if they are still energetic in all their pursuits and have found a real balance not only between work and life but between their journalistic and entrepreneurial roles. As MacDonald et al. point out, "increased levels of job satisfaction would be associated with reduced levels of burnout" (2016, p. 39).

> One thing is good about this job. If you're not completely done, it keeps your head running, it won't let you get rusty because every story is different. When I talked about it with doctors, they said of course, the brain is a muscle, and you need to train it. So I've taken this job as a cure. I go on vacation, and I'm connected to the newspaper online and when I have a moment I work on the newspaper, but I don't suffer from it. I have physical work, do sport, so if I feel pressured, I'll do those. In the last thirty years, there have been times when the company owned me body and soul, but you can't be a slave for thirty years, you'd be dead by now, so of course I took breaks too. (journalist-entrepreneur Cyril)

One of the key parts of the journalist-entrepreneurs' habitus is their social capital in terms of their relationships and the balance they achieve in the management of the newspaper business. Those who are on their own generally struggle far more with precariousness and burn-out. Unsurprisingly, the balance can take different forms. Nevertheless, the attempt to achieve it can also be seen as a manifestation of peer recognition, which is an important element of journalistic work and symbolic capital. Bourdieu considers one of the principles of legitimisation in the journalistic field to be internal peer review (1996). As Wiik adds, "the identity-making of journalists: they have to achieve legitimacy in the eyes of their peers" (2009, p. 354). Elena Raviola points out that there is "the logic of journalism, where legitimatization is gained through peer recognition" (2012, p. 934). Julia Evetts considers part of the journalistic occupational professionalism to be "discourse constructed within professional groups themselves that involves discretionary decision-making in complex cases, collegial authority" (2006, pp. 140–141).

> A former owner who transformed the title after the revolution was the driving force at the time and experienced the golden age of the nineties. He's such a mentor, we talk to each other several times a year. (journalist-entrepreneur Filip)

> [*Are you able to distinguish your roles as editor-in-chief and owner?*] Well, not after all these years. There are two of us entrepreneurs here, my colleague takes care of the printing, the typesetting. I'm the editor-in-chief, so theoretically I should have the last word, but we always talk about things together. [Having two owners] is an advantage. There were times when I thought it was tough, but we always put things straight again. The advantage is also that when I want to go on holiday, I know that I can be away for two weeks, and everything will be fine. (...) Sometimes [we had disputes] regarding the future development of the company, whether we should buy another property, go into debt, or buy other technologies and further develop the printing business. And we didn't agree on these things, but we were able to figure it out and move on. (journalist-entrepreneur Ota)

Those interviewees who work together as managing couples also agree about how the balance of responsibilities should be defined. It is not just a matter of having more people at work and everyone doing their part but also of not interfering in the work and responsibilities of one's partner and thus not destroying the nomos of the journalistic field, journalists' cultural capital, symbolic capital, and the related symbolic capital of the newspaper. As Julien Duval (2005, p. 138) points out, "economic and journalistic logics are not always at odds. Editorial independence is frequently a selling point" and "firms and practices directed exclusively by either economic or journalistic logics appear doomed to fail".

This "meeting in the middle" reflects the doxa of four pairs of co-workers of different kinds who are trying to achieve a mutual balance and therefore set the nomos. Interestingly enough, they are trying in different ways. After years of cooperation Marie and Josef built a solid wall between the commercial and editorial parts of the publishing company, and on top of that they share in an understanding of the importance of the newspaper's symbolic capital. However, from a long-term point of view, the first of these partnerships, which was mindful of the symbolic and thus also the economic capital of the newspaper and kept the journalistic nomos safe from interlocutors, seems to be the most sustainable:

> The business manager and me as a journalist and an owner had big fights at first because he got various "advantageous" financial offers from advertisers. But he gradually understood when I said no because it affects the credibility of the newspaper. We can try to compromise, but it doesn't work. I think that without him as a business manager I wouldn't have been able to do it for very long. (…) It's simply no longer possible for one person to do all that single-handed. (journalist-entrepreneur Marie)

> We still run into problems, there will always be a struggle, but we're pulling the same length of rope. I started to work for the newspaper to help her, but I had no experience, so she taught me. (…) It's important to separate her work and mine because I can easily afford what she can't. I would never persuade her to write nicely about an advertiser because it has only a short-term benefit, it's an ad hoc solution and it destroys the good name of the newspaper. (manager Josef)

Ema and Pavel were on their way to creating a similar balance until they were affected by the economic crisis and its fall-out, which shifted the balance towards the economic side of the business:

> From the beginning we argued a lot, I admit that. (…) We argued before we found our roles. We split responsibilities, he just runs the newsroom and I'm in charge of advertising. Since then, I'd say it works. (manager-entrepreneur Ema)

> She threw herself into growing the business and gaining advertising. (…) Sometimes it's harder, it's better when there's only one owner, for example if you can't make a decision because it's her responsibility and she's not here. (…) We really had it sorted but when the economic crisis came with all its consequences, it got more difficult. We've now agreed that we don't write articles about topics which could be paid advertising, but it's a bit of a shame, the newspaper is impoverished by it. (journalist-entrepreneur Pavel)

Cyril and Ben are an example of a balance based on differences of age, experience, cultural, social, and symbolic capital. Journalist-entrepreneur Cyril appreciates the fresh ideas from his younger colleague, journalist Ben: "it gives me a jolt, so it helps". After being "orphaned" when his two former colleagues with whom he started the newspaper left, "I was confronted with for the first time in my life. I was in a newsroom with people I understood but found myself in the same boat as people I hadn't shared experiences with in the past, and it was kind of a bit tricky." Cyril didn't feel good about it, but luckily replaced it by making Ben an assistant, while they understand each other.

Finally, Marta and Martin decided to divide their responsibilities on the basis of their own social capital, which in their particular locality seemed more important to them than a division of responsibilities into editorial and commercial, with a wall between them. The journalist Marta is in charge of advertising, because, as entrepreneur-journalist Martin reflects, "there's social contact and social capital in her case, because she knows people and I think she has a better chance of arranging things, of persuading people". On the other side, Marta considers entrepreneur-journalist Martin to be "good for investigative journalism, I don't like to write about politics in general, it's really not for me. And he's really good at accounting and distribution."

The importance of stability, cooperation and peer recognition between partners and colleagues is also shown by examples of relationships whose problems were caused by disagreements over money. These illustrate the relationship between the social, cultural, and economic capital of the actors.

> There were three of us. The company was in my name, normally the three of us shared it, but I managed it financially. And that's where the trouble began: we couldn't divide all [the money] because you always have to think about the "back wheels" of the business. And they couldn't understand that very well, so we lasted four, five years and then we broke up. (journalist-entrepreneur Barbora)

> At first we had eight shareholders, and everyone worked here. There were times when the money had to be brought in because there was no money, so they had to get it and not everyone had it … And me and my colleague, we did the most. They were working here, but only me and her were still putting something in, we invented new projects. And the rest said, you can do it, but if it makes a loss, you two will have to bear it, and

I got so upset that we were even shouting at one another. (...) It was a matter of principle, so we said: enough. It was clear that the two of us were on the same page and the others were just following us. So then we had a peace meeting and said goodbye to them. When you want to do something with eight people, it's crazy. (journalist-entrepreneur Pavel)

Considering another part of journalist-entrepreneurs' social capital, the journalist-entrepreneurs do not have any relationship with and/or knowledge of their audience; in this regard, they are similar to the journalists already explored. This reoccurs, despite all the newspapers I researched having similar, traditional business models built on revenues from advertising and readers. It also runs against what we would expect from understanding the role of the audience in shaping the field. Bourdieu (1996) points out that journalistic workers derive their legitimisation from the audiences, as well as from their peers. However, Bourdieu (1996, pp. 24–25) at the same time reminds us there is "an effect typical of the field: you do things for competitors that you think you're doing for consumers". Many entrepreneurs said they neither know who their audience is nor are they interested in changing their conception of what their audience looks like: to paraphrase Anderson, the picture "remains locked in place and unable to change". Anderson argues that "local journalism's image of the public is grounded in a vision that sees the public as a unitary, structural, or even interlocking entity that journalists can either confidently speak to or call into being" (2013, pp. 165–166). This means that the authority of journalism and of the journalists and entrepreneurs becomes "deeply problematic" (Anderson, 2013, p. 166). Nevertheless, as scholars stress, the audience is, from an entrepreneurial point of view, a foundation of two kinds of capital – legitimacy and revenue:

> It is the audience who judges the legitimacy of the journalistic field and it is the audience's attention that is monetized in the form of subscription and advertising revenue. Thus, journalists have found themselves in a complex relationship with news audiences. (Vos et al., 2019, p. 1009)

Journalist-entrepreneurs gradually fall back on the only information about readership they possess: opinions obtained from special surveys. Hence like journalists, they have only individual and anecdotal information about who the readers are. Journalist-entrepreneur Ota calculates the readers' tastes merely from the actual number of copies sold: "As I distribute the newspaper, I see which issue was less successful and that's our feedback. And salespeople in the newsagents tell us, you've got to put something decent in to sell it." Similarly, journalist-entrepreneur Ivo observes: "We have a lot of obits and memorials in our newspaper, from which you can see how the newspaper appeals to the readers." Journalist-entrepreneur

Cyril sums up: "There was once a reader survey that confirmed what we'd already thought." However, the more active they are and the more they try new things, the more they are handicapped by their lack of information about the audience.

> Local newspapers have the great disadvantage that they are here in the locality, it's such a little pond, with both big fishes and small fishes. The local [newspapers] aren't watchdogs, we're slaves to democracy. Everybody thinks that we should publish whatever the public wants and if we don't publish it, it's immediately wrong and they throw stones at us. We helped many people, and they couldn't bear to be grateful to us. (…) I think I'm a hero. But no one appreciates it. (journalist-entrepreneur Dana)

> They rarely come when they're in trouble, far more often when they want to hurt someone and use a newspaper to do it. It happens with both individuals and political parties. (journalist-entrepreneur Cyril)

While readers cannot in general be partners for journalist-entrepreneurs, as part of their social capital, the latter do regard as important their relationships to individuals with economic or symbolic capital in a respective locality – members of the *local field of power* who are fellow business people. As journalist-entrepreneur Lucie believes, "if I just approach a businessman today and say hello, I need help, I know he won't let me down". This relationship can be considered as an acknowledgement of peer-entrepreneurs.

> There's certainly [a tradition of working with local entrepreneurs] here. For their part, it will also involve some nostalgia because they built a printing house which created our newspaper. (journalist-entrepreneur Filip)

> When we started there was one computer in a town. Someone had it at home, and another person across the street had a printer, so the person with the computer allowed us to rewrite our material at some agreed time. Then we waited for the other person when he got back from work, he'd let us use the printer. (journalist-entrepreneur Ota)

> We mostly sold it at newsagents, we could count on its regional appeal because we knew the newsagents. We delivered it ourselves, so we were actually at the sellers every week, everything worked, because fortunately they felt that it was also their newspaper. (journalist-entrepreneur Ivo)

The power that a journalist-entrepreneur gains as a businessperson and owner of a newspaper is the result of the extra activity and effort they give. How they deal with the power is related to the values and principles they apply at work (doxa), and it can be twofold. On the one hand, journalist-entrepreneurs articulate their values of public service and responsibility more strongly than others. For example, journalist-entrepreneur Marie mentions an internal ethical code which is applied in her newsrooms. As has been pointed out, "the journalistic field's commitment to a public service role and to ethical decision-making has been a source of (...) journalistic capital. Legitimacy and revenue are two forms of capital – capital that news organizations have had to keep in balance" (Vos et al., 2019, p. 1009).

> I always give a voice to the weaker members of society. I want them to be heard. I am aware that the power of a newspaper could annihilate someone. I've never wanted that to happen. With this in mind, I didn't even want the paper to be a tabloid. (journalist-entrepreneur Barbora)

> When I think about fucking up the newspaper or shutting it down, I always remember those people who ask when the next issue will be published. They're interested. The discontented, the loud-mouthed and the moaners are mostly the ones who are heard, decent people are not heard. That decent folk will get together and put the rude ones in their place will never happen. (journalist-entrepreneur Dana)

> Me and my business partner, we are right-wingers because to this day we are self-employed. Back then we were very cheeky, but it was fun with us. People were waiting for what would be in the newspaper, what we would write about next. When I read it back today, I see that we were terrible, I say to myself: you fool. It was strong stuff, but the people enjoyed it. (journalist-entrepreneur Ota)

On the other hand, their efforts to change their locality for the better and their frustration that journalism does not always bring visible and immediate changes may prompt them to become involved in local politics. At the same time, this can compromise the journalist-entrepreneur's impartiality (Deuze, 2005), her symbolic and concurrently economic capital (cf. story of journalist Milan; story of journalist-entrepreneur Marie). Nevertheless, it doesn't mean that everyone is aware of it. For example, to the question, "Given the political history of the newspapers do your readers perceive you as an independent newspaper?" journalist-entrepreneur Lucie answered: "Well, it never occurred to me to consider how people see us ..."

Some of my communication partners reflected that their involvement in politics was largely possible mainly due to the then missing professional journalistic rules, either explicit (nomos), or implicit (doxa). This could be due to their particular cultural capital – a lack of education in the field, a lack of rules in the newsroom; and the changing nomos of the journalistic field, normative expectations during the media transition of the 1990s. During periods of upheaval, the "complex and controversial relationship between journalistic practices and norms" is called into question, where "the ethical frameworks that constitute journalism's cultural capital" are associated with the transitive nature of the post-socialist media system (Vos & Singer, 2016, p. 144).

> I started with the idea, like probably everyone who was new in the newspaper, that I would change the world. We don't have power, we have influence, and that's the end of it. We can't change a lot of things that would be worth changing. (journalist-entrepreneur Cyril)

> My colleague is now a member of the city council. I was on it too, I was a member of a municipal board, until I found out that the situation was impossible. And the current deputy mayor is our former colleague. So the way we've resolved it is that a colleague here on the council writes about a neighbouring town, and I've lived in another village for a while now, so I'm writing about this town. It's always occurring to someone here [to run for local politics]. (journalist-entrepreneur Ota)

> I was on a city council and municipal board till I became editor-in-chief, because until that point it was possible. But it was still a bit of a problem because when I was on the municipal board, something was discussed in a way which was completely different from how it was discussed in the city council, and I knew all about it and had to write it up. But it was still in a wild era, today's standards are different, you have to look at what happened then through the eyes of the time. It wouldn't be possible today but then I didn't see it as a conflict of interest. That occurred to me only when I became the editor-in-chief. (journalist-entrepreneur Pavel)

Considering the meaning journalist-entrepreneurs ascribe to the job, their disillusionment with their role as both journalist and entrepreneur is apparent in the stories told by those of them who have reverted to the singular role of journalist. They grew tired of responsibility or felt abandoned by their business partners, whereas now they are mostly satisfied doing the job for which they felt a passion from the beginning. For example, journalist Robert sold his newspaper, but later gave financial help to restart it because of the responsibility he felt for his former employers and because of his affinity with the journalistic profession: "The newsroom revolted and quit because the new owner became active in local politics and very controversial. When they left, I helped them financially and I continued to help them with the content of the newspaper." At the same time, in the stories of the journalist-entrepreneurs, it becomes clear they have ceased to be active and begun, rather, to passively accept the general tendency of the newspaper and the business; and/or they have reached the limits of their business acumen.

> It was an evolution. At first there were four of us as partners/entrepreneurs. One died, another left, and then there were two of us. The last partner wanted to retire in her 70s, but I didn't have the money to buy her out. So we sold our shares to a new owner. But this wasn't the only problem – we were no managers or entrepreneurs, just journalists. We made the managerial and organisational decisions sideways, so to speak, we were never experts at it, we just ran it somehow. (…) But the new owner is good in the field

you asked about, the managerial stuff, he has time for this, and I have time for journalism. (journalist Emil)

I never funded the newspaper as a shareholder and by selling our shares we sheltered under the wings of a large publishing company that publishes other local newspapers, among other things. So I reckon that, if nothing else, they will help us financially. And I'm not dealing with economic development any more: having sold the shares, I regard it as someone else's job to take those decisions. (journalist Eva)

I published and managed the newspaper for five years, and then I wanted to do other things, so I sold it. Every time I've perfected something in my life, I've stopped enjoying it. And local journalism is problematic when you do it the way I did. Basically the whole town hated me for three years, because you very quickly find that everyone you write about is your distant relative. (…) So I sold it and actually cut myself off from it. (journalist Robert)

By far the most important topic, related to the very significance of the job and mirroring doxa and illusio, was a journalist-entrepreneur's transfer of the newspaper's ownership and management to somebody else.[20] Although this topic proved to be sensitive during the interviews, and was eventually discussed by almost all my communication partners, for the most part it was initially unspoken and had to be elicited. They saw their success as a journalist-entrepreneur as an outcome of their collected social, economic, and – mainly – symbolic capital. Within the confines of their own localities, they had become part of the *field of power*, as the sum of renowned journalist and entrepreneur. As Bourdieu explains, the field of power

> is the space of the relations of force between the different kinds of capital or, more precisely, between the agents who possess a sufficient amount of one of the different kinds of capital to be in a position to dominate the corresponding field, whose struggles intensify whenever the relative value of the different kinds of capital is questioned (…) especially when the established equilibrium in the field of instances specifically charged with the reproduction of the field of power is threatened. (1998a, p. 34)

Most of the interviewees received a buyout offer during their career; nevertheless, they were either unwilling to sell their newspaper to a chain (e.g. journalist-entrepreneur Dana); or they received it at a time when they were young and had enough energy to continue to run it; or both. Journalist-entrepreneur Cyril summed it up this way: "A chain wanted to buy us, but I was about 40 and I enjoyed working here. I always had one rule, that while money can bring you happiness, it isn't necessary. And the job at least occasionally brought that feeling of happiness. I'd rather do what I wanted, than just sitting on a pile of money. I don't regret it."

The hardest thing for a journalist-entrepreneur appears to be admitting that after a career of nearly thirty years, she has serious trouble finding a successor. This is the case for journalist-entrepreneur Dana, for whom one of her children, when asked about succession, said: "I'm not going to bury myself here in a small town and in the local newspaper." And for that journalist-entrepreneur, the lack of a successor will mean that the newspaper will cease to exist or be up for sale (similar to the story of journalist-entrepreneur Marie). As for journalist-entrepreneur Ota: "If we hoped to preserve the family tradition, I'm afraid it won't work. We know that we will have to close it in a few years or sell it to someone."

> Well, we've already started talking about it, but we can't solve it yet because we're at the same situation with the kids, so I thought that my grandchildren, perhaps, would take over. We'll have to deal with it in the next few years, we're still busy, we still solve problems, we catch up on things, and we don't address these things much yet … (manager-entrepreneur Ema)

> We're so careful because the journalists are scared of every change. They worry because they are employed here and may want to take out a loan and they're afraid of ending up on the pavement. (…) it's not even necessary yet, because I will retire in … six or seven years, so it's not urgent just yet. On the other hand, [a fellow editor-in-chief from a nearby local newspaper] has just had a stroke and is in the hospital … (journalist-entrepreneur Pavel)

> It would be ideal if I found a new partner, and I contact people and ask, and their advice is always similar: on the one hand, don't even think about doing it all yourself; on the other hand, think carefully about who you'll take on. (journalist-entrepreneur Cyril)

Given the importance of the handover topic for the interviewees who are journalist-entrepreneurs, it is remarkable that there are only two examples of a successful handover among them: in both cases it was a handover to the journalist who was editor-in-chief at the time. There is also one example of a problematic and only ostensible transfer to the child of a journalist-entrepreneur:

> I'm sorry in the sense that I've been publishing the newspaper for thirty years and it's been a lot of work. And I thought that at least one of the grandchildren would take it on. I think that my newspaper will die with me. I'm already preparing for it. (journalist-entrepreneur Barbora)

This again illustrates not only the difficulty of finding a suitable successor but the (un)willingness of journalist-entrepreneurs to give up their "baby", and their related doxa, illusio, symbolic capital and economic investment, all at once (Vos & Singer, 2016).

The example of journalist-entrepreneur and former editor-in-chief Filip[21] shows the ambivalence of the successor's position and an emerging habitus of the journalist-entrepreneur, shaped by: passion for the journalistic job but no business experience and a related naivety; low symbolic and economic capital which has, however, significantly increased as a result of the transfer; and the refusal of the former owner to sell the paper to a chain. What often remains is the feeling that not everything has gone as it should, but it is suppressed by the strong relationship of the new owner to the profession and the newspaper:

> Well, there was such strong nostalgia on my side, I swear at it every morning (laughs), but ... I don't know, I just thought I'd save it. It was handed over and everything was solved in half a year. I resisted for a long time and there were various options, for example to sell it to the chain, that would have been the most logical. They'd wanted to buy it a year before, but the former owner didn't want to sell it and he offered it to me. (...) It was a bit of a scam on me, I was naive, but somehow, I put up with it. I wouldn't like to analyse myself on this matter. I don't regret it. Readers were the most important reason not to close it and also our relations with the printers, our traditional partner. (journalist-entrepreneur Filip)

Working practices of a journalist-entrepreneur

Three types of practice characterise the work of journalist-entrepreneurs and their doxa and illusio. The first type is purely journalistic: proposing, corroborating, and writing stories (journalist-entrepreneur Pavel); editing articles and doing layout (journalist-entrepreneurs Lucie; Karel); and being the leader of their colleagues (journalist-entrepreneur Karel). The second type is initially a joy for journalists, but constant repetition makes it an annoying routine. The most frequently mentioned examples are searching for a potential journalist within the limited possibilities of the periphery (journalist-entrepreneur Lucie) and teaching the basics of the craft (journalist-entrepreneur Karel). As Pavel points out – "You can't really write anything yourself because you always have to teach the newcomers again and again." The third type of practice, which journalist-entrepreneurs perform daily and usually dislike, is related to the ambivalence of the managerial function. On the one hand, there is a responsibility to preserving the medium and the business, for example, preventing and/or addressing lawsuits (journalist-entrepreneur Pavel); raising money and fighting for survival year after year; managing business administration; dealing with losses; and managing loans (journalist-entrepreneur Karel). On the other hand, when the journalist-entrepreneurs are unable to delegate tasks, they are also subbing literally all the jobs in the newsroom, as Siegelbaum and

Thomas (2016) have also found – where their roles include reporting, advertising and sales, distribution (journalist-entrepreneur Ivo).

> When I joined the newsroom, it still worked the way it should work, there was hierarchy, succession, and leadership, but in my view that's now unsustainable in local newspapers. And it's wrong that I should have to combine all these functions, it's clearly wrong, but it's not possible to do it in any other way. (journalist-entrepreneur Filip)

> No benefits. On the contrary, as a self-employed person you bear all the responsibility for absolutely everything. Whatever happens, you're first in line, shafted by the state. (journalist-entrepreneur Dana)

The interviewees who acted less as journalists and assumed more responsibilities as entrepreneurs were the most tired of their job and generally exhausted. The happiest ones either found a balance between the above-mentioned types of responsibility or they stayed active (Smethers et al., 2017), kept inventing new projects, both journalistic and entrepreneurial. For Ivo, this is planning a further expansion of his business; for Ota it is his business's self-sufficiency and sustainability: "We did a lot of regional projects, for example we published some regional books, so we tried hard. Rather than saving money, we always did something extra. If you can, keep everything in your own hands, as soon as you let it go, you just don't know anything."

Habitus, capitals, and practices of an entrepreneur-journalist on the margins

Story of entrepreneur-journalist Jan

I somehow didn't have a problem with writing, I was quite interested in those things, but I studied something else. My parent studied journalism, however, after he was excluded from the Communist party, they prevented him from finishing school. After the year 1990 I naturally kept a closer eye on what was happening in the town. There was a question at that time of whether my town should again be the district town. I learned that the district newspaper was going to close so I contacted them and came up with the idea that when these people knew the job and they were locals, I'd hire them and publish the newspaper.

I was an entrepreneur at that time, I owned several buildings in the town, and later I added other businesses. And at the same time, they gave me problems with the local municipality. This is how my whole life has been, people either love me or hate me, there's nothing at all in between. So I moved the newsroom of the local newspaper, which had formerly been owned by the district municipality, to one of my properties and we published the first issue in 1992. On the front page it had a map of the former district, we basically wanted to help re-establish the facilities of the district and somehow link the information to the municipalities and the people. Nevertheless, we didn't succeed in re-drawing the district. In the enthusiasm of the time, I had a logo done which included the sign of the Velvet revolution, which was then a bit of an anachronism. I even went so far as to register it as a trademark.

I enjoyed owning a newspaper: I saw it as providing a service. It was nice when people sent good wishes to you at Christmas. It started with enthusiasm, we tried to do everything differently and better, and offer critical comment. It wasn't long before my wings were clipped: a lady filed a civil lawsuit and criminal complaint against me. I understood that local newspapers can't afford to criticise much because then no one will talk to you, you won't get any information and it has consequences for your personal life, but at least I understood how it works.

My original thought was that I made solid money as a businessman, so I didn't really want to make money from publishing a newspaper. I'm probably weird because everything is supposed to be done with the aim of making money. In the beginning, when it was profitable, it was pleasant. I liked the feeling that I was creating something, that I had something in my hand. Making money is nice, but if you just pile it up you have to invest it and take care of what you've invested, but here you had a product. And it's a public thing. So I came to like it and, moreover, I felt as if we were revivalists, delivering newspapers through snow-covered roads to remote villages. But later on, when we had to count every penny, it became pointless.

To be honest, I bought a newspaper so that I could have a bit of influence, I'm not going to hide it. There was my interest in the political situation, it was good that we had democracy, but I just wanted to direct it somewhere and I didn't want the old guard, I wished the new ones well. I have to admit that sometimes we lacked objectivity, though on the other hand, when the Communists did something good here, we wrote about it, only not so enthusiastically (laughs). Nevertheless, my relationship with the municipality didn't develop in the best way, and it upset me so much that I put together a political group and became a local politician on the city council. I was there for one term. Well, it was hell combining this with publishing a newspaper because of course you're not objective, so I tried to detach myself from the newspaper as far as possible, I basically dealt only with operational matters.

At the beginning I had a whole journalistic team in the newsroom, but gradually I started to do the work of the reporter and editor which I quite enjoyed while learning on the job. When the journalists left it was getting harder and harder to find replacements. So it more or less came down to me, there were times when I basically did the newspaper all by myself. It was exciting and it was always a struggle to get a journalist *to do the job. My rescue was a relatively large network of freelancers and cooperation with municipalities, which gave me information about what was new. And when I got someone to do the journalistic job, they had the whip hand over me. Whenever I blamed this person for anything, she could just tell me she was quitting straightaway. So it was a bit difficult, but it still functioned.*

Then business generally started to get complicated. The admin grew to such an extent that I didn't have time for normal work. The number of problems also increased: economically, from falls in advertising, and there were more and more people whom we'd given a kicking in the newspaper who wouldn't talk to us. But we could still operate because I regarded the business from the start as a non-profit activity, I didn't need to make money on the newspaper itself. I wanted it to break even, nothing more. I was willing to devote everything to it, my time, all my strength, but only until it cost me money I had to find from somewhere else. And it happened in the end. In a quarter of a century, you form a relationship to it, I know that sentiment doesn't belong in business, but it's a bit different with a newspaper.

I was thinking for five years about winding it up. But when I used to bring fifteen, twenty thousand Czech crowns of my own into the newsroom every month, it was no longer possible. It really didn't work, so I tried to at least make it last for twenty-five years, a purely arbitrary period, but in the end, I had no choice but to close it. I tried everything I could, because I enjoy making money and I know how to make money. I didn't want to make money on the newspaper, but I didn't want to lose money on it either. No one was interested in buying the business, and even if they had, then frankly it would have annoyed me that I could no longer influence it after I'd sold it. For the same reason, I didn't even want to cooperate with anybody. To this day, the closure of the paper brings tears to my eyes. But as I used to say, feelings don't make money.

The last class of actors and last habitus that I will analyse is that of the entrepreneur-journalists. Using the same thematic groups and subtopics – the motivation to become and stay an entrepreneur; the meaning of the job; the working practices of an entrepreneur – I focus on the similarities and differences between the different kind of entrepreneurial actors.

The motivation to become and continue as an entrepreneur-journalist

Unlike the similarity between a journalist and a freelancer, the difference between a journalist-entrepreneur and an entrepreneur-journalist starts with the illusio, the initial motivation. An entrepreneur mostly buys a newspaper as a potentially profitable business (perhaps even several newspapers) or as a tool of influence (cf. story of entrepreneur-journalist Jan) and does so without any previous experience of journalism. She acquires journalistic skills and experiences as she is socialised within the newsroom, gradually building her journalistic cultural capital from there. Nevertheless, her initial motivation is mostly financial. This reflects Raviola's (2012, p. 934) finding of an opposition "between the logic of journalism, where legitimatization is gained through peer recognition, and the logic of markets, where numbers measure legitimacy".

On top of this, these entrepreneurs often had no experience of business in the early 1990s. As manager-entrepreneur Ema, who applied for the position of accountant in the local newspaper in the early 1990s, "but the lady who was leaving didn't tell me that it was due to close in two months". The entrepreneurs were local business people but also students, teachers (journalist Radim) or money-lenders (entrepreneur-journalist Artur).

> I didn't see the economic potential in publishing a newspaper, I was just interested in doing it, mainly for political but partly journalistic reasons. Although I don't really consider myself a journalist in the true sense of the word – I wouldn't call myself one – I really enjoyed it. And the fact that it is profitable is just a plus. (entrepreneur-journalist Martin)

> I took the newspaper over to save it, it would have gone under, it wasn't working out economically. So as a local patriot I took it on in the hope of reviving it somehow and thought it might partially support my business activities. (entrepreneur Petr)

> When the revolution began, I wanted to get into business like all my ancestors, but I didn't know how. (…) I remembered that I'd read that the government was offering 18 thousand Czech crowns to anyone who was willing to start up their own business, so I said I'd start a business … well, I thought, I'll publish a newspaper. They gave me the green light and I went out, I said to myself: 'Jesus Maria', I'm such a jerk, what have I just done, I'm going to be a journalist and I don't know a thing about it. (entrepreneur-journalist Max)

> The original owner of this newspaper started to pay badly, so the whole newsroom left and founded another newspaper, but they couldn't manage it because they didn't know anything about how a company works. So they sold it to a man who published it but he eventually lost the newspaper in a game of roulette. (…) I wanted to help them financially. I was quite successful at the time, so I got into the company and bought it. (entrepreneur Mirek)

While the initial motivation of these entrepreneurs is primarily financial, later their illusio transforms, and the motivation to become journalists becomes more interesting and worthy of consideration within the context of the journalistic field. According to my interviewees, there are two dividing lines which determine whether an entrepreneur will or will not become an entrepreneur-journalist. The first is between rationality and emotionality. To draw a line between journalists and entrepreneurs by claiming that the former are professionally motivated, and the latter are financially motivated would be an over-simplification. I do not rely on the definitions of "profession" and "professionalism" as outlined by some scholars[22] but rather point to Evetts's (2003, 2006) distinction between two contrasting forms of professionalism – *organisational* professionalism and *occupational* professionalism.[23] This offers a schematic understanding of differences between journalists and entrepreneurs, the former emotional, the latter rational (cf. Örnebring, 2009). As Evetts (2006, pp. 140–141) defines it, "organizational professionalism is a discourse of control used increasingly by managers in work organizations" and "incorporates rational-legal forms of decision-making, hierarchical structures of authority, the standardization of work practices, accountability, target-setting and performance review and is based on occupational training and certification". On the contrary, occupational professionalism "involves a discourse constructed within professional groups themselves that involves discretionary decision-making in complex cases, collegial authority, the occupational control of the work and is based on trust in the practitioner by both clients and employers"; "it is operationalized and controlled by practitioners themselves and is based on shared education and training, a strong socialization process, work culture and occupational identity, and codes of ethics that are monitored and operationalized by professional institutes and associations".

There is no simple or stereotypical divide between "rational entrepreneurs" and "emotional journalists". During the interviews journalists often described their passion for the job – understandably so because they chose it – whereas the entrepreneurs decided to run a profitable business whose precise nature was largely unimportant, at least initially. However, over time some of them built a passionate relationship with journalism, whether they started writing or editing for their newspaper (Schapals, 2022). The inclination to a rational or emotional perspective thus depends more on life history and temperamental predisposition (habitus) – on the cultural capital of the agents (their skills and experiences) and their social capital (their relationships with various actors on the periphery in general and in the newsroom in particular), than on their position in the field – whether they are on the editorial or commercial side (Bourdieu, 1998a). How these two types of actors may differ is illustrated by the journalist Milan while describing two owners of the newspaper he worked for:

> One of them had an interesting vision, he knew that he was buying an independent local newspaper, the one that people bought, so it could have an impact on the locality, on the socio-political situation. (…) In the end, because the newspaper didn't pay for itself, he added other businesses so that he could continue to finance the newspaper from the earnings of his other companies. The other is such a passionate, dedicated

individual. (…) He remained faithful to his newspapers and participated in every aspect of their production for twenty-two years. (journalist Milan)

Considering the "rational" motivation of the entrepreneurs, it is likely that they will offer more reasoned responses than journalists to the question, "If your newspaper were a human being, what it would look like?" They identify the newspaper not with themselves but rather with a presumed reader-consumer: "A slightly older person, but he would still be a vital individual who wants to learn new things and still wants to work well" (manager Anna); or with an ideal product (Wolfgang & Jenkins, 2018).

> Maybe a woman, she'd be more talkative, I've never thought about it like that ... Well, because they call us gossips it probably should be a woman (laughs). Not the malicious type, she should be sympathetic. (manager-entrepreneur Ema)

> I rather think of a guy. I look at it from an investigative point of view because I think there is a real need for directness, determination, and uncompromisingness which I dare say are male qualities. Of course, that doesn't exclude a female, it's just that I saw a man there. (entrepreneur-journalist Martin)

> I think someone very objective and unscrupulous, measuring everything by the same standard, as in life. (entrepreneur-journalist Dan)

Similarly, the agents in the commercial part of the newsroom may reflect their strong relationship with the newspaper – for instance, by speaking about it as if it were a child. Nevertheless, the entrepreneur-journalists' illusio is (at least partly) influenced by rational, especially economic, motivation.

> I can't throw something out of the window that I built for 15 years. I didn't devote 15 years of my life, which I could have enjoyed in a completely different way, to take my child and throw it in a cesspit. [*Are you now utterly devoted, dedicated to the newspaper?*] No, you're confusing being devoted with being idiotic ... Yes, it's my baby, I helped make it grow, and having put that effort in, I want the child to develop further. And, of course, I also expect some financial reward from that, only an arsehole works for free. (manager Josef)

The second dividing line is between willingness to take responsibility for the newspaper and willingness to take responsibility for the business. My interviewees could be divided in the following broad way considering the illusio: while *journalists* feel passion for their job; *journalist-entrepreneurs* feel passion for the journalistic profession and they struggle with entrepreneurial requirements, particularly the welfare of the staff and the economic health of the company; and *entrepreneur-journalists* manifest their passion for the job primarily by shouldering their entrepreneurial responsibilities. This is well illustrated in the remarks of the former journalist-entrepreneur and current journalist Robert, who now understands this as a responsibility, as opposed to a freedom (Waldenström et al., 2019):

> I'm actually happy now when I just write for the newspaper, I'm the happiest I've ever been. I can do it without worries, I write freely about what I want and do something that is nice, that is good. And the worries with advertising are handled by the publisher, so I really don't care. (journalist Robert)

Similar motivation can be observed in all my communication partners with respect to the question, why do they still stay in the field? Over the years and with a gradual immersion in the journalistic field which has provided them with both entrepreneurial and journalistic experiences, their relationship with newspapers has developed as well as their habitus. Sometimes the formal role of an entrepreneur-journalist becomes so much a part of a person's identity that, though she has other business activities, this identity remains the strongest, especially after doing so for decades. Entrepreneur-journalist Artur puts it simply: "If I didn't do this, what would I do?" The emotional relationship has its counterpart in a newspaper's financial profitability: while profit is a primary goal, entrepreneur-journalists deepen their relationship with the newspaper over the years. A deteriorating economic situation contributes further to it, for instance, when it obliges them to be the sole occupant of the newsroom.

> Until recently, it was profitable and now we work on auto pilot. (…) Sometimes I enjoy the job when I see some of the dickheads, local politicians, when we make their lives a bit harder. It's clear to the paper when someone is (not) taking pleasure in the job. (entrepreneur-journalist Dan)

> [*Why do you stay?*] I don't know, because when we founded it, we were trying to build something: we moved, then we bought some premises, we still seemed to be building something, we paid off our debts and now we are actually more stable. I don't know what else has changed … maybe we've changed (laughs). (manager-entrepreneur Ema)

The level of motivation to stay in the job also depends on the degree of struggle for the newspaper's survival. The more the entrepreneur-journalists face challenges, overcome obstacles, and have to fight for the newspaper, the more motivated they become (cf. the story of entrepreneur-journalist Jan). However, they're not just fighting for the newspaper as such, but also (and sometimes above all) for their reputation, their symbolic capital, as local entrepreneurs.

> If I'm alive and well, the newspapers will be published, unless of course something happens that you can't predict. If someone's going to make a problem, I'm having less fun. (entrepreneur-journalist Max)

Well, sometimes it was horrific, but it's good to remember what we overcame and what we did well (smiles). (entrepreneur-journalist Jan)

I bought a newspaper because I wanted to help the original owner financially. I was doing quite well at the time as a businessman, so I got involved in it with members of my family. We all helped financially so that it wouldn't go bust. But then we found out that the former owner had backed out and stuck it all on us. It turned out that there were more than a million hidden debts and I signed with a notary to take over everything because I thought I could somehow handle it. (entrepreneur Mirek)

Overcoming obstacles as an entrepreneur and possessing related economic capital helps to explain why entrepreneur-journalists gain their symbolic capital more from their entrepreneurial than their journalistic identity. As former entrepreneur and current journalist Robert reflects: "I like being both, but the older I get, the more I appreciate things that exist for a long time. If I had to choose, I would pick a business over publishing newspapers." In their own localities the entrepreneur-journalists are mostly better known as "the entrepreneur" and "the newspaper owner" rather than an author of journalistic content. Moreover, a business failure in publishing could impact on their other businesses or at least result in a loss of entrepreneurial pride. Hence entrepreneur-journalists seldom speak of themselves as journalists (Harlow & Chadha, 2019). As entrepreneur-journalist Dan sums up: "I'm not a journalist! I've only been producing a newspaper for 30 years. I write it, edit it, publish it, distribute it, and do the administration."

Meaning of the job

When comparing the motivation of entrepreneur-journalists and other actors (journalist-entrepreneurs, owners, managers), it is important to focus on the interweaving of both their identities, entrepreneurial and journalistic. In terms of the meaning of the job, entrepreneur-journalists do not deny that the purpose of entrepreneurship is to make a profit (Raviola, 2012). There are entrepreneurs who continue to do well, affirming the lasting economic success of the papers they run on the margins of the media industry. Nevertheless, most of them are in a situation where they are financially supported or support the unprofitable publication of their paper from their other business (cf. the stories of entrepreneur-journalist Jan and journalist Milan). The entrepreneur Petr justifies the loss of seven million Czech crowns which he incurred in publishing a newspaper because he believed in the investment:

I didn't want to lose seven million there, I thought, I'll put two million into it, I can afford it, I'm doing quite well as a businessman. Then the business got worse, so the

> resources weren't available any more. When we started, it still seemed promising. If it lost only a couple of hundred thousand a year, then maybe I could hang on to it. If for two hundred thousand a year I could give three people a job, it would be worth it. (entrepreneur Petr)

Interestingly enough, it was only after it became clear to them that their publication of newspapers would not be a successful business that the entrepreneurs began to talk about the other reasons, they had bought the newspaper – to fulfil their journalistic dreams and/or talents, or at least to derive power from it as their entrepreneurial symbolic capital declined. Manager Anna now views it with a certain detachment: "Owning a newspaper is probably interesting for every entrepreneur. Sometimes it gives her influence, but it's probably not even completely possible to operate a private newspaper without being influenced by the owner." If we continue to follow entrepreneur Petr's story, we can trace that development and see how, with the best of intentions, there was considerable entrepreneurial illusio in terms of acquiring influence and making synergies with other businesses that he confused with editorial independence.

> I liked it and it benefited my ego that we kept it independent. I could tell everyone to go to hell. I said look, you're a Communist, and you want to publish something here? I don't censor articles, but there'll be another piece alongside yours offering a counter-opinion. (…) I didn't become a journalist, but I funded it, and I was a guarantor of political, democratic independence. (entrepreneur Petr)

The meaning that the interviewee attaches to his role of "guarantor of independence" appears to be mistaken – even if economic conditions forced him to close the paper, he kept as a secret weapon the possibility that he might reopen it, and from this he still draws power and potential social and political influence. It emerged from our conversation that even though he has not published his paper for several years, he still uses it as a lever, a means to negotiate his position within the locality. He is not completely candid, or self-reflexive, about this since he tries to hide his strategy behind the oft-repeated sentence: "I'd give the newspaper to anyone for free."[24] But it is just a ploy. Using these strategies is probably nothing new in business but it brings new ways of creating and using various forms of capital. Declining economic capital is balanced on the one hand by an apparent effort to deepen cultural capital by using traditional expectations about journalism; and on the other hand, by strengthening social capital, using the newspaper as a means of coercion. The attempt to acquire symbolic capital is therefore in direct conflict with a loss of economic capital. On top of this, the attitude to their business of the entrepreneur-journalists is generally motivated by their effort to make a name for themselves, to build and maintain a positive *brand* (Wolfgang & Jenkins, 2018). In relation to newspapers, they express it mainly when talking about selling or closing the newspaper down.

> The brand is connected to us in some way, and if we sold it and then it developed along different lines it might cast a bad light on us, even if we had nothing to do with it. (entrepreneur-journalist Martin)

> [*Did you want to sell it?*] My name is connected to the newspaper, so I didn't want to ruin my name. (entrepreneur Petr)

If we think about them as individuals with more than two occupations, the entrepreneur-journalists' pragmatic approach to publishing newspapers is more understandable. While journalist-entrepreneurs become frustrated and exhausted by managing two different sets of responsibility – those of a journalist and those of an entrepreneur – the entrepreneur-journalists are much more immersed in business and usually responsible for more than one company. Thus, while journalist-entrepreneurs complain about having less time for the journalism they love, entrepreneur-journalists regard journalism as a reward for, or recreation from, their main work. This may be another reason (next to using the newspaper as a weapon of power) that, despite their pragmatic approach, entrepreneur-journalists perceive their newspaper business with the illusio which differs it from other businesses. Even if it loses money, it supports their "hobby".

Their description of their work-life balance is similar to that of the journalist-entrepreneurs: it ranges from those who are recharged by the pressure (entrepreneur Mirek); through those who finish their shift in the newsroom and start work in their other business(es), sometimes on a night shift (entrepreneur-journalists Dan, Artur, Max); and those who enjoy journalism as fun or as relaxation (entrepreneur-journalists Max, Artur) or as an emotional release during hard times (manager Anna); to those with serious health problems as a consequence of insecure job conditions and burn-out (MacDonald et al., 2016).

> As the workload increased, my health went downhill. I'm already tired. (entrepreneur-journalist Artur)

> I'm trying not to look at the computer at all right now because my eyes are already damaged. It bothers me because I'm fed up with the job, well, I've been doing it for a long time. (…) A month ago, I had shingles from overwork. (entrepreneur-journalist Dan)

Thinking about power and influence in the context of the significance which entrepreneur-journalists attach to their job raises the question of whether they feel any responsibility for it, and if so, whether it is a different kind of responsibility from that which they feel for their other businesses? Two types of doxa are discernible: The first is that of the entrepreneur who asserts her independence but admits that she gains power from the newspaper.

> I told everyone that once I started to play in the colours of a political party, I would stop being independent and would not be able to write anything against them any more. But I wouldn't like that. Until now I've always considered myself to be an impartial and objective person. (entrepreneur-journalist Max)

> I'm not into politics at all. If the newspaper is independent, it should rely only on me! (entrepreneur-journalist Artur)

The second attitude to responsibility is that of the entrepreneur who wishes to exercise his power more widely, for example, as a local politician or representative of the local municipality. Like journalist-entrepreneurs, some of the entrepreneur-journalists regard their engagement in politics as a logical step in "helping their respective localities".

> I admit it openly, we're a medium of opposition. Against the criticism that we're politicians and looking after our own interests, I say: yes, it's true, and why not when people buy it and want to read it? We're a privately-owned medium, we can argue about [independence] and talk philosophically about whether it's right or not. (entrepreneur-journalist Martin)

> I've been in local politics for three terms, so I know how it all works. I was an independent candidate. [*Was it a problem for your work?*] It bothered the other politicians, not me. As a "politician" I pushed for transparency, to ensure nothing secret was going on. And in the newspaper, when something needed to be written about the town, I didn't write it but I gave the materials to my colleagues so they could write it. So the politicians couldn't accuse me of wielding influence. (entrepreneur-journalist Dan)

Neither type of entrepreneur-journalists considers this behaviour to be problematic in terms of journalistic norms and rules, reflecting nomos of the peripheral journalistic sub-field. Like most journalists they rarely talk about doxic values, norms, and rules per se, and some see rules as applying only to their subordinates, and in a somewhat simplistic way. For example, entrepreneur-journalist Dan understands the values of truth and public service as key: "You have to write the truth, because if you write an outright lie or some nonsense and you meet that person the next day in a self-service shop, he'll punch you in the mouth"; and criticises competition: "Our competitors get their information from press releases while we get ours from people, so the competition can't provide the service we provide."

On the other hand, entrepreneur Petr was one of the few to mention the importance of journalistic ethics: "We have always been independent, we were in no one's pocket. We just didn't care. I kept this line from the beginning: we didn't favour anyone and we always remembered the journalistic … I would like to say, ethics." But the same interviewee Petr also believed it is important to point out that the newspaper he owned was activist:[25] "We once organised a petition here, it got sixty thousand signatures, and managed to stop the sale of a property here in the town centre because we raised such opposition. The newspaper showed that it was wrong and prevented it." In a similar vein he spoke openly about supporting various individuals in the locality: "Several times we were a great stabilising element in the area, a guarantee of democratic civic development because we stood up for someone."

Nevertheless, there is one part of the doxa that emerged without prompting from the interviewer, a type of rule related to the independence of a newspaper which some of the entrepreneur-journalists consider important. Because of their entrepreneurial character they consider it unacceptable to receive any money or subsidies from the state or municipality. They understand this as inimical to freedom and were alone among my communication partners in mentioning this topic.

> People don't understand what it is to be an independent newspaper, they think that we are as objective as God, but it doesn't work like that. (…) People don't understand that independence is fundamentally an economic matter. (entrepreneur-journalist Dan)

> When I hired people who were registered at a labour office, I could get twenty thousand Czech crowns per person. I never did it and I had a lot of employees. (…) It was the same with the town hall, I had a feeling they'd want something from me in return. (entrepreneur-journalist Jan)

Considering social capital, the relationships that entrepreneur-journalists form with other actors in the journalistic field are unique and their peculiarity emerges in almost all stories that are told by my interviewees. It is caused by the fact that they are very much lone wolves, relying on themselves not because they are left alone, as journalist-entrepreneurs sometimes are, but because they choose it, and it suits them (Harlow & Chadha, 2019). Unsurprisingly, entrepreneur-journalists talk about three other kinds of actor with whom they have a relationship: their partners and colleagues in a newsroom; the people within a particular locality; and the members of the local field of power, especially politicians. Nevertheless, these relationships as the entrepreneur-journalists depict them are mostly unbalanced: they are not a partnership, but a power relationship.

Speaking about a managerial balance in the newsroom, entrepreneur-journalists differ from journalist-entrepreneurs in being either mostly alone or in partnership with someone who has less power and responsibility than they have. Entrepreneur-journalist Max described how he acquired the fixed idea that he could do the job himself: "Then I contacted a colleague from my former job and hired him, today he is my deputy here." Even if they realise that doing it alone is not a wise option (entrepreneur-journalist Dan), the entrepreneur-journalists carefully consider who they let into their business, partly because of occasional bad experiences with business partners. "From time to time I advertise for a business partner, I was even with one of them in a notary's office, but I had to call it off. Either they've no experience or they're scammers," said entrepreneur Mirek. The problem appears to be a lack of trust in business matters which prevents them from relying more on their colleagues or family members.

In the case of entrepreneur-journalists, a power relationship typifies their dealings with colleagues – their subordinates in the newsroom. On the one hand, there are managers who even after many years have not come to terms with the peculiarities of journalistic culture; on the other, there are managers who judge the abilities of their colleagues only as these do, or do not, conform with their own requirements.

> [Working in a newspaper] is terrible for me! The people here are unmethodical, people who don't understand anything. Before this I basically worked all my life with professionals. Those people who don't understand maths are completely stupid. (manager Josef)

> My newspaper works because my secret is that I can suss people. People have been working for me for fifteen or twenty years. (entrepreneur-journalist Artur)

> I know how to organise my time and my hobby is to organise other people. I've always organised it so that everyone has a job. I can't understand people who do everything themselves, I did the opposite. (entrepreneur-journalist Max)

With respect to their relationships with people in their locality, entrepreneur-journalists value their own social capital because it can be transformed into economic and symbolic capital – the position of themselves, their colleagues, and their newspaper in a locality – and this consolidates their position within the field of power. Entrepreneur-journalist Martin expressed this in an appreciation of the social and economic capital of his editor-in-chief: "I think that her social capital played a role, because she worked here for twenty years, so many of the advertisers and correspondents knew her very well. And it outweighed those who were against us." Similarly, the entrepreneur-journalist Jan mentioned the importance of personal ties with other local business people with respect to advertising.

Beyond this, however, entrepreneur-journalists are not particularly concerned about their relationship to the readership, neither about the audience-centred public service perspective, nor about the market-centred perspective. Nor are they particularly concerned about the advertisers. What they define themselves against are the local political representatives as other members of the field of power (entrepreneur-journalist Dan; entrepreneur Mirek). It could be seen as part of the power negotiations in a respective locality and also of the ambivalent attitude of entrepreneur-journalists to the field of power. For example, entrepreneur-journalist Dan mainly criticises the politicians' lack of vision and preoccupation with making money: "They are only about money, money, money", which is almost as if he was pointing the gun at those in his own ranks.

In line with their descriptions of their relationships, the entrepreneur-journalists address the topic of handing over a newspaper less frequently than the journalist-entrepreneurs. This is probably a result of their more extensive experience of business and therefore of a far more rational attitude to it (cf. illusio). Unlike the journalist-entrepreneurs they do not dream of handing the newspaper over to their family: instead, they think about the abilities and merits of whoever will succeed them.

> [For the handover] I can see only one colleague in the newsroom as a candidate. But he's terribly lazy and unreliable, he says he'll come on Tuesday, but he doesn't say which month, so it's hopeless. (entrepreneur-journalist Dan)

> I envy previous generations, how they passed a business on, how it went from father to son, I would really like that, but it won't happen for two reasons: I don't have children and even if I did, nowadays it's very unlikely that kids will want to do what their father did. (…) In any case, I wouldn't pass it on to someone who didn't in the slightest degree deserve it just because I felt he could carry it on. Because I think a person into whose lap it falls won't appreciate it, so it won't take long before the newspaper disappears. (entrepreneur-journalist Max)

Working practices of an entrepreneur-journalist

Describing the daily practices of entrepreneur-journalists is complicated by the fact that among my interviewees, the business people were those who least liked to talk about their work practices openly.[26] Moreover, these practices differ radically from what they do in their other businesses – for example, when (for economic reasons) they don't take any money for the work they do in the newsroom (entrepreneur Petr; entrepreneur-journalist Dan). In addition to their entrepreneurial and journalistic work in a newsroom, entrepreneur-journalists usually run other businesses. They struggle with bureaucracy and administration on a daily basis, as well as having responsibility for journalistic content.

> The state is killing us with its bureaucracy. I basically spend two days a week just working for the state, I fill out all sorts of reports, it's terrible. I write at least one article

for the newspaper, the editorial. It totally exhausts me. I have been doing it for thirty years and you have to write it every week. (entrepreneur-journalist Dan)

Nevertheless, the interviewees speak more about freedom, which they regard as closely associated with their practices. Even if they do not mention it explicitly,[27] their stories emphasise their ability to do what they want and use their own judgement about what is important as part of the doxa. It is related to the responsibility they feel towards their business in general and the publishing business in particular.

> In the beginning, there was stress. Every week it looked like we were going to close. We came up with the slogan "Only ours is ours." They laughed at us because we were doing it badly. And we *were* doing it badly. We worked on the principle that although we were doing it badly, we were doing it in our own way. The competition, they were pros. I thought we couldn't fight them. But it turned out that, yes, it mattered to the readers that we were local. After a year, we started to be more successful than the competition. I picked up a larger share. (entrepreneur-journalist Artur)

> I hate cell phones, I haven't had one in a long time, everyone asks me how I can do business without one. I was perhaps the last person in the country to have a mobile phone and I still don't have a car. I go everywhere on foot, by bus or by train. [*That's quite unusual for a journalist and an entrepreneur* …] (Laughs) Exactly! And I tell everyone, do it like me, because that's the only way you can get to know people, you can get to know where you really are, and you won't be living in a greenhouse. (entrepreneur-journalist Max)

From an economic point of view, interviewees exploit their publishing companies for synergies with their other businesses or to look for further business opportunities (entrepreneur Mirek). Nevertheless, emotion and affinity – the illusio – play a big part for those who have crossed the entrepreneurial boundaries shared with journalism. Their stories clearly reflect their life histories and the interweaving of two different habituses:

> I ended up being a journalist twenty years ago and thanks to our new project I came back to it. I really enjoy it and I'm sticking with it. I have a good impression of it, much better than if I wrote the advertising texts I used to write, because now I can write freely, as I wish to write. Moreover, I enjoy it because I can afford to work on an article for three days. (entrepreneur-journalist Max)

To conclude, the habitus of the class of entrepreneurs on the margins – their attitudes, perceptions, discourses, behaviour, emotions, ideals, values, skills, and the historical trajectory of their career – is clearly identifiable and distinguishable from other agents in the journalistic field. Although it might seem from the previous chapter that a simple distinction holds good between emotionally driven journalists and rationally motivated entrepreneurs, this is not the case. On the contrary, a key element in the habitus of a journalistic entrepreneur resembles that of the journalists in being an emotion, the journalistic illusio. Nevertheless, it is manifested differently: as a *desire for change and power*, which is visible in the motivation to become an entrepreneur; visible in the struggle to achieve change either in the newspaper or in local politics and society; or in a reluctance to give up the role. The affective dimension of the entrepreneurs is evident in the different forms of capital they possess, mainly in symbolic capital and their relationship with a field of power. Power was a frequent topic among my communication partners.

Even though entrepreneurs are on the margins of the journalistic field, in that space where it encounters an economic field, in terms of my broad definition and the nomos of the peripheral journalistic sub-field, both journalist-entrepreneurs and entrepreneur-journalists can be considered as *journalists*. Both can be considered either as actors on the edge of the journalistic field "who claim to belong to [it], but who also recognize institutionalized boundaries" (Maares & Hanusch, 2021, p. 274) or as interlopers, who "do not consider their activities journalism per se, [but who] acknowledge their contributions to news production" (Holton & Belair-Gagnon, 2018, p. 74). This perception is based on their self-understanding, a bottom-up approach focused on

> how entrepreneurial journalism is a process of becoming-with on the level of everyday practices. (...) to tease out how discourse, activities, materialities, and different sorts of affect are constructing practices of entrepreneurial journalism together, trying to create an understanding of how practices work, rather than what they are. (Brouwers, 2017, p. 218)

Or, as Vos and Singer (2016, p. 145) describe, with the rise of entrepreneurialism as an acceptable type of journalistic practice, there is also a change of cultural capital in the journalistic field, based on new beliefs and practices, particularly "pull of economic capital". Nevertheless, this merging of two previously distinct roles of a journalist and an entrepreneur can bring about a change in a norm of the field.

There are clear boundaries between a journalist and an entrepreneur and between a journalist-entrepreneur and an entrepreneur-journalist. Interestingly enough, their motivations are similar and can be considered as the illusio – ideals about changing society or a locality, whether by writing about it or by accumulating enough symbolic capital to exert an influence on it; or by policy-making and political decisions. Conversely, their initial motivation weakens in different ways: while journalists can afford to dissipate their original activity by adopting a passive approach to their job, entrepreneurs either remain active or close the newspaper.

There are some visible parallels and similarities between this definition of the identities, habituses, and practices of journalist-entrepreneurs and entrepreneur-journalists and the suggested typologies of entrepreneurs in general and entrepreneurs in media. Fauchart and Gruber (2011) define three types of entrepreneurs' identities: Darwinians, Communitarians, and Missionaries. Nevertheless, they note that these categories are not mutually exclusive, they are overlapping and fluid: "Darwinians are founders driven by self-interest, wanting to create a profitable, successful firm. They see themselves as professional business people, and others as competition they want to distinguish themselves from. Success is measured in terms of financial gain and being the best"; "Communitarians desire to support and be a part of a community. They see themselves as contributing something valuable, and they look at counterparts as potential allies, rather than competition. Success is equated with being a useful and respected member of a community"; "Missionaries are founders who want their product to advance a social or political cause. They see themselves as agents of change and desire to lead by example. Success involves convincing others to follow their political or social vision to make the world a better place" (Harlow & Chadha, 2019, p. 895). Harlow and Chadha tested this typology on Indian entrepreneurs in journalism and added a fourth category, the Guardian: "This category was necessary because while these founders valued profitability and competition, much like Darwinians, they also exhibited the Communitarian trait of offering something valuable to the community, and the Missionary ideal of wanting to make the world a better place"; "what distinguishes Guardians from the other categories is the founders' emphasis on producing quality journalism, regardless of profit, community, or mission" (2019, p. 897).

The habituses of a journalist-entrepreneur and an entrepreneur-journalist are interesting and distinctive because of their two interconnected elements. These elements reflect the life histories of the actors since they develop gradually. Their starting points within the journalistic field are wholly different, but the journalist, almost by definition, sits in the middle of the journalistic field, and the entrepreneur on the edge of that field, one which intersects with the economic field, gradually drift towards each other. Unlike journalists and freelancers, whose life histories are parallel, journalist-entrepreneurs and entrepreneur-journalists converge from opposite positions. Hence their position is ultimately on the borders of the journalistic field and the economic field but closer to that of the journalist than that of the entrepreneur.

Notes

1. Russo (1998) observes that her survey respondents reported a stronger identification with the job than with the newspaper they worked for.
2. I analyse the stories of journalists and journalist-entrepreneurs in terms of *journalistic* habitus, since the journalist-entrepreneurs built their journalistic before their entrepreneurial habitus.
3. An interviewee's dissident past and particular circumstances during the Velvet Revolution were also important elements in the development of particular media organisations.
4. For more about dissent and its social and cultural capital see Možný (1991).
5. It can be also understood as an ambivalence between journalism-as-duty and journalism-as-work which could be one of the reasons for spiralling job dissatisfaction, depicted by Siegelbaum and Thomas: "The theory of alienation, as articulated by Marx (1867), holds that under capitalism workers lose control over their work by surrendering its surplus value to capital and becoming anonymous cogs in the capitalist machinery. This results in workers losing their autonomy and becoming alienated" (2016, p. 391).
6. Reinardy's burn-out definition is based on English slang, where "to burn oneself out" means "to work too hard and die early" (2011, p. 34).
7. For more about journalists' involvement in local politics see chapters "Habitus, capitals, and practices of a journalist-entrepreneur on the margins" and "Habitus, capitals, and practices of an entrepreneur-journalist on the margins".
8. I understand the close relationship between journalists, audiences, and sources not as exclusive to local journalism, but rather as characteristic of the limited, often peripheral, spaces of journalism where there is also a limited number of actors from various fields (cf. *interlocutors*, Marchetti, 2005).
9. The communication partner then agreed to the recording and use of this portion of the interview.
10. I understand journalists' practices to consist not only of their reflections on where and how they work (Hovden, 2008) but their position in the field with respect to other actors (Benson, 1999).
11. For an analysis of the spatial dimension of journalistic practice, see, e.g., Usher (2019).
12. I define freelancers as any kind of *atypical worker*, who works for a media organisation without "[regular] income, job security, health benefits, maternity leave or other benefits attached to permanent jobs" (Gollmitzer, 2014, p. 827), and is involved in the content production.
13. See the example of a newsroom's "patchwork structure" as described by journalist-entrepreneur Marie in the chapter "Journalists".
14. Among my communication partners there are exceptions that prove the rule: two journalist-freelancers work for significantly distant newsrooms located in different regions.
15. Cf. the *passivity of journalists* discussed above (Goyanes & Rodríguez-Gómez, 2021).
16. For a critique of emotion in journalism as "an epistemological blind spot", see Wahl-Jorgensen (2019, p. 674).
17. As I defined them above in accordance with my findings from the interviews and observations.
18. For more about the media transition see Chapter 4 (cf. Jebril et al., 2013; Paletz & Jakubowicz, 2003).
19. One of the new political parties after Velvet Revolution in November 1989 (see Možný, 1991; Paletz & Jakubowicz, 2003).

20 The problems involved in handing over a newspaper – its dependence hitherto on a single person and on her solutions – are closely connected to the depicted "fragility" of organisations on the margins. For more about this topic see Chapter 4.
21 The second example is the story of journalist-entrepreneur Monika, to whom a local businessman and politician sold the newspaper when she was editor-in-chief.
22 I understand journalism not as a profession but an ideology, focusing on the ways that journalists make meaning from their work (Deuze, 2005; cf. Jenkins, 2016; for more see Chapter 1). Bourdieu himself criticised "profession" as Hovden (2008, p. 29) points out: "'Profession' is a folk concept which has been uncritically smuggled into scientific language and which imports into it a whole social unconscious. It is the social product of a historical work of construction of a group and of a representation of groups that has surreptitiously slipped into the science of this very group (…). The category of profession refers to realities that are, in a sense, 'too real' to be true, since it grasps at once a mental category and a social category."
23 Cf. the clash of professional and managerial discourses (Andersson & Wiik, 2013; Waldenström et al., 2019; for more see Chapter 4).
24 A similar strategy was employed by entrepreneur Mirek.
25 This topic was discussed only by the freelancers and can be associated in these two classes with a similar shortage of cultural capital and different doxa in terms of journalistic norms and rules. For more see chapter "Habitus, capitals and practices of a journalist on the margins".
26 Compare this with the journalists' reluctance to talk about money.
27 Compare this with the journalists' emphasis on their freedom.

References

Ahva, L. (2017). How is participation practiced by "in-betweeners" of journalism? *Journalism Practice, 11*(2–3), 142–159.

Anderson, C. W. (2011). Blowing up the newsroom: Ethnography in an age of distributed journalism. In D. Domingo & C. Paterson (Eds.), *Making online news – Volume 2: Newsroom ethnographies in the second decade of internet journalism* (Vol. 2, pp. 151–160). Peter Lang Publishing.

Anderson, C. W. (2013). *Rebuilding the news: Metropolitan journalism in the digital age*. Temple University Press.

Benson, R. (1999). Field theory in comparative context: A new paradigm for media studies. *Theory and Society, 28*(3), 463–498.

Benson, R., & Neveu, E. (Eds.). (2005). *Bourdieu and the journalistic field*. Polity Press.

Bourdieu, P. (1984). *Distinction. A social critique of the judgement of taste*. Harvard University Press.

Bourdieu, P. (1996). *On television*. The New Press.

Bourdieu, P. (1998a). *Practical reason: On the theory of action*. Stanford University Press.

Bourdieu, P. (1998b). *Teorie jednání* [*Theory of action*]. Karolinum.

Bourdieu, P. (2005). The political field, the social science field, and the journalistic field. In R. Benson & E. Neveu (Eds.), *Bourdieu and the journalistic field* (pp. 29–47). Polity Press.

Bowd, K. (2005). Country newspaper journalists' perceptions of the influence of 'localness' on professional practice. *Australian Journalism Review, 27*(2), 105–117.
Brouwers, A. D. (2017). Failure and *understanding-with* in entrepreneurial journalism. *Journal of Media Business Studies, 14*(3), 217–233.
Curtin, M., & Sanson, K. (Eds.). (2016). *Precarious creativity: Global media, local labor.* University of California Press.
Cushion, S. (2007). Rich media, poor journalists. *Journalism Practice, 1*(1), 120–129.
Deuze, M. (2005). What is journalism?: Professional identity and ideology of journalists reconsidered. *Journalism, 6*(4), 442–464.
Deuze, M. (2007). *Media work. Digital media and society series.* Polity Press.
Deuze, M. (2019). What journalism is (not). *Social Media + Society, 5*(3), 1–4.
Deuze, M., & Witschge, T. (2020). *Beyond journalism.* Polity Press.
Dopita, M. (2007). Peirre Bourdieu o umění, výchově a společnosti. Reflexe sociologie praxe Pierra Bourdieua v české sociologii [*Peirre Bourdieu on art, education, and society. Reflection of Pierre Bourdieu's sociology of practice in Czech sociology*]. Univerzita Palackého v Olomouci.
Duval, J. (2005). Economic journalism in France. In R. Benson & E. Neveu (Eds.), *Bourdieu and the journalistic field* (pp. 135–155). Polity Press.
Ekdale, B., Tully, M., Harmsen, S., & Singer, J. B. (2015). Newswork within a culture of job insecurity: Producing news amidst organizational and industry uncertainty. *Journalism Practice, 9*(3), 383–398.
Eldridge II, S. A. (2018). *Online journalism from the periphery. Interloper media and the journalistic field.* Routledge.
Eldridge II, S. A. (2019). Where do we draw the line? Interlopers, (ant)agonists, and an unbounded journalistic field. *Media and Communication, 7*(4), 8–18.
Erzikova, E., & Lowrey, W. (2017). Russian regional media: Fragmented community, fragmented online practices. *Digital Journalism, 5*(7), 919–937.
Evetts, J. (2003). The sociological analysis of professionalism: Occupational change in the modern world. *International Sociology, 18*(2), 395–415.
Evetts, J. (2006). Short note: The sociology of professional groups – new directions. *Current Sociology, 54*(1), 133–43.
Fauchart, E., & Gruber, M. (2011). Darwinians, communitarians, and missionaries: The role of founder identity in entrepreneurship. *The Academy of Management Journal, 54*(5), 935–957.
Gaziano, C., & McGrath, K. (1987). Newspaper credibility and relationships of newspaper journalists to communities. *Journalism Quarterly, 64*(2–3), 317–328.
Glück, A. (2016). What makes a good journalist?: Empathy as a central resource in journalistic work practice. *Journalism studies, 17*(7), 893–903.
Gollmitzer, M. (2014). Precariously employed watchdogs?: Perceptions of working conditions among freelancers and interns. *Journalism Practice, 8*(6), 826–841.
Goyanes, M., & Rodríguez-Gómez, E. F. (2021). Presentism in the newsroom: How uncertainty redefines journalists' career expectations. *Journalism, 22*(1), 52–68.

Harlow, S., & Chadha, M. (2019). Indian entrepreneurial journalism: Building a typology of how founders' social identity shapes innovation and sustainability. *Journalism Studies, 20*(6), 891–910.

Hepp, A., & Loosen, W. (2021). Pioneer journalism: Conceptualizing the role of pioneer journalists and pioneer communities in the organizational re-figuration of journalism. *Journalism, 22*(3), 577–595.

Holton, A. E. (2016). Intrapreneurial informants: An emergent role of freelance journalists. *Journalism Practice, 10*(7), 917–927.

Holton, A. E., & Belair-Gagnon, V. (2018). Strangers to the game? Interlopers, intralopers, and shifting news production. *Media and Communication, 6*(4), 70–78.

Hovden, J. F. (2008). *Profane and sacred. A study of the Norwegian journalistic field* [Unpublished doctoral dissertation]. University of Bergen. https://bora.uib.no/bora-xmlui/bitstream/handle/1956/2724/Jan%20Fredrik%20Hovden.pdf?sequence=1

Jebril, N., Stetka, V., & Loveless, M. (2013). *Media and democratisation: What is known about the role of mass media in transitions to democracy*. Reuters Institute for the Study of Journalism.

Jenkins, J. (2016). Public roles and private negotiations: Considering city magazines' public service and market functions. *Journalism, 17*(5), 619–635.

Kleinsteuber, H. J. (1992). The global village stays local. In K. Siune & W. Truetzschler (Eds.), *Dynamics of media politics: Broadcast and electronic media in Western Europe* (pp. 143–153). Sage.

Kotišová, J. (2017). Cynicism ex machina: The emotionality of reporting the "refugee crisis" and Paris terrorist attacks in Czech Television. *European Journal of Communication, 32*(3), 242–256.

Lamour, C. (2019). The legitimate peripheral position of a central medium: Revealing the margins of popular journalism. *Journalism Studies, 20*(8), 1167–1183.

Le Cam, F., & Domingo, D. (2015). The plurality of journalistic identities in local controversies. In R. K. Nielsen (Ed.), *Local journalism: The decline of newspapers and the rise of digital media* (pp. 99–115). Reuters Institute for the Study of Journalism; I. B. Tauris.

Maares, P., & Hanusch, F. (2021). Exploring the boundaries of journalism: Instagram microbloggers in the twilight zone of lifestyle journalism. *Journalism, 21*(2), 262–278.

MacDonald, J. B., Saliba, A. J., Hodgins, G., & Ovington, L. A. (2016). Burnout in journalists: A systematic literature review. *Burnout Research, 3*(2), 34–44.

Mathisen, B. R. (2023). *Journalism between disruption and resilience: Reflections on the Norwegian experience*. Routledge.

Možný, I. (1991). *Proč tak snadno ... : Některé rodinné důvody sametové revoluce: sociologický esej*. [*Why so easily ... : Some family reasons for the Velvet Revolution – a sociological essay*]. Sociologické nakladatelství.

O'Neill, D., & O'Connor, C. (2008). The passive journalist: How sources dominate local news. *Journalism Practice, 2*(3), 487–500.

Örnebring, H. (2009). *The two professionalisms of journalism: Journalism and the changing context of work. Working paper*. Reuters Institute for the Study of Journalism.
Örnebring, H. (2013). Anything you can do, I can do better? Professional journalists on citizen journalism in six European countries. *The International Communication Gazette, 75*(1), 35-53.
Örnebring, H., & Möller, C. (2018). In the margins of journalism: Gender and livelihood among local (ex-)journalists in Sweden. *Journalism Practice, 12*(8), 1051-1060.
Paletz, D. L., & Jakubowicz, K. (2003). *Business as usual: Continuity and change in Central and Eastern Europe media*. Hampton Press.
Pihl-Thingvad, S. (2015). Professional ideals and daily practice in journalism. *Journalism, 16*(3), 392-411.
Raviola, E. (2012). Exploring organizational framings: Journalism and business management in newspaper organizations. *Information, Communication & Society, 15*(6), 932-958.
Reinardy, S. (2011). Newspaper journalism in crisis: Burnout on the rise, eroding young journalists' career commitment. *Journalism, 12*(1), 33-50.
Reinardy, S. (2013). Depleted resources causing burnout for layoff survivors. *Newspaper Research Journal, 34*(3), 6-21.
Rivas-Rodriguez, M. (2011). Communities, cultural identity, and the news. In W. Lowrey & P. J. Gade (Eds.), *Changing the news: The forces shaping journalism in uncertain times* (pp. 102-117). Routledge.
Rosenlund, L. (2009). *Exploring the city with Bourdieu*. VDM Verlag Dr. Müller.
Russo, T. C. (1998). Organizational and professional identification: A case of newspaper journalists. *Management Communication Quarterly, 12*(1), 72-111.
Ruusunoksa, L. (2006). Public journalism and professional culture: Local, regional and national public spheres as contexts of professionalism. *Javnost – The Public, 13*(4), 81-98.
Schapals, A. K. (2022). *Peripheral actors in journalism: Deviating from the norm?* Routledge.
Scott, M., Bunce, M., & Wright, K. (2019). Foundation funding and the boundaries of journalism. *Journalism Studies, 20*(14), 2034-2052.
Schultz, I. (2007). The journalistic gut feeling: Journalistic doxa, news habitus and orthodox news values. *Journalism Practice, 1*(2), 190-207.
Splendore, S. (2020). The Dominance of institutional sources and the establishment of non-elite ones: The case of Italian online local journalism. *Journalism, 21*(7), 990-1006.
Siegelbaum, S., & Thomas, R. J. (2016). Putting the work (back) into newswork. *Journalism Practice, 10*(3), 387-404.
Smethers, S. J., Bressers, B., & Mwangi, S. C. (2017). Friendships sustain volunteer newspaper for 21 years. *Newspaper Research Journal, 38*(3), 379-391.
Steiner, L. (2012). Failed theories: Explaining gender difference in journalism. *Review of Communication, 12*(3) 201-223.
Tandoc, E. C. Jr. (2019). Journalism at the periphery. *Media and Communication, 7*(4), 138-143.

Usher, N. (2018). Breaking news production processes in US metropolitan newspapers: Immediacy and journalistic authority. *Journalism, 19*(1), 21–36.

Usher, N. (2019). Putting "place" in the center of journalism research: A way forward to understand challenges to trust and knowledge in news. *Journalism & Communication Monographs, 21*(2), 84–146.

Vos, T. P., Eichholz, M., & Karaliova, T. (2019). Audiences and journalistic capital: Roles of journalism. *Journalism Studies, 20*(7), 1009–1027.

Vos, T. P., & Singer, J. B. (2016). Media discourse about entrepreneurial journalism: Implications for journalistic capital. *Journalism Practice, 10*(2), 143–159.

Wahl-Jorgensen, K. (2009). News production, ethnography, and power: On the challenges of newsroom-centricity. In E. S. Bird (Ed.), *The anthropology of news and journalism: Global perspectives* (pp. 21–35). Indiana University Press.

Wahl-Jorgensen, K. (2019). Challenging presentism in journalism studies: An emotional life history approach to understanding the lived experience of journalists. *Journalism, 20*(5), 670–678.

Waldenström, A., Wiik, J., & Andersson, U. (2019). Conditional autonomy. Journalistic practice in the tension field between professionalism and managerialism. *Journalism Practice, 13*(4), 493–508.

Wiik, J. (2009). Identities under construction: Professional journalism in a phase of destabilization. *International Review of Sociology, 19*(2), 351–365.

Wiik, J. (2015). Internal boundaries: The stratification of the journalistic collective. In M. Carlson & S. C. Lewis (Eds.), *Boundaries of journalism: Professionalism, practices and participation* (pp. 118–133). Routledge.

Wolfgang, D. J., & Jenkins, J. (2018). Crafting a community: Staff members' conceptions of audience at a city magazine. *Community Journalism, 6*(1), 1–20.

Zelizer, B. (2017). *What journalism could be*. Polity.

CHAPTER 4

Newspapers on the margins

Despite, or perhaps because of, the fact that the media are a product of people, it is important to consider not only individual actors but the organisation as an agent in the journalistic field. In parallel with the individualistic tendencies of journalists on the margins, the newspapers they work for are also loners, precluded within their respective localities. They are outlying islands in the journalistic archipelago, mostly lacking contact, or cooperation with others. It further underlines the fragility of local media and at the same time highlights the importance of telling their stories.

Viewing the journalistic field as it were from above, we can see that it is wholly the product of individuals and organisations, their mutual interplay, hierarchy, and the logic of their existence. No matter if one individual embodies an entire newspaper (as is often the case on the media periphery), the organisation is as much a part of the journalistic field as the individual actor and the class of actors.

Following my bottom-up approach, my aim in this chapter is to situate specific types of organisations on the margins in terms of two kinds of relationship and their dynamics, in light of the *path-dependency* approach (Benson & Neveu, 2005): the relationships between those within the organisation, and those the organisation forms with other agents in the journalistic field.

The internal dynamics of an organisation are based both on the individual actors – their habituses, capitals and practices – and on the history and culture of the organisation, its capitals, and practices, and therefore on the organisation's *disposition*. The external dynamics encompass relationships with other agents in the journalistic field while recognising certain boundaries, and therefore establish the organisation's *position* (Benson, 1999). Both kinds of dynamic can be perceived in terms of the premise that in order to understand a *macrocosm* – the journalistic field – we must first understand the *microcosm*, the individual actors within it.

Peripheral organisations

The importance of newspapers which operate on the journalistic margins can be illustrated by the story of a woman in a small Czech town. She failed to obtain relevant information from the municipality, and she could not comment on local issues in the municipal press,[1] so she decided to publish a "supplementary newspaper" – one which was irregularly issued but complemented official information. The municipality labelled her a "local troublemaker", but she persisted in publishing and distributing her newspaper to the mailboxes of all the citizens of the town. Two issues of her newspaper cost her around 23 thousand Czech crowns (approx. 900 Euro) to produce, but she commented: "Money plays no role in this, I was just upset, and I was mainly prompted by the need to inform citizens about what is happening at the town hall" (Menšík & Prchal, 2017).

This story highlights an important aspect for the existence of peripheral media organisations: there respond to a void, where a limited number of professional communication channels exist; where some of the media are biased by their very nature (e.g. the municipal press); and where topics and events taking place on the periphery are not of interest to the national media. The consequence of these obstacles may result in a lack of relevant information for people who live away from the main centres of population.

When considering the boundaries of the journalistic field, one can easily overlook the newspapers in the localities: from the national level they are almost invisible, because they are dispersed in their respective localities. They are entirely dependent on peripheral structures and individuals – from their readership, through those who work for them, to the publishing structure (printing house, distribution, newsstands, etc.). In a word, they are vulnerable organisations which have to fight constantly for their space within the journalistic field.

As in previous chapters I will focus here on these peripheral organisations – local newspapers in the Czech Republic – as a homogeneous group. During my fieldwork, I visited or spoke with representatives of all currently published local newspapers and with several owners of some that are defunct. In line with Bourdieu's distinction, I focus only on *segmented media*, not *omnibus media*, as newspaper groups or chains:[2] "the category of 'omnibus' extends to all media outlets

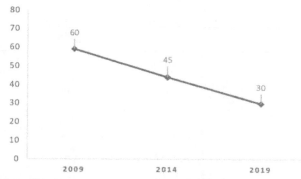

Figure 1: Number of local newspapers in the Czech Republic
Credit: The Author.

which 'maximize their clientele by neutralizing their product' (…) such as most regional newspapers" (in Benson & Neveu, 2005, pp. 8, 22). Based on my survey, in 2009 there were 60 local newspapers in the Czech Republic; in 2014 there were 45, and in 2019 30 (see Figure 1 and lokalnik.cz/localmedia.cz).[3]

These local newspapers were never part of the *Czech Publishers' Association* (2020) or audited by the *Audit Bureau of Circulations* (2020), unlike the regional newspaper chain and the national dailies, so there is no publicly available data about them. Even so, local newspapers still have a powerful position within the journalistic field, the total printed copies of these titles in 2019 were estimated in the survey at 190,000 per week.[4] A gradual reduction of the size of these peripheral newspapers is apparent when we compare their basic characteristics in this decade to those in the last – distribution area; frequency of publication; readership; type of ownership; and tradition of publication. Their features have become bland – their diversity of content has disappeared, and the individual titles have retreated to their safest means of survival by focusing on the most profitable area of a district distribution, publishing weekly rather than daily, and resorting to a corporate type of ownership (see Table 2 and Figures 2–6).

Table 2: Comparison of local newspapers in the Czech Republic

	2009	2019
Distribution area		
Municipality with extended powers	11	6
District	35	24
More districts	11	0
County	3	0

(continued)

Table 2: *Continued*

	2009	2019
Frequency of publication		
Fortnightly	6	3
Weekly	51	25
Biweekly	3	2
Copies sold per issue[8]		
Up to 2,000	6	10
Up to 6,000	28	12
Up to 10,000	5	4
Up to 15,000	6	4
Up to 25,000	1	0
Type of ownership		
Self-employed owner	16	3
Corporate	44	27
Longevity of publication		
Up to 5 years	18	2
Up to 10 years	6	1
Up to 20 years	36	7
Up to 30 years	0	20

Credit: The Author, first used in Waschková Císařová (2023b).

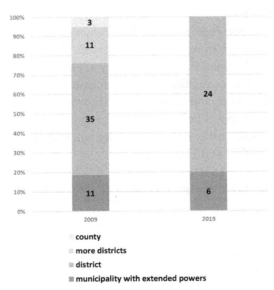

Figure 2: Distribution area
Credit: The Author.

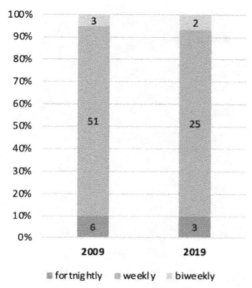

Figure 3: Frequency of publication
Credit: The Author.

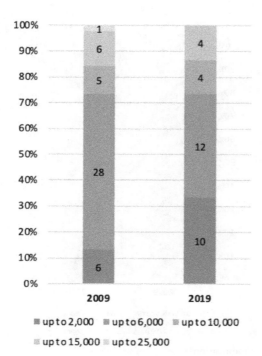

Figure 4: Copies sold per issue
Credit: The Author

110 | THE MARGINS OF JOURNALISM

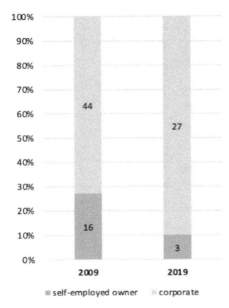

Figure 5: Type of ownership
Credit: The Author

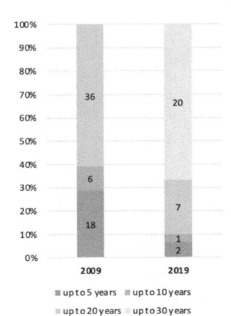

Figure 6: Longevity of publication
Credit: The Author.

Organisational dynamics of the peripheral organisations

In this chapter, I will develop a field theory approach to the organisations as peripheral agents in the journalistic field. My aim is to interconnect the individual and organisational actors, suggest the different types of organisational dynamics and the forms of capital distributed among the peripheral organisations, and analyse the structure of the marginal journalistic field. But this time from a macro-level perspective.

There are two important agents at the micro level of the journalistic field – the individual actors, journalists, manifesting their "personal and professional characteristics", and organisations with their particular "organization dynamics" (Benson & Neveu, 2005, p. 17). Individuals and organisations are both agents in the field, which is a network of relationships, and it is important to consider their dispositions (capital), their positions in the field, and the two-way connections between positions. As Benson and Neveu (2005, p. 4) stress, "fields are arenas of struggle in which individuals and organizations compete, unconsciously and consciously, to valorize those forms of capital which they possess". In short, it is crucial to think *relationally*:

> organizations or individuals who dominate a field are generally those who successfully convert one form into the other, and in so doing, amass both "social capital" of friendship and colleague networks, and "symbolic capital" through which their dominance is legitimated. (Benson & Neveu, 2005, p. 4)

Nevertheless, the key part of the analysis is to develop an understanding of the margins of journalism at macro level. As Benson and Neveu point out, it is here that the main difference between the field theory and the organisational approach is apparent:

> in its more systematic attempt to incorporate empirical data on individual journalists, newsbeats, and media organizations into progressively larger systems of power. (...) "field" opens up a new unit of analysis for media research: the entire universe of journalists and media organizations acting and reacting in relation to one another. (2005, p. 11)

The key elements of organisational dynamics are the different forms of capital, internal functioning, external relations, and historical trajectory. I understand *organisational dynamics* at the *micro level of individual organisations*: as "influences arising from characteristics of journalists as individuals (social and educational background) and as a corporate group defending (and struggling to define) a professional identity" (Benson & Neveu, 2005, pp. 11–12) – habituses, practices, doxa, forms of capital[5] (Bourdieu, 2005), and hierarchy (Örnebring et al., 2016); as journalists' relationships to the organisation (Goyanes & Rodríguez-Gómez, 2021); as competition and distinctions among journalists – the relational construction of journalistic identity (Lamour, 2019); and as organisational path dependency.

Concurrently, I understand organisational dynamics at the *macro level of interorganisational field*: as the competition/cooperation of organisations; as "changes in the relative prestige of news organizations" (Benson & Neveu, 2005, pp. 11–12); as "both the differing organizational cultures and the distinct past trajectories of the staffs and their publications" (Erzikova & Lowrey, 2017, p. 920); and as boundaries and hierarchies (Bourdieu, 1995).

The capitals that agents possess, and their related practices, are similarly important for organisational agents (see Table 3) as for the individual agents (see Table 1). They are based on the same essence of the four capitals (social, cultural, economic, and symbolic) and practices, but take on specific forms based on organisational dynamics. To depict them more specifically, an organisation's *social capital* reflects "a durable network of more or less institutionalized relationships of mutual acquaintances and recognition" (Benson & Neveu, 2005, p. 21), especially in terms of relations of individual actors inside the organisation and the organisation's relations with other actors in the peripheral journalistic sub-field (e.g. other individuals: readers, sources; other organisations: newspapers, organisations ensuring production, advertisers). Considering an organisation's *cultural capital* entails focusing both on the cultural capital of the individual actors inside the organisation and on the organisation's institutional rules and norms, knowledge, tradition of existence and related experiences and built brand. It can be converted

Table 3: Capitals on the organisational level

Capital	Definition
Social capital	Relations of individual actors inside the organisation, organisation's relations with other actors in the field
Cultural capital	Cultural capital of the individual actors inside the organisation, organisation's institutional rules and norms, knowledge, tradition of existence and related experiences and built brand
Economic capital	Property size, numbers of circulation, subscription, advertising revenue and the overall financial condition of the organisation
Symbolic capital	Considered legitimate and/or prestigious, recognition from a group

Credit: The Author, based on definitions above.

to *economic capital*, property size, numbers of circulation, subscription, advertising revenue and the overall financial condition of the organisation. Therefore, "any of these forms of capital might be converted to symbolic capital when it is deemed legitimate and/or prestigious in a certain field" (Erzikova & Lowrey, 2017, pp. 922–923); and manifested "through the recognition, institutionalized or not, that [one] receive[s] from a group" (Benson & Neveu, 2005, p. 21).

One can also consider an organisation's *practices*, what is the work it performs, how it approaches key dilemmas, which roles it plays in the field, the volume and composition of capital and dynamics of the specific field in which the social practice takes place (Hovden, 2008).

Newspapers

To understand a *newspaper* as an organisation is to connect the micro and macro levels of its operations. As Deuze and Witschge (2018, p. 173) point out, the studies on organisations are changing from the original emphasis on the organisation as "macro-structural entity", to the more recent view of the organisation with both micro and macro level structures. Scholars working in this direction stress the need to more fully comprehend the spectrum of internal processes related to the organisation: to understand the organisation as a framework for analysing journalistic work, to understand cooperation within the organisation, and capture internal "personal networks" (Deuze & Witschge, 2018, p. 174).

Others regard as important the structures established by entrepreneurs and organisations and their economic functioning (e.g. business models; Jenkins & Nielsen, 2020). And yet others focus on the *newsroom* as a place located or relocated in, or missing from, a particular space, a "material space of journalistic labour" and using technologies while providing a place for relationships (even with readers), cooperation, competition, and creativity (Usher, 2015, 2019). It is also a place of life histories (Wahl-Jorgensen, 2019); affections (Kotišová, 2017) and relationships (e.g. between journalists and managers; Raviola, 2012). Scholars also stress that journalists should not be "blinded" by routine organisational processes which, according to Cottle (2007, p. 10), can be caused by a "focus on 'organizational functionalism' [which] privileges routines and patterned ways of doing newswork over differentiation and divergence". In short, the analysis of a newspaper should encompass all those important elements of organisational dynamics – personal, spatial, temporal, and emotional – which exist, in Deuze and Witschge's (2018) phrase, "beyond journalism", but which I prefer to describe, since they are not new, as *alongside* journalism.

An organisation is a community of people and ideas with its own historical development and memory. Its processes are at the same time based on the individual actors and on the "collectivities that experience and react to sweeping change" (Wahl-Jorgensen, 2019, p. 672). This approach allows us "to see journalists both as individuals who have distinctive and embodied experiences", and "as members of a rapidly changing sociological category". And these actors – individual and organisational – have different dispositions and occupy distinctive positions in the journalistic field, which form their reaction to the change, "their ability to adapt and thrive under challenging circumstances", which means, that some journalists and organisations are "better equipped with material and emotional resources to adapt to processes of 'creative destruction' currently shaking up the industry", "whereas others are structurally positioned to fail" (Wahl-Jorgensen, 2019, pp. 672–673). This ability to respond to a change is also affected by structural conditions and power relations – journalists working for local media face the same challenges and changes as journalists working for leading news organisations, but the latter are in a better position to deal with them.

Journalistic field

To think about an organisation as an agent in the journalistic field is to think about the full spectrum of its relationships with other external processes which emerge from a negotiation of boundaries: organisational collaboration (Hatcher & Thayer, 2017), that is, a shared collectivity "by which reporters engage in cultural discussion and argumentation across news organizations" (Zelizer, 1993, p. 221); organisational authority (Anderson, 2013); organisational dependency on other actors on the periphery; and organisational competition (Jenkins & Nielsen, 2020).

Moreover, the journalistic field in the Czech Republic is unique in its post-transitive nature following the move away from socialism and the adoption of democracy (Surowiec & Štětka, 2019). The transformations of society, politics, and the functioning of the media in the transitive and post-transitive phases have set the basic framework for the functioning of the journalistic field in the Czech context (for more, see Waschková Císařová et al., 2024). This has undoubtedly also had an influence on its periphery. From the perspective of those newspapers situated on the margins of the journalistic field, particularly local newspapers, the rigid character of the journalistic field before 1989 has changed to a field dominated by the national media with the local media regarded as merely peripheral players. Where before 1989 there was a clear and stable niche for local newspapers, since then the systematic acquisition of local newspapers and the concentration of ownership into one publishing chain have marginalised these media further to the margins of the field. This contributed to the disintegration of the media system and the further marginalisation of local newspapers as lone, fragmentary units well-nigh invisible in the larger journalistic field. Subsequently, as chains moved from the local to a national level, they further dislocated the boundaries of the journalistic field (Waschková Císařová, 2017).

The current situation of local media in the Czech context is as follows: newspapers based on the traditional business model are the traditional carriers of local news (Waschková Císařová, 2023b). Apart from them, there is a strong presence of municipality-owned media in all localities (Waschková Císařová, 2015). These are mainly print media, but they also include television; nevertheless, these media can be mostly understood as an organ of political PR for local political representatives (Oživení, 2023). The Czech local journalistic environment is marked by its hesitation in undergoing a digital transition (Waschková Císařová, 2023a), and the almost non-existence of online pure players or hyperlocal media (Harte, 2019). Late into the second decade of this century, there were only a few such media who focused on producing their own news coverage, rather than generating content from other sources (Sýkorová & Waschková Císařová, 2024). In 2019, there were 24 different media organisations[6] in the sub-field I am developing here as the sub-field of local newspapers on the margins.

Other media are operating above the local level[7] in the Czech journalistic field. Setting aside those local media owned by central media chains at the national level, regional news is covered by public service media such as Czech Television and Czech Radio, but their space for such content and the range of topics they cover is limited (Sýkorová & Waschková Císařová, 2024). At the national level, where operations are centralised in the capital, Prague, there are five commercial daily newspapers, two of them which would be categorised as popular tabloids. There are three public service media, operating on radio and television, and the Czech Press Agency. There are also three commercial television channels; and dozens of radio stations, which are networked but lack their own news production.

If we consider only the formal, quantitative coverage of localities, there are no *news deserts* in the Czech Republic (Abernathy, 2018; Lindgren et al., 2019) because publishing chains own local dailies in almost every part of it. However, the centralisation and delocalisation of chains' functioning and content mean that people living on the periphery fail to receive relevant local information (Waschková Císařová, 2016, 2017). As Penelope Abernathy (2018) explicitly defines, a news desert is not about quantity but quality of media coverage, stating that it is "a community (…) with limited access to the sort of credible and comprehensive news and information that feeds democracy at the grassroots level".

The situation of local newspapers in the Czech Republic has been reflected by the *European Federation of Journalists* in their report, which stressed that Czech local media "are in a very difficult position, leaving a big part of the citizens without real independent impartial information on local interests, which has a negative impact on participation in local debates and democracy" (Fact-finding Mission to the Czech Republic, 2019, p. 2). A recent research report focusing on news deserts specifically, and which looks not only at the state of local media in the Czech Republic, but compares results across Europe, shows that the state of Czech local media is one of the worst in Europe – the risk scores for all indicators were either high or very high (Sýkorová & Waschková Císařová, 2024).

From the survey, interview, and participant observation data I have collected in studying local newspapers, it become obvious that the characteristics of an organisation's size reveal certain development trends, albeit only shallow ones at a descriptive level. I therefore take its *success* as the second and more important indicator. These data show that size does not automatically mean success, or a stable position in the journalistic field. To ascertain success, we must focus on the (lack of) specific capitals – social, cultural, economic, and symbolic – which a particular organisation might possess. In respect of these we can speak about three kinds of newspaper organisation: (1) achievers; (2) survivors and (3) leavers.

Based on the reflections of the interviewees themselves and on my observations, I distinguish between different classes of organisation according to the extent and stability of their capital. There were, of course, interviewees who exaggerated the position of their organisation, but in the whole complex of capital reflection there were still visible signs that the actual situation was different and there were recognisable boundaries between the different groups of organisations.

The *achiever-organisations* possess all kinds of capital, and their position is stable, and not just economically. This does not mean that they do not have partial excesses in their history that have weakened their capital, but they were able to overcome these and gain the greatest recognition of other actors in the journalistic field and the local field of power, and therefore acquire the strongest symbolic capital.

In the case of the *survivor-organisations*, occasional excesses became a trend that further destabilised them. At the same time, they resigned from certain things and their passivity further deprived them of capital. Nevertheless, within this group two sub-groups were discernible from the perspective of acquired kinds of capital – one that tends more towards being achievers and the other which moves slowly towards being leavers.

The *leaver-organisations* took the form either of newspapers that have closed or those that are heading for closure, either openly or so far covertly. Two organisations from this group were not aware at the time of the research that they were closing their papers: one of them now publishes online news only, the other has sold its name to a publishing house which transformed it into a freesheet. Unsurprisingly, the middle group of survivors with average results was the most strongly represented with fourteen organisations. Among the achievers were five organisations; among the leavers seven.

Notes

1. Media owned and published by local (village, town) or regional municipalities, paid for by local taxes, in which the local/regional political leadership often uses public money to promote themselves or does not want to let the opposition into the content of the media. For more, see Waschková Císařová (2015).
2. E.g. publishing chains like VLM newspapers (cf. Waschková Císařová, 2020, 2017a).
3. There is one publishing chain, VLM (70 dailies covering almost every district of the Czech Republic) which is not covered by these statistics because its structure is centralised and its content delocalised (for more see Waschková Císařová, 2016).
4. By comparison, the best-selling national daily, tabloid *Blesk*, sold in 2019 183,206 copies per day according to Audit Bureau of Circulations (Audit Bureau of Circulations Czech Republic, 2020).
5. As explained in Chapter 1.
6. There were 30 newsrooms owned by the 24 organisations. Two of them were small-scale chains with 4 newspapers each.
7. Local media operate in the space of districts, regional in regions. There are 14 regions and 76 districts in the Czech Republic (for more, see Sýkorová & Waschková Císařová, 2024).
8. In 2009, only 45 newspapers provided information on the number of sold copies per issue.

References

Abernathy, P. M. (2018). *The expanding news desert*. Hussman School of Journalism and Media: Center for Innovation and Sustainability in Local Media. www.usnewsdeserts.com

Anderson, C. W. (2013). *Rebuilding the news: Metropolitan journalism in the digital age*. Temple University Press.

Audit Bureau of Circulations Czech Republic. (2020). https://www.abccr.cz/en/

Benson, R. (1999). Field theory in comparative context: A new paradigm for media studies. *Theory and Society, 28*(3), 463–498.

Benson, R., & Neveu, E. (Eds.). (2005). *Bourdieu and the journalistic field*. Polity Press.

Bourdieu, P. (1995). *The rules of art. Genesis and structure of the literary field*. Stanford University Press.

Bourdieu, P. (2005). The political field, the social science field, and the journalistic field. In R. Benson, & E. Neveu (Eds.), *Bourdieu and the journalistic field* (pp. 29–47). Polity Press.

Cottle, S. (2007). Ethnography and news production: New(s) developments in the field. *Sociology Compass*, *1*(1), 1–16.
Czech Publishers' Association. (2020). http://www.unievydavatelu.cz/cs/home
Deuze, M., & Witschge, T. (2018). Beyond journalism: Theorizing the transformation of journalism. *Journalism*, *19*(2), 165–181.
Erzikova, E., & Lowrey, W. (2017). Russian regional media: Fragmented community, fragmented online practices. *Digital Journalism*, *5*(7), 919–937.
Fact-Finding Mission to Czech Republic. (2019). Media freedom rapid response. European Federation of Journalists, Syndicate of Journalists of Czech Republic, European Broadcasting Union, Nordic Association of News Publishers, European Centre for Press and Media Freedom. https://europeanjournalists.org/wp-content/uploads/2019/10/Czech-Republic-fact-finding-mission.pdf
Goyanes, M., & Rodríguez-Gómez, E. F. (2021). Presentism in the newsroom: How uncertainty redefines journalists' career expectations. *Journalism*, *22*(1), 52–68.
Harte, D., Howells, R., & Williams, A. (2019). *Hyperlocal journalism. The decline of local newspapers and the rise of online community news*. Routledge.
Hatcher, J. A., & Thayer, D. (2017). Assessing collaboration in one media ecosystem. *Journalism Practice*, *11*(10), 1283–1301.
Hovden, J. F. (2008). Profane and sacred. *A study of the Norwegian journalistic field* [Unpublished doctoral dissertation]. University of Bergen. https://bora.uib.no/bora-xmlui/bitstream/handle/1956/2724/Jan%20Fredrik%20Hovden.pdf?sequence=1
Jenkins, J., & Nielsen, R. K. (2020). Preservation and evolution: Local newspapers as ambidextrous organizations. *Journalism*, *21*(4), 472–488.
Kotišová, J. (2017). Cynicism ex machina: The emotionality of reporting the "refugee crisis" and Paris terrorist attacks in Czech Television. *European Journal of Communication*, *32*(3), 242–256.
Lamour, C. (2019). The legitimate peripheral position of a central medium: Revealing the margins of popular journalism. *Journalism Studies*, *20*(8), 1167–1183.
Lindgren, A., Jolly, B., Sabatini, C., & Wong, C. (2019). *Good news, bad news. A snapshot of conditions at small-market newspapers in Canada*. Local News Research Project, National NewsMedia Council. https://portal.journalism.ryerson.ca/goodnewsbadnews/wp-content/uploads/sites/17/2019/04/GoodNewsBadNews.pdf
Lokálník – Local media. Database of local newspapers in the Czech Republic. lokalnik.cz / localmedia.cz.
Menšík, J., & Prchal, L. (2017, December 17). Kouřimská radnice zakázala důchodkyni psát do obecních novin. Za vlastní peníze začala vydávat své. *Aktualne.cz*. https://zpravy.aktualne.cz/domaci/radnice-kourimi-zakazala-zvedave-duchodkyni-psat-do-obecnich/r~7cf37d3ae1a811e7af7dac1f6b220ee8?redirected=1513606589
Oživení. (2023). *Krize lokální žurnalistiky v zemích V4 a specifická role radničních zpravodajů* [*The crisis of local journalism in V4 countries and the specific role of municipal newspapers*]. https://oziveni.cz/wp-content/uploads/2023/02/Policy-paper_Oziveni_CZ.pdf

Örnebring, H., Lindell, J., Clerwall, C., & Karlsson, M. (2016). Dimensions of journalistic workplace autonomy: A five-nation comparison. *Javnost/The Public, 23*(3), 307–326.

Raviola, E. (2012). Exploring organizational framings: Journalism and business management in newspaper organizations. *Information, Communication & Society, 15*(6), 932–958.

Surowiec, P., & Štětka, V. (2019). Introduction: Media and illiberal democracy in Central and Eastern Europe. *East European Politics, 36*(1), 1–8.

Sýkorová, L., & Waschková Císařová, L. (2024). Czech Republic. In S. Verza, T. Blagojev, D. Borges, J. Kermer, M. Trevisan, & U. Reviglio (Eds.), *Uncovering news deserts in Europe. Risks and opportunities for local and community media in the EU. Research Project Report* (pp. 41–47). European University Institute. https://cmpf.eui.eu/wp-content/uploads/2024/02/CMPF_Uncovering-news-deserts-in-Europe_LM4D-final-report.pdf

Usher, N. (2015). Newsroom moves and the newspaper crisis evaluated: Space, place, and cultural meaning. *Media, Culture & Society, 37*(7), 1005–1021.

Usher, N. (2019). Putting "place" in the center of journalism research: A way forward to understand challenges to trust and knowledge in news. *Journalism & Communication Monographs, 21*(2), 84–146.

Wahl-Jorgensen, K. (2019). Challenging presentism in journalism studies: An emotional life history approach to understanding the lived experience of journalists. *Journalism, 20*(5), 670–678.

Waschková Císařová, L. (2015). Comparing Czech and Slovak council newspapers' policy and regulation development. *Media and Communication, 3*(4), 62–75.

Waschková Císařová, L. (2016). Czech local press content: When more is actually less. *Communication Today, 7*(1), 104–117.

Waschková Císařová, L. (2017). Should we consider local newspaper chains local media? Development of the local press chain in the Czech Republic. *Mediální studia, 11*(2), 112–128.

Waschková Císařová, L. (2020). Local media owners as saviours in the Czech Republic: They save money, not journalism. In A. Gulyas & D. Baines (Eds.), *The Routledge companion to local media and journalism* (pp. 214–225). Routledge.

Waschková Císařová, L. (2023a). We were innovators, but we gave up: The muted digital transition of local newspapers. *Digital Journalism, 10*(3), 1–18.

Waschková Císařová, L. (2023b). Backed into a corner: Structural changes that lead to local news deserts. *Media and Communication, 11*(3), 1–9.

Waschková Císařová, L., Jansová, I., & Motal, J. (2024). Delayed reflections: Media and journalism data deserts in the post-socialist Czech Republic. *Media and Communication, 12*, 1–14.

Zelizer, B. (1993). Journalists as interpretive communities. *Critical Studies in Media Communication, 10*(3), 219–237.

CHAPTER 5

Disposition and position of a newspaper on the margins

This chapter builds on the earlier focus upon individual agents in the journalistic field both logically and inductively. It is similarly based on the self-understanding and self-definition of my communication partners and considers not only individual but organisational actors on the margins of the field. The stories will now focus much more on the interplay of the individual and organisational agents but still adopt a bottom-up approach.

My aim is to focus on *organisational dynamics* both at the micro level of individual organisations and at the macro, inter-organisational level. To keep the same approach and format, I will begin with typical stories of three particular organisations based on the success indicators, their relative possession of the specific capitals – social, cultural, economic and symbolic. Moreover, based on a consideration of these forms of capital, I will speak about three types of newspaper organisations: *achievers*, *survivors*, and *leavers*. To capture the interplay between individual agents, the stories are told from the observer's perspective and subsequently supplemented by the views of my interviewees.

Disposition and position of a successful newspaper on the margins

Story of an organisation: The Achiever

To be an achiever doesn't automatically bring happiness. When an entrepreneur builds a stable position after almost thirty years in business and beats all the competition and when, in his own words, the position of his district weekly "has never been better", it looks from the outside as if the organisation has found a sustainable business model for a local newspaper. It seems like an example to be followed. Nevertheless, a deeper insight into its organisational dynamics reveals that at both the intra- and inter-organisational levels it has achieved some things that can be emulated – but others to avoid.

At the level of individual agents and their relationships, it is as if everyone is telling a different story. The journalist-entrepreneur was used to having colleagues-friends he could count on in previous newsrooms. They were a group of old friends with mutual trust and clearly distinguished roles. Moreover, when they chose outside collaborators, they turned primarily to those they knew were of like minds. They formed a team of colleagues with similar capitals, goals, and enthusiasm, which further strengthened their relationship to the organisation. "I just wanted to be a journalist, but one of us had to be a manager and it was OK for me to do it, none of my colleagues were keen to do it. I ended up being an entrepreneur and director." On the other hand, the owner still remembers the wrongs done to him by his journalist subordinates: "Sometimes I was surprised at how much the journalists hated us as their bosses." This is absent from the present newspaper: he lost a whole network of contemporaries with similar knowledge, experience, and approach to work. Aged nearly sixty, he feels old and considers his priorities differently. "I have a colleague responsible for the economic and administrative functioning of the organisation. I could pass it on to her." She is one of the few whom he considers to be his teammates in the organisation, and what they have in common is that they are all colleagues from the past: editor, graphic designer, ad-man. It seems as if he values his other colleagues, most of them about a generation younger, insufficiently. He lacks confidence even in the editor-in-chief and puts himself in the role of an indispensable director of the newspaper's daily operations: he leads meetings, decides on content. As a result, he also feels a loss of relevance and fights burn-out: "I don't want to do the donkey work any more. You caught me while I'm trapped here, but I get my pleasure from elsewhere, I'm just going through the motions."

The journalist-entrepreneur's long-term collaborators have a specific position in the newsroom. It stems partly from their job positions and years of experience, partly from the trust of the owner and their close relationships. These actors in the organisation have an advantageous position and feel satisfied with their job. "I still enjoy the job, I'm affected by it," notes the graphic designer. The owner asks him about his health and holiday plans, in contrast with his distanced relationship with the editor-in-chief and two reporters. What is most apparent is his low opinion of the editor-in-chief, who rapidly adjusts his views to those of his bosses. The boss even snapped at him during an editorial meeting in front of reporters: "Don't argue with me foolishly."

The journalists are surprised and envious when the owner offers to make me coffee. They comment on it: "He's never offered something like that to us." Journalists are used to going for a beer together after the newspaper's weekly deadline. But when I ask if it involves the whole team, the editor-in-chief answers: "No, not the boss. He doesn't drink and that's probably part of the problem." Nevertheless, some journalists in the team talk more about their hobbies than the job itself, and how convenient it is that a weekly publication allows time for them. Or they add: "A weekly is better than a daily, there's no danger of burn-out." Conversely, others enjoy the job: "The job still gives me more than it takes, even though I must commute every day."

Interpersonal relationships are also complicated by the fact that the team meets in the newsroom only at the time of deadline, otherwise they work from home. To sum up, the interplay of individual actors is more combative than cooperative. The owner does his job "with all his heart, with all his soul and with all his abilities", but his distrust of certain subordinates affects the whole organisational dynamic, the journalists' relationship to their work and to the newspaper.

On top of that, individual relationships in the organisation influence practices and responsibilities. With rich experience of various local newspapers and even of a publishing chain, the owner continues to represent the weekly as a successful project: "The newspaper makes a living without any problems and generates a decent profit. We achieved what is historically our highest average sales last year, and this year we are maintaining the same numbers." Interestingly enough, he considers that the main reason for their success is that the "newsroom" is doing the job with all its heart: "You need such an attitude to succeed. This has no direct bearing on quality. There are mistakes in our newspapers, proofreaders fluctuate, reporters have linguistic bad habits. But I believe the readers know that the newsroom wants to give them as much truthful information as it can, especially the news that some people want to hide. And they especially appreciate it when we do it with courage and without regard to the possible consequences. I think that's what shocked them all – not only our readers but the advertisers. They've never seen anything like this before. And then there's something I'll keep to myself."

Nevertheless, there are more concrete and less secretive reasons to regard the organisation as an achiever in terms of its practices and operation. For his publishing strategy, the entrepreneur draws on thirty years of experience in the locality. He has decided to focus on the print issues of the weekly rather than on online news or social media: "On the day we publish the new print issue we put only headlines and leads from the front page on the web. We have Facebook, but it is run by ad-people, we don't put journalistic content there. The readers don't complain, they are mainly older."

The everyday production of the journalistic content, despite difficult relationships among colleagues, works smoothly. Routines and hierarchies are clear, the deadline doesn't bring much stress, the journalists reduce stress by mutual teasing and humour. In the end colleagues are grateful to one another for their part of the work. The owner no longer intervenes at the deadline after he checks the main features of the new issue, hence the mood in the team is much more relaxed. This anomaly is reflected by the subsequent planning meeting, which is chaired by the owner. The owner leads the meeting strategically while the editor-in-chief has an overview of specific topics, but the discussion shows that the editor-in-chief sometimes lacks basic local knowledge or research for a topic. This creates an atmosphere in which reporters are torn between fear of an authoritarian owner and disgust with an editor-in-chief who lacks authority and who quickly trims his opinions according to those of the owner. It visibly affects reporters and their ability to introduce interesting topics and to be courageous and creative, all of which impacts on the organisation and on the content of the newspaper.

At the macro level of inter-agent dynamics, the declared main partner for the organisation is the reader. Nevertheless, it is more of a declaration, a business attitude, than a real relationship: "We provide special content for our readers, such as a regular supplement for seniors; supplements about air quality. We still have to come up with something new. These supplements are also a specialised advertising space," says the owner. The weekly has a popular character with a colourful title page suggesting that it is a part of the yellow press but with more restrained content inside, thus giving the impression that the weekly is more tabloid than it is. But it clearly works for the target audience of older readers. When a reporter got information from people on the street about an unexplained death, they said: "We expect to read everything about it in your newspaper." The organisation has no information about the readership profile of the weekly. The editor-in-chief considers the people queuing for a fresh issue in front of the newsroom as "a typical sample of readers": nevertheless, he can't define them as other than "seniors". However, some thought about the readership yields clearer answers: "We have to have a newsroom in the city centre for our readers and advertisers. And if it's upstairs, we'll need an elevator," says the owner. It may also be important to maintain the tradition of newsboys selling the weekly on the streets.

In terms of inter-organisational dynamics, there is one indisputable cause of the organisation's success: for years the weekly fought off strong competition, there were several traditional local newspapers but only this weekly survived. The competition made it stronger while the space left by its defunct rivals was free to fill. With a dwindling *number of local newspapers, one would expect the owners to think about cooperation, but the owner of an achieving weekly sees no point in that. From the position of a successful operator, he is willing to deal only with similarly successful actors, and curiously, he despises the less successful solo operators among local newspaper entrepreneurs.*

Having analysed the stories of my interviewees and the information from my participatory observations, I will focus on selected elements of the organisational dynamics including the relational construction of internal organisational dynamics – relations within a team; relations between journalists and managers; journalistic professional identity; organisational hierarchy – and the relational construction of the organisation's position in the journalistic field – relations with other players as readers and sources; the competition and cooperation between organisations. Jenkins (2019, pp. 1070–1071) encourages, "assessing the organizational level reveals the systems of power, such as owners, that shape policies, norms, and behaviors, as well as the motivations, often economic, driving them", while at the same time recognising that "the extra-media level is important, as it examines external institutions shaping content, such as advertisers, sources, and other media organizations". Moreover, these levels have an impact on journalists' identities – e.g. conflict between journalistic ideals and commercial interests of the organisation; or journalists' autonomy – how their boundaries are negotiated with other actors, e.g. audience and sources.

The relational construction of internal organisational dynamics

The intra-organisational dynamics of peripheral newspapers are formed by the characteristics and interactions of individuals and their classes. At this level, what determines the success of a particular organisation is varied, but include a close relationship to the job, and members of organisations who achieve this level of success consider this to be key element of the journalistic illusio. They speak not only of the diligence, willingness, and energy of their colleagues, whether superiors or subordinates, but mainly of an indefinable bond to the job: of "having it in their heart".

This corresponds to the view of Reinardy (2011, p. 34), who found "journalists are highly committed to their profession and define such commitment as loyalty, pride in their work, getting facts correct, providing multiple sides of a story and playing the role of governmental watchdog". Similarly, Tracy Callaway Russo (1998, p. 74) adds that "journalists have potential affective attachments both to their profession and its mission of discovering and presenting news to readers, and to the organization that makes that presentation possible". Wahl-Jorgensen (2019, p. 675) finds this as well, arguing journalists can be "emotionally attached to the news organizations they work for, the actual work they do, and the idea of bringing news to the public", but this attachment "varies according to social, economic and material circumstances", and is therefore related to the kinds of capital the organisation possesses. Within my own study, journalist-entrepreneur Marie explains why her colleague, a former journalist now at the age of retirement, still goes to the newsroom if only to make up the proofs: "It's about the smell of the newsroom, she needs it at least once a week, otherwise she misses it."

Surprisingly, my interviewees valued attachment to the profession more than they did their relationships between colleagues. Russo (1998) suggests that journalists experience attachments to profession and organisation, and that journalists also feel a strong attachment to their co-workers. Nevertheless, the community of journalists on the periphery is limited, and so too are these attachments: after a thirty-year history of rivalry some journalists become colleagues only later. An extreme example is the story of one district weekly whose employees decided to destroy it before they moved to a competing local newsroom, doing so at the moment of the deadline. As their former boss Marie recalled, "we were actually in a life-and-death struggle with these people". Nevertheless, some of them are still sitting in her newsroom today: "These people love the job, so maybe they don't care who they work for, they just want to do it and we are the last newspaper here. (…) And I am able to rise above the past," Marie thought. A team of colleagues which sticks together, doesn't change too often and above all, has a common goal and some success in reaching it is more important for journalists than calling a team a family:

> We founded the organisation in the nineties and our first colleague left us twelve years ago … and some people have already retired. I think we're such a cohesive bunch here. (journalist-entrepreneur Ota)

The individuals' identities and mutual relationships are, nevertheless, affected by three things related to the stability of an organisation – a shrinking newsroom; journalist-employees who have become journalist-freelancers; (non)existent newsrooms and working from home. Nevertheless, achiever-organisations still manage to balance these developments (Ekdale et al., 2015). For example, when seeking to make economies, the owners of these organisations understand that changes and redundancies in the journalistic workforce are the last thing they should be considering (manager Josef; journalist-entrepreneur Oto).

> I would have to be a complete moron if I fired a man who goes in the direction, I want him to. He gets money for it, he's happy and I'm happy. (manager Josef)

In these organisations there are still journalists who are employees or who work as internal self-employed persons. It depends on them what form of contract they have (journalist-entrepreneurs Ota, Marie). As Marie adds, in her organisation there is no place for freelancers – "If our journalists want to make money, they have to write. So the newsroom has one or two freelancers."

All the achiever-organisations still have newsrooms. Nevertheless, in some of them journalists work more often from home and meet each other less and less frequently, while other newsrooms remain the centre of the organisation. As Anderson (2011, p. 160) points out, "the newsroom remains a central space in which the work practices, rhetoric, and technologies of journalism intersect to create an occupation".

> I saw that our rivals began their decline by closing their local newsrooms. So I know how important the newsroom is for local people, to know that someone is still sitting there. (journalist-entrepreneur Marie)

> Our newsroom is open from 7.30 to 16.30. Two people are there every day, even if they just sit there and swing their legs. If it closed, our readers and news sources wouldn't visit us next time. (entrepreneur-journalist Artur)

> Having a newsroom is uneconomical, but it's more about the social contact. A group of people actually exists there, they come because of the personal contact. (entrepreneur-journalist Martin)

Marie observes that one of her subordinates left a newsroom because she missed being in a collective. This reflects Örnebring's (2013) observation that group work shows the importance of the professional collective and a shared organisational culture, or what Russo (1998, p. 72) describes in terms of the pressure introduced by the "increasing physical separation of employees from other organizational members and especially from others in their functional reference group". Therefore, the doxa in the achiever-organisations is still based on the cooperation of internal journalists in the newsroom. Since they are the most powerful actors in the sub-field, the newsroom can be considered part of the law of the field, the nomos.

> My journalists haven't even gone for a beer together because they have no time for it. We meet once a year and otherwise we just call each other. I consider it our handicap that I'm not able to provide it for those people. (journalist-entrepreneur Marie)

As I have shown, the organisational dynamic can be constructed as a team or as a hierarchy. Thinking about the organisation hierarchically, journalists have to be accountable to their superiors in a way that acknowledges the journalists' professional autonomy (Waldenström et al., 2019). With regard to the hierarchy of achiever-organisations, all those examined in my sample from the periphery are owned and controlled by journalist-entrepreneurs or entrepreneur-journalists. They all consider it important to lead by example (cf. *managerialism*; Waldenström et al., 2019) and they are also those with a strong bond to the profession (e.g. entrepreneur-journalist Artur). As manager Josef said, the most important motivation is confidence in the project; journalist-entrepreneur Marie stressed confidence in colleagues and pointed out that a strong hierarchy and team spirit were created during hard times:

> When we're doing well, we're open to our subordinates. When we're not doing well, we air the problems adequately, of course, because I can't panic: I want these people to stick it out. But during the hard times, they knew I was paying them even if I didn't take any money myself. And I think that may have held them. (journalist-entrepreneur Marie)

> The point is that people who stay here are loyal to the company, I wouldn't say it's just about the money. I hate lazy people and I hate making excuses, but everybody from the outside has to treat my journalists very respectfully. I'm the only one who can yell at them, they're my people. (manager Josef)

This seemingly ideal version of an organisational hierarchy can be understood with the help of Raviola (2012, p. 952), who observed that relationships between journalists and managers can be characterised in three ways: (1) "they are coexisting, none of them setting a clear cut opposition between the two logics nor delineating a clear trend of supremacy for one or other"; (2) "they represent different 'times' (past, present and future) quite consistently over time"; and (3) "technology plays a role in narratively justifying this representation of different times". As she adds, the first organisational framing is "a sort of foundational myth in newspapers, often sustained as a lost paradise by editors and as a wasteful luxurious original sin of old times by a few managers" and "represents an ever-present legacy from the past"; while the second framing "is associated with current actions taken to remedy the potentially fatal consequences of the original sin and contributing to the survival of newspapers"; and the third "is associated with the future, shaping actions for new projects or processes". It is thus not surprising that these leaders have their doxa: rules and demands they place on their subordinates to structure the organisational hierarchy – from workload, through quality control, to the journalists' safety and responsibility.

> When someone new comes, I tell him you will work on Saturdays, Sundays and evenings and she says: what if I'm sick? I say, no one is sick here, just lie down for three days from Wednesday to Friday, but the newspaper just has to come out. (journalist-entrepreneur Marie)

> I started to control people and I started implementing data measurement – when I don't measure, I don't manage. We have some clear rules for our people. When they oppose us, I reply: you can think what you like, but (…) convince me it's not right what I think, and I'll adjust the decision. (manager Josef)

All the interviewees from the achiever-organisations regard money as the least important element in motivating their teams. As Josef notes: "It's not just about the salaries, I'm not saying that the salary is irrelevant. It's very relevant, the salary has to satisfy me, but it's not just about that." Money is not the reason why people leave these organisations. As journalist-entrepreneur Ota points out, "we like people who seem to be able to take care of themselves and not go somewhere holding their hands out". Paradoxically, the economically uncertain periods united the team. Similarly, Ekdale et al. (2015, p. 383) point out that "a culture of job insecurity has a limiting effect on newsroom change as those who fear their jobs are in danger are unlikely to risk altering well-understood practices, while many others who perceive job security would rather accommodate than initiate change".

> It's interesting that in those difficult times we really pulled together, and when things suddenly relaxed, the relationships were no longer the same. Everyone started to look harder at each other, as is logical when you survive. (journalist-entrepreneur Marie)

The cultural capital of organisations (Rosenlund, 2009) is built on tradition or the organisation's operation; on internal rules and norms (Cornia et al., 2020); on institutional knowledge; and on development and learning (Erzikova & Lowrey, 2017). In the case of an organisation on the journalistic periphery, the tradition (Bourdieu, 1995) is mainly formed from the duration of its existence and the maintenance of its brand (Ali et al., 2020). The brand encompasses the cultural capital of an organisation, and its ability to convert this to economic capital, thus raising its symbolic capital (Erzikova & Lowrey, 2017). The span of existence isn't just a matter of longevity (Smethers et al., 2007), but the volume of cultural capital possessed by the organisation and its representatives. Most of the achiever-organisations have almost thirty years' history:

> The weekly was founded in the 1990s and witnesses remember how newsboys sold it here. It's a hegemon, it was here, it is here now, and it will be in the future. The salesperson at the newsagent doesn't even ask what newspaper you want on the day the newspaper is published, just hands you this. (journalist Leo)

Nevertheless, the organisation's longevity is also associated with the cultural capital of its owner in the locality and its important links are more than merely temporal, as can be seen in two instances. In the first instance two organisations were founded in 2001, when there was a significant concentration of the ownership of local newspapers. They thus entered a monopolised market and faced strong competition in the form of a chain of local newspapers (Waschková Císařová, 2013). One of the reasons these new organisations were able to assert themselves was that the owners were already experienced and well-known entrepreneurs and publishers of local newspapers. Hence their cultural and social capital counted for more than their organisations' longevity and forged their traditions differently. As Bourdieu (1995, p. 243) illustrates, "the entrance fee to be paid by any new entrant is none other than the mastery of the set of achievements which underly the current problematic".

The second instance is even more striking. It relates to a weekly which is less than five years old but can be considered an achiever. The editor-in-chief of a local weekly was forced to resign after the intervention of local politicians. The weekly had more than twenty years of history and followed a local newspaper with an even longer tradition. The politicians wanted to get rid of the editor-in-chief and also changed the weekly to a monthly. Their intervention was a big cause and provoked strong civic resistance, so the former editor-in-chief decided to act: she not only left but started her own newspaper which immediately eclipsed the former weekly.

> We just took over the weekly cycle without a break, and we had a week in which to do it. If we'd started later, it might not have worked. People were used to getting their weekly and this habit was the reason we succeeded. (journalist Marta)

According to my interviewees from achiever-organisations, brand maintenance, including the newspaper's name, layout, colour, or content direction, is part of an organisation's tradition. They themselves often deprecate some of these elements as anachronistic but show their understanding of the importance of brand building and immutability. This can be at the same time understood as a form of *nostalgia*. Jenkins and Nielsen (2020b, pp. 484–485) have pointed out that journalists' "interest in preserving what has traditionally distinguished their brands – historical presence, professional values, and reader trust". Nikki Usher (2010, p. 914) adds, that "nostalgia operates to create vivid associations with a past that envisioned a world of legacy journalism as 'work that had meaning'". Nevertheless, nostalgia can at the same time prevent organisations from further development, from innovation: "nostalgia also masks reality" and it can mean that journalists are "failing to consider what it means to be professional journalists during this transitional time and are instead mourning the past". They sustain themselves "through conversation about traditional values and conceptions of identity of traditional newsrooms rather than being future-oriented" (Usher, 2010, pp. 914, 924).

> The format was then created according to the printing house, so we stuck to it. The brand doesn't change. And the newspaper has the same colour of header to this day because we invented it then (manager Josef)

> We also considered whether to completely reduce the format, but we said that we wouldn't risk it because people are used to it. Same thing, we're black and white, we could just send it to a colour printing house, too. But we said no, we're going to stay in our conservative format, and advertisers don't mind as long as we're actually conservative and still doing the same things. (journalist-entrepreneur Ota)

Similarly, the organisations' representatives understand that newspapers have a high profile in the place where they are published (Bowd, 2014) – from the visible newsroom in a local town (journalist Leo), through billboards and signs with a newspaper's brand (entrepreneur-journalist Artur), to catchy slogans used for self-promotion (journalist-entrepreneur Ota; entrepreneur-journalist Artur).

A newspaper's rules and norms, reflected not only in ethical and professional expectations but in choice of content, are part of the organisation's cultural capital and the actors' doxa. As Katie Artemas et al. (2018, p. 1004) acknowledge, "institutional norms play a significant role in shaping practices and symbol systems; just as institutionalized practices and symbol systems influence norms". To have a clear mission, unequivocal internal barriers and be consistent about what and how one wants to communicate with readers is part of the institutional knowledge. However, these rules and principles are often just doxic, unconscious assumptions, a "set of professional beliefs which tend to appear as evident, natural and self-explaining norms of journalistic practice" (Schultz, 2007, p. 194). Hence to the question, what are the internal rules of the newsroom?, only one of my interviewees from the achiever-organisations replied that they had their own code of ethics.

> We have our own code of ethics, everyone receives it with the contract: they sign it as a part of the contract. I probably haven't published it, I created it from the ethical codes of the big media. We specify in the code that our people must not work for anyone who competes with us. (…) They can do PR for anybody if it doesn't compete with us. (…) Last May, I fired a journalist who absolutely refused to accept that we had any rules here … he made his own policy, so I terminated his contract with immediate effect. (…) I want my colleagues to be outside politics. (journalist-entrepreneur Marie)

Marie adds that she could see how their rules and independence made them competitive: "We were never attached to any interest groups, which the other weekly newspapers were (…). There were people working who had sympathies, antipathies, but we always tried to be above it. Our newspapers sold very well; we could afford the impartiality."

Other interviewees referred to implicit organisational norms and rules rather generally and vaguely, without having an internal codification of them. As journalist-entrepreneur Ota summarises: "Well, I guess, we kind of understand each other here." It is particularly interesting when we consider the overall law of the journalistic field, the nomos, from the point of view of the most successful, therefore the most powerful, organisational agents in the field.

It is not uncommon for other journalists to be involved both in their newspaper and in local politics, including at the same time. This is unacceptable from a normative point of view of an independent press, nevertheless it is a visible part of the nomos of the Czech peripheral journalistic organisations. Bourdieu (1996, pp. 76–77) stresses both the autonomy of journalists and the distance between them and other actors, for example, politicians, "it will be greater or lesser, more or less difficult to cross, and more or less unacceptable from the point of view of democratic principles". Roman Hájek et al. (2015, p. 47) add that these patterns of behaviour were acceptable in the 1990s, but no longer: "a friendship between journalists and politicians is currently considered a potential threat to mutual trust". Jenkins (2019, pp. 1071, 1083) explains the situation of some local journalists, who are members of "more than one interpretive community [which] may also create contradictions, such as when journalists must balance a geographic loyalty with a dedication to professionalism". They must then determine "when to privilege one identity over another, as well as [considering] the needs of the company".

> I entered politics to solve a political problem here, and we succeeded. But then I didn't want to be in politics any more. (journalist Marta)

> A colleague is now on the city council, I was even in the municipal government until I found out that it was not possible. The current deputy mayor … is our former colleague and a member of my family. So everyone is aware of it. (…) But while we were here on the newspaper, we were not party members, we were always independent candidates and somewhere at the bottom of the list of candidates, but since the people knew us from the newspaper, we always got the most votes. (journalist-entrepreneur Ota)

Some of the interviewees seem to have abandoned all rules, and they are the ones whose newspapers tend to be tabloids or pseudo-tabloids. In fact, they tended to focus on the organisation's position of power.

> It is not a surprise that everyone here in the locality is connected to everyone else. (entrepreneur-journalist Artur)

> The newspaper has served for years as a propaganda tool of the town hall coalition. When the politicians needed to get rid of someone, they did it with the help of the

newspaper. A second group of politicians set up a rival weekly, which was a defence against it, so they kept each other in check. The two wings of the same political party, who did not like each other, each had their own newspapers, and those newspapers served as a tool in the internal party struggle (...). They also had a problem with racist articles, which were addressed a lot ... The mayor has his editorial in the newspaper. (journalist Leo)

When creating the newspaper's content, interviewees mentioned the set of doxic principles they seek to apply in the long term. As journalist-entrepreneur Ota points out, for the content of a successful newspaper, it is important to be both conservative and innovative, or in short active: "Here and there we introduce a new section, then we end it and come up with another one. But the structure of the newspaper remains the same, people already know what's on the front page, the second page, the third page ..."

Thinking about key topics, interviewees mention the need to be "interesting, lively, a bit controversial, to come at the problem from various angles, to pick catchy and investigative topics" (journalist-entrepreneur Ota); "we have always believed that we should also write about the countryside. Newspapers must be for everyone, and everyone must have space here" (journalist-entrepreneur Marie); or "you can always read there something about what is happening in the city" (journalist Leo). Manager Josef sees it in more detail: "There were very popular firefighting competitions and we started to cover them all. We were the first local medium to start paying attention to the firefighters, it was an amazing journalistic coup. And it became a phenomenon, everyone started imitating us."

Journalist-entrepreneur Marie adds three more rules understandable as part of the journalistic doxa, which are related to content production: journalists should keep a distance; journalists shouldn't be exalted above the readers; and journalists should get out into the field. This aligns with findings from Kristy Hess (2013), Liesbeth Hermans et al. (2014), and Kathryn Bowd (2011), who position similar rules as boundaries for the field.

> I'm always pleased when a journalist is not from the town that she's covering, because the local journalist doesn't want to deal with problems in the place she lives. (...) I want journalists to be like normal people so that they don't feel like part of an elite, which happened here in the 1990s when they began to think they ranked alongside the mayor. That's why I force them to deal with small, village topics, because I know that's what people want to read, and I also want them to be close to ordinary people. (...) [*How do you force journalists to report from the field not a desk?*] And where else should they be? We have readers because we are out in the field. (journalist-entrepreneur Marie)

As I mentioned earlier, an important part of an organisation's cultural capital is its traditions and capacity for further development and learning. In journalistic organisations, this mainly concerns technological innovation and in newspapers it means the *digital transition* (Waschková Císařová, 2023a). Entrepreneurs brag about how trendy they were in the 1990s, calling themselves innovators or pioneers: "we were the first of the small newspapers to send newspapers by wire" (entrepreneur-journalist Artur); "in 1992 we were so advanced that we had a computer and I think the programme was called Ventura ... it was completely unique" (journalist-entrepreneur Marie). They remember these times as "mythical golden ages" (Nielsen & Levy, 2010, p. 138); or "the good old days" (Andersson & Wiik, 2013, p. 709).

Nevertheless, even achiever-organisations among local newspapers struggle to see themselves as innovators any longer. Instead, they highlight the general decline of print newspapers overall. As entrepreneur-journalist Artur puts it: "Paper newspapers are no longer the force they once were." But when the trend was current in the Czech Republic around 2008, they were enthusiastic about the digital transformation of their newspapers. Most of them later resigned during the digital transition because they lacked the time and expertise to find an economically sustainable way of producing local news online. During and after the economic crisis most of the achiever-organisations were also unable to get money either from online readers or online advertising, so they began to understand online news as something that print pays for. As the newspaper industry generally weakened, the achiever-organisations, with few exceptions, preferred to end their online presence rather than endanger the print newspaper.

The findings I've outlined here are similar to those of other scholars, who found in studying similar journalistic actors and organisations that slow-paced digital adaptation, notably the "slow adoption of digital tools"; "tactical missteps" which include "giving away online content for free and the relatively late implementation of online strategies"; proved to be "an obstacle to profitability" (Ali et al., 2018, pp. 1, 2). This behaviour can be seen as a manifestation of *nostalgia*, a description which, according to Usher (2010, p. 924), can be "used here as an umbrella term for the panoply of feelings that these journalists have about the print industry's shrivelling away". However, as Nielsen and Levy (2010, p. 138) draw attention to, "even in times of otherwise profound change, innovation in most cases seems to happen at the margins of the business of journalism (as it has historically)", therefore "amongst young entrepreneurs, disgruntled professionals, minorities dissatisfied with prevailing norms, alternative media ventures". Erzikova and Lowrey (2017, p. 934) interconnect "stunted innovation in digital journalism at these regional papers" with the low capitals – *cultural* capital: "poor professional education within news organizations and limited understanding by advertisers"; *economic capital*: "weak markets, disinterested owners and local businesses, scarce budgets, shortage of reporters, and minimal investment in analytics tools"; and *symbolic capital*, which "digital online journalism possesses". There is a notable disparity between how the interviewees think about the innovations (illusio), how active they still are, and how much they do, or don't, want to learn (doxa), which also shows different levels of cultural capital.

> We have web pages and we have Facebook, but we're somewhat limiting the web pages in favour of Facebook, because we haven't found a way to charge for the news. (…) We prefer to stick to the printed version as long as we can and we're not looking for a route to the reader on the Internet. (…) Ten years ago, we developed the web … we didn't leave it, but we don't develop anything new on it. (…) We're still unable to make money other than through the sale of the printed newspaper … (journalist-entrepreneur Ota)

> We have a website and we have Facebook. (…) But I believe that what feeds us is the print. (…) So I change the online title page only once, twice a week and our original topics are not online at all. During a weekend I put the most interesting topics on Facebook, so I can see how it spreads and from the analytics what was read the most. (journalist Marta)

Among all my communication partners there is only one organisation which considers its online presence to be an integral part of its economic success, and which therefore understands its development of cultural capital as an opportunity to raise its economic capital (Ali et al., 2018). Nevertheless, the interviewees stress the importance of learning continuously (Lindgren et al., 2019) and being active (Goyanes & Rodríguez-Gómez, 2021). As manager Josef crisply puts it: "We keep learning by trial and error. The mistakes move us forward. (…) All my mistakes were later lessons learned in everything."

> For a long time, we stuck with the newspapers, but as the older readers die off and young people don't tend to read so much, we noticed that we had a decline, compared to ten or fifteen years ago. Nevertheless, we counted up and we're very happy that we've got a bigger number online than we lost in print, but they're a different group. We know that readers of printed newspapers are 40 plus or 35 plus, but in contrast, people have been viewing us online since they were 16, and of course the old ones are not online as much. (journalist-entrepreneur Marie)

> We absorbed the new trends slowly, no one understood them at first. We created our online presence by chance because we expected that online news would be competition for the print titles! (…) No one understood it here, and of course a discussion began about competition between newspapers and the web, and a rule was

formulated: we write news for the newspaper and a week later we put the news on the web. (manager Josef)

One of the key characteristics of the performance of achiever-organisations is economic stability and profitability. Interviewees and communication partners from the participatory observation admit to making a profit, but speak about it rather reluctantly (Abernathy, 2018). As manager Josef says: "We make little profit, but we do make one." Journalist-entrepreneur Ota adds: "We've never run at a loss, so we could say that we're still okay, that we still have it under control." Their attitude is in keeping with the tradition that money and success are not talked about. Some of the journalists have learned from the competitive pressures that they have to keep the reasons for their success to themselves. As journalist Marta points out: "The reason we are in the black is our know-how. Everyone would like to know it … We really just live from advertising and sales."

But as well as the "secret ingredient", there are more pragmatic and banal reasons for their economic success (Cestino & Matthews, 2015). These include simple logic – "I can only spend as much as I have in my pocket, and that applies to the whole newsroom" (manager Josef) – and careful economic judgement before starting a business – "I can count, so it was clear to me that it could make economic sense. Of course, many people wondered about it and questioned whether it would be possible. (…) We simply earned money from advertising and newspaper sales" (entrepreneur-journalist Martin). It was also said by Tibor, that "we were an example of a regional newspaper that 'somehow just survives'. We survived in the 1990s, to this day it is a miracle that we did. When we started, newspapers had to cost half their production costs. Now the situation is incomparably better." The publishing house "makes a living without any problems and generates a decent profit. We achieved what were historically the highest average sales last year, this year we are at the same numbers" (journalist-entrepreneur Tibor).

That the situation is now stable does not mean that these newspapers have never had economic problems. Rather, it means they were able to actively overcome these (Smethers et al., 2017): "There were times when we had to put our own private money into the newspapers. Fortunately, that's no longer the case" (manager Josef); "I fear that our economic stability could again be threatened by the next economic crisis, if the advertising dries up" (journalist-entrepreneur Marie). Or that they will have to sacrifice something: "We used to have a specialist for the culture page, but somehow, we weren't able to meet their financial requirements. That's another problem, as salaries grow in the public sector and everywhere else, here you only get the money you earn: the package isn't limitless" (journalist-entrepreneur Ota). This supports Anderson's (2013, p. 145) thesis that "success seems to be no guarantee of stability in the new media world".

The business model of the achiever-organisations is without exception traditional: it is built on revenue from the sale of newspapers and advertising,

> based on a dual market-place logic whereby content is sold to audiences, audience attention to advertisers, and where a positive feedback loop exists so that large audiences enable higher advertisement rates, which in turn underwrite content production that creates more income from audiences. (Olsen et al., 2020, p. 200)

Maintaining this traditional business model can be driven by the nostalgic and conservative attitude of the journalists: "managers and editors suggested a nostalgia for a time when display advertising and subscriptions sustained their editorial practices, and they value the readers who prefer this format" (Jenkins & Nielsen, 2020b, pp. 484–485). Similarly, Joaquín Cestino and Rachel Matthews (2015, p. 2) mention the problems of newspapers to invent a new business model and "often path dependency has been argued to furnish a plausible theoretical explanation to the locked-in-dominant-business-model in legacy newspapers". Steve Paulussen et al. (2011) add to the discussion different point of views of managers and journalists, how to approach innovation – managers trying to find new sustainable business model and journalists considering potential improvement of quality of their work. In any event, my communication partners cannot imagine another business model for their media. They resemble Jenkins and Nielsen's (2020b, p. 473) interviewees, who "recognize that the traditional business model for local news no longer works (but feel they must preserve it to continue their work)".

> We can only spend what we earn from advertising and selling newspapers. The traditional model still works for us. (journalist-entrepreneur Marie)

> If I raise the price per copy to 25 Czech crowns, I must produce something for which the reader is not sorry to give the money. But I really can't answer, I can't imagine any other revenue for newspapers than from sales and advertising. (manager Josef)

An interesting difference, however, exists in one form of entrepreneurship: a significant group of entrepreneurs in the peripheral press have started their business as self-employed persons, not a firm. Entrepreneur-journalist Martin explains that being self-employed is more advantageous to him than running a company because he has no employees, his only colleague works for him on invoices (Ekdale et al., 2015). "The company would be more convenient if we had employees, it would probably be better, but we don't have sales in the millions here … Though I guarantee the business with all my property." Nevertheless, most owners later switched to a limited liability company, as journalist-entrepreneur Marie explains: "If you incur debts as a self-employed person, no one will protect you from them. If you have a limited liability company, you can just put it into insolvency, which our competitor has done about six times already."

In a world where the traditional business model for media is called into question, the achiever-organisations on the margins have still successfully built on that framework. For their being more stable in terms of economic capital than similar organisations, one reason can be adduced. Their work is primarily *an activity*, not only in terms of economic self-sufficiency and entrepreneurial initiative, but which on a broader level requires perseverance and courage (Ekdale et al., 2015). An organisation's economic self-sufficiency can be understood as the active minimisation of risks arising from external influences and the organisation's external relationships. But at the same time, it supports the individualisation of an organisation and disrupts the interdependence of the actors on the margins and therefore their social capital (Beck & Beck-Gernsheim, 2001). As journalist-entrepreneur Marie notes about her newspapers' improving finances: "It also works because we have our own means of distribution, and it simply wouldn't be possible without it. If I had to pay thirty-nine per cent of an issue to an external distributor and still wait sixty days for them to send us our money, it would destroy us. We still have to deal with the Czech Post, it's just crazy."

An extreme case of economic efficiency is found in one newspaper which, from its beginnings, was almost entirely self-sufficient. As journalist-entrepreneur Ota points out, it owns the building in which it is located – "We bought the house in the 1990s, so we pay rent to no one. No one wants 80 thousand Czech crowns from us every month, which would then mean that we had no money for wages." They also own their own printing apparatus – "We have a printing machine in the house, so we can print our newspaper along with external orders." – and they distribute the newspaper themselves. As the owner adds:

> When we had to pay for services it was a lot of money and, moreover, we were always a customer. So although a regular one, matters were outside our control. It happened that the newspaper came out a bit later or the distributor paid us late. But here the newspaper comes first, we come first. And we have it under control here. ... At the time we bought it we probably didn't even realise what we were going to gain. We found out that many of the other printing offices belonged to a chain, and many of the local newspapers were fooled. (journalist-entrepreneur Ota)

As well as self-sufficiency, an important aspect of an organisation's economic health is its entrepreneurial initiatives. It is visibly reflected in the efforts of companies not to solve economic problems by cutting their operations, but by developing other assets (Ali et al., 2020). As journalist-entrepreneur Ota explains, "rather than cut the budget, we always did something extra" – for example, organising local cultural and sporting events (journalist-entrepreneur Marie; manager Josef; journalist-entrepreneur Ota); producing and publishing thematic advertising supplements (journalist Marta; journalist-entrepreneur Tibor); producing and publishing locally oriented non-fiction and fiction books (journalist Marta; journalist-entrepreneur Ota); organising the rental and sale of local real estate (entrepreneur-journalist Artur).

At the same time these side initiatives of media organisations on the margins manifest an intention to gain all types of capital within the locality. In the eyes of manager Josef, they nevertheless have their limits: "I can do business in other things but not the publishing house. If I involve the publishing house in something else, it could become vulnerable, it would be under outside influences."

The relational construction of the organisation's position in the journalistic field

The inter-organisational dynamics among the actors on the periphery, based on the organisation's position in the journalistic field, consists of relations with other actors, the competition and cooperation between them. Being part of the class of achiever-organisations means that a newspaper has a specific position in the field based on the possession of its various forms of capital, its power, and therefore it can participate in the formulation of the fundamental law of the field, the nomos (Bourdieu, 1998). In the bigger picture of the journalistic field, there are several actors who play their roles in the field. Generally speaking, they are either individuals (audience members; sources; advertisers; cf. *interlocutors*, Marchetti, 2005) or other organisations (other media; cooperating production organisations) (Bowd, 2014). By reflecting on the position of the other actors, the interviewees staked out the position of their own organisations. The interrelationships reflect the organisations' symbolic capital, which they acquire through recognition by the other actors in the field and from the volume of capital they possess.

My communication partners emphasised that they regard their organisations as unique. Nevertheless, they did not associate power with size, as one might expect: on the contrary some of them believe that the smaller the better. Although most of the publications in question are traditional district weeklies and small chains within an achiever-organisation, the interviewees emphasise the uniqueness and strength of the smallest newspapers, typically serving a non-district town (mostly of five to ten thousand inhabitants) and its immediate surroundings. As journalist-entrepreneur Marie sees it, even the smallest newspaper is special and unique. Moreover, interviewees are able to perceive the capital behind the uniqueness, mostly social as well as economic. The small newspaper is often built on tighter social links with the locality (Hess & Waller, 2016, 2017).

> I think the local was important here, that I was from here and so the people accepted me as the publisher. (…) Moreover, the town used to be the district town and so it suffers from a kind of jealousy of the current district town. It deserves its own local newspaper. (journalist-entrepreneur Marie)

> I think that social capital played a role, because my colleague worked here as a journalist for twenty years, so many of the advertisers and correspondents knew her and they also needed the newspaper to represent the community. (entrepreneur-journalist Martin)

> There is less competition in the smaller towns. (…) And the local entrepreneurs want to advertise in the local newspapers not because they need to but because they want to show that they have the money for it. (manager Josef)

According to my communication partners the relationships with other actors are based on two conflicting motivations – cooperation and competition. Those sections of the public which impinge on the journalistic field, such as audiences, news sources and advertisers, are considered cooperating actors. Mutual relations are based on a pragmatic and realistic conception of what these actors seem like. Unlike most of my communication partners, the interviewees from the achiever-organisations have clearer ideas about who their audience is. They do not confirm the finding that "regional journalists know very little about their readers" (Ewart, 2000, p. 3); but from their knowledge one can see that "the gap between journalism and its audiences is widening" (Hermans et al., 2014, p. 642).

> Once we did a huge survey of our readers at the end of the year and we rewarded them. We found out who they were and what they wanted to read. We did it once. It confirmed what we knew that these were people of thirty-five plus. (…) Well, of course, we all talk about who our reader is, everyone knows that the topics we'll write about flow from this awareness. (journalist-entrepreneur Marie)

> We used to do [surveys of readers] more than we do now. Our audience is 30+ people … now it's older … it has shifted: young people don't read anything, so we now have readers our age and older [which means 45+]. (journalist-entrepreneur Ota)

At the same time, the public is the group without whose support the very existence of newspapers would not be possible. It is therefore clear that the achiever-organisations' relations with this group of actors are mostly positive and stable. As Ragnhild Kristine Olsen et al. (2020, p. 20) stress, what is important is not only the audience's size but its demographic: "A smaller, more engaged audience may be more valuable for advertisers and thus generate more revenue for media organizations than a large, fleeting one." Newspapers gain their recognition (symbolic capital) mostly by selecting the right, locally relevant, topics and fulfilling the preconditions for quality journalistic work, as well as by economic incentives – in other words, when they match the nomos of the field and use their social, cultural, and economic capital.

> People read the newspaper a lot in the villages hereabouts because they don't have anything else and our journalists dedicate themselves to it, they just go round the villages and write up what's going on there. (journalist Leo)

> We have readers because we're there, we're in hockey, we're in football, we're visible in the field. (…) We couldn't break through there for a while, and we got the saving idea that we should do classified ads for free. And so the number of sold copies jumped perhaps one hundred per cent and at that point the newspaper quite simply established itself. (journalist-entrepreneur Marie)

Even if the relationship is disturbed, a cooperation which arises from the symbolic capital of the achiever-organisation eventually prevails.

> Whenever our newspapers got more expensive, the readers always grumbled for a while, they swore terribly, but within a month they always came back to us, they just got used to it. (journalist-entrepreneur Marie)

> The town hall's clerks were forbidden to provide us with information for some time … So we had to deal with everything through the [Freedom of Information Act]. Then the mayor said that the office was paralyzed, which was of course nonsense. I told him, if you didn't forbid them, they would tell us without any problems: they'll tell us anyway, but because they're scared, they want to cover themselves by getting us to ask through legal and official channels. (entrepreneur-journalist Martin)

> We had a problem with the previous town hall representatives, whom we helped into their political grave, so then it became hard. But now, thanks to the opposition winning the election, it's okay here again. We have a good relationship with the police, with the firefighters, with rescuers, with the court … we have gained key partners on our side and our relationships have stood the test of time, so we have no problem with that. (journalist-entrepreneur Ota)

Over the past thirty years, organisations on the margins have faced various types of competition: from similar weekly newspapers, from newspapers owned by pressure groups or politicians, or the municipal press (Hájek & Carpentier, 2015; Waschková Císařová, 2015) and from the concentration of local media into the singly owned chain and a related "cleansing" of the market (Lindgren et al., 2019). Today there is talk of "sandwich pressure", the strongest form of competition from both bottom and top – from the municipal press and the chains of local newspapers. As Bourdieu (1996, pp. 24–25) reminds us there is "an effect typical of the field: you do things for competitors that you think you're doing for consumers". But precisely because of their stable position in the journalistic field, the achiever-organisations don't consider the competition fatal. As manager Josef sums up: "The competitive newspaper people thought they would destroy us. They were shocked at what happened, we really bit into them. And within a year and a half they went under. Because if I have an opponent, I'll stamp him into the ground."

> I don't think [the municipal press] creates competition for us, I think readers perceive it as a kind of mouthpiece whereas we are independent. (journalist-entrepreneur Marie)

> As a competitive weekly I felt we would be inferior. Eventually I bought that competitive publishing company and then put my feet up on the table and smoked a cigar. But then I suddenly found out that I was losing motivation! (entrepreneur-journalist Artur)

> There were some newspapers published here, but always only for a while, the daily chain is published here somehow, but they basically don't do regional activity any more. The municipal press is no competition for us. (journalist-entrepreneur Ota)

Being an achiever means not only becoming more resistant to the competition but experiencing a certain kind of loneliness at the top of the field of peripheral journalism. Newspaper organisations often act as solitaries, but because they are perceived as the strongest, most powerful actors and often approached by other local newspapers for cooperation (Jenkins & Graves, 2019). Recognition by their rivals, and through it a strengthening of their prestige and reputation, are part of the achiever-organisations' symbolic capital (Benson & Neveu, 2005). However, they either do not really cooperate with, or somewhat look down upon, the rival organisations (Hatcher & Thayer, 2017).

> We used to cooperate with [a nearby district weekly] a long time ago, because they were our friends. We had a pretty good relationship with them, but they've already stopped the weekly. (…) Another editor-in-chief quite caught my eye, but it's a long time ago … it's all gone now … Recently we were asking colleagues from [a distant district weekly] various questions, they somehow picked up the story there, so we also promised them a visit, then it didn't happen. (journalist-entrepreneur Ota)

Deuze and Witschge (2018, p. 173) conclude that "media professionals and their audiences are increasingly (expected to be) working together, to converse and co-create. This process accelerates the flow of people, processes, and ideas through the networked enterprise that journalism becomes." In contrast, Hatcher & Thayer (2017, p. 1286) are aware of the problems that may arise from cooperation, when "hesitations with partnerships on behalf of the journalists themselves have also been described as a trust issue". Another reflection of the symbolic capital of organisations was their involvement in the attempt to establish an advertising network consisting only of local newspapers. Achievers were key to such a business (journalist-entrepreneur Ota; manager Josef), but when the whole idea failed, it further deepened their distrust of cooperation. Therefore, cooperation among agents is not part of the nomos.

Nevertheless, there is one specific type of agency which every organisation requires and, in the opinion of my interviewees, with which even achiever-organisations must cooperate. These are the ancillary organisations (e.g. printing offices, distribution firms, newsstands) which are involved in the newspapers' production and publication, and which operate in the same locality as the newspapers themselves. The relationship between them reflects the co-dependency of agents in the peripheral part of journalistic field as well as the importance of the relationship which newspapers on the margins must make with those in the local field of power. But it also shows the fragility of the whole production system on the periphery, something which contributes to the fragility of newspapers' position (Waschková Císařová, 2023b).

When these ancillary organisations disappear from the market, the newspaper will either have to take over all aspects of the production itself (journalist-entrepreneur Ota; journalist-entrepreneur Marie; journalist Marta) or risk dependence on national corporations or chains. Bowd (2009, p. 50) confirms changes in the operation of the peripheral newspapers, e.g. the concentration of printing facilities: "Whereas once most local newspapers had printing presses on site and supplemented their income by taking on outside printing work, now most papers are printed in another town or city", which has "the potential to loosen the ties between newspaper and community of circulation". Nevertheless, some matters, such as selling points or subscription delivery, cannot be resolved by the newspapers' organisations themselves:

> We started years ago with a significantly higher number of sold copies. Since then, twenty-two village stores have closed and no one in the village will stock it. The people would read it but they've nowhere to buy it! (journalist Marta)

> When we started, there were perhaps fifteen hundred newsagents, and because of them we used to start distribution at four o'clock in the morning. It was really a network, four newsagents on each road. We miss that, the sales structure has completely changed. We communicated a lot with those novice businesspeople who opened a

> shop in the village and today the locals are happy that at least the [national grocery chain] has stayed in the village. And this is actually now our main partner. (…) If it weren't for that, I wouldn't know where we would sell the newspaper. And in some places, there are convenience stores owned by Vietnamese. Thanks to this we can cover the countryside. (journalist-entrepreneur Ota)

The general dissatisfaction among the interviewees is with the large national companies, with which the local newspapers don't have sufficient symbolic capital to cooperate. Even the achiever-organisations were not "good enough" to be respected business partners for the big monopolistic companies.

> Distribution through large national companies destroyed one of my newspapers. We couldn't ensure that they met their contractual conditions, and they were late in giving us the money from our newspaper sales. (journalist-entrepreneur Marie)

All the interviewees mentioned the Czech Post, the state postal monopoly, which is the only organisation to distribute the newspaper to subscribers. They speak about feelings of inferiority and of being trapped in this partnership. Such powerful actors, external to the journalistic field, can nevertheless influence it and change its nomos, its fundamental law (Bourdieu, 1995).

> We do everything ourselves except subscriptions, which are unfortunately in the hands of the Czech Post, a terrible partner. It's a monopoly. (…) We tried to find an alternative, but it doesn't exist. So we basically had to nod at the new contract and they raised the price for us again by two crowns per copy. You can appeal on the basis of thirty years' cooperation and how much money we've already brought them, but they don't want to know. (journalist-entrepreneur Ota)

> We only have those subscribers who live somewhere outside the district and are keen not to lose contact, otherwise we don't have subscribers because they have to pay nineteen crowns for a postage stamp. That's more expensive than the newspaper, so it's completely pointless for them. (journalist Marta)

The organisational dynamics of the achiever-organisation is based on the long-term and on a laboriously built *balance* at all levels: thanks to their powerful position, they also set the nomos. Internally, it rests on teamwork, a clear hierarchy, a consistently maintained wall between the editorial and commercial part of the newsroom and formulated journalistic rules and norms. Externally it is built on maintaining relationships with relevant, often similarly peripheral actors and avoiding the influence of monopolistic actors; and on a combination of different forms of capital. Nevertheless, this balance is not given or passively accepted: it must be repeatedly, actively, and tirelessly re-created.

Disposition and position of an average newspaper on the margins

Story of an organisation: The Survivor

When viewed both from outside and inside the local newspaper community, this organisation appears to be a clear achiever. Moreover, if I were to categorise organisations on the margins purely by size, this would be among the strongest. Yet on closer inspection I found clear signs that its success is qualified by a whole set of problems of varying degrees of seriousness, and this places it within the group of survivor-organisations.

My entry into the newsroom for participatory observation coincided with the anticipation of some bad winter weather: it was literally the moment of silence before the storm. And later the storm struck. My relationship with the people in the newsroom developed similarly – from the initial maintenance of a façade, when the journalists suspected me of being an agent of the management, to a deluge of disclosures from both journalists and managers. On my first glance at the intra-organisational dynamics, everything seemed neat and tidy. With its own house it looked self-sufficient: it boasted a stable editorial team of journalists who still meet every day in the newsroom, and a whole team of graphic designers, distributors, and advertising sellers.

Even the second glance revealed more positives than negatives. Journalists spoke about their colleagues in the newsroom as a family, managers reflected that despite problems after the economic crisis, the organisation was now stabilised. "The best part is that we have a good bunch here," said the editor with enthusiasm. She is the kind soul of the company. She not only organises the logistics of the newsroom and arranges newspaper production, but mediates in disputes, makes the newsroom cosy, and sometimes even sings. Nevertheless, she is an authority only in the eyes of her younger colleagues: "They are like my children, I probably got used to smoothing or finishing everything for them. When I'm sick or on vacation, it's awful, they keep writing to me and calling and complaining that I'm not there … The editor-in-chief won't forgive them anything." An older colleague with the reputation of the hardest worker frightens the editor – "I can't even change headlines in his articles." In this way, more subtle elements in the working relationships began to emerge.

Each journalist is in charge of their own pages in the newspaper, whether culture, crime or politics. The editor-in-chief is responsible for the title page and the opinions. "I do the rest, writing fillers, preparing supplements; inventing competitions for readers and adding posts on social media. I really enjoy it," the editor sums up. The journalist who has worked in the newsroom for more than twenty years enjoys the work as well: "I have my section, I have my freedom and I'm loyal too. The job is seventy per cent routine, but the other thirty per cent means you meet interesting people." The editorial team has remained the same for a couple of years. It is complemented, in this case in the roles of proofreaders, by colleagues of retirement age who once worked as journalists in this newsroom.

Nevertheless, a third and most searching look at the intra-organisational dynamics shows that beneath the surface there has been a radical change in the dynamics of the organisation, in respect of two factors: the aftermath of the economic crisis, specifically the decline in advertising revenues and the number of readers; and the traditionally exalted position of the organisation, which had hitherto not been obliged to deal with such problems. Formerly, the money "just went to it". While weaker but in the end more successful organisations were gradually preparing for this change and helped themselves by taking a more proactive approach, this originally achiever-organisation got cold feet and "solved" economic difficulties by destabilising the relationship between the editorial and commercial parts of the organisation. At the top of the hierarchy there are the two co-owners of the newspaper – one the editor-in-chief and one the manager – who have divided the organisation along the wall that stands between its editorial and commercial parts. But as a result of fears for the organisation's survival, the necessary balance between these parts of the organisation has been disturbed.

The consequences seem negligible, but their real impact is explained by the journalists. Changes included an order to keep a precise record of the hours worked between 8 and 16.30: "We have to record all our arrivals at the newsroom and departures from the newsroom. We have to sit here for eight hours, everything is checked"; and decisions about news content are made only from the perspective of advertising: "Advertising determines how pages focus on the smaller towns in our region. We just add texts to the advertisements." The organisation's strategic decisions are not adequately explained to the newsroom: "No arguments are made here; decisions are just handed down."

The manager's strategy of saving money, accumulating functions, and withdrawing behind the wall of "doing things the old way" is in direct conflict with the efforts of journalists to enjoy their work by being creative. The internal conflict is generational – between the (older) owners, who defend themselves against uncertainty by doing things in the old way, and the (younger) journalists who want to follow new trends but lack the mandate to do so. As one of the journalists observes: "The manager has got stuck in the '90s because of being terrified of change, of people coming up with anything new. So everything stays the same, except that no one wants to advertise in the supplements about cars and housing any more. There is a saying here that if this is journalism it could be done by pulling a man off the street. It's always bubbling here, then there's 14 days of tension and then we move on again. What can the manager do to us? If they fire me, the newspaper would collapse round their ears. I'm loyal to the brand, that's why I'm doing it. They own it, but the manager just belittles my efforts."

The situation isn't helped by the fact that the director never goes directly to the newsroom. Decisions are conveyed to the journalists by the editor-in-chief, who, however, does not seem to be on their side, and this erodes his authority in the newsroom. "The editor-in-chief is duped by the manager," says one of the journalists. "The editor-in-chief is a kind person, the director is a mean bastard, and the editor-in-chief retreats," adds another journalist. Nevertheless, the journalists still consider the editor-in-chief to be their last line of defence: "When the editor-in-chief and the manager argue, we are terrified that the editor-in-chief will give up and leave."

The owners themselves – the editor-in-chief and manager – see the situation from their points of view. The manager states pragmatically that if the newspaper doesn't make sufficient money, it won't exist: the editor-in-chief is aware of the problem, but he is between two millstones. The positions of the manager and the owner are fundamentally the same, however. The editor-in-chief being at the same time an owner of the newspapers sits on two chairs. "I have struggled with burn-out and I know that I don't give nearly as much to the job as I used to." Thus, the journalists are denied any delegated responsibility and faced with a prospect of passivity.

This distribution of forces within the organisation is reflected in both jobs and the product itself. The meeting to plan the next issue starts as a professional one: the editor-in-chief leads the meeting and plans the issue, the editor supports him, and the journalists pitch their ideas. But with further meetings, the façade begins to crumble – nobody discusses the topics or participates in the planning but rather passively ticks off the tasks to be performed. The topics are outdated even for the newspaper's publishing span; the smaller towns in the area are ceded to freelancers; advertising considerations dominate the editorial meetings more than is customary; and there is no public evaluation of how well the journalists are doing their job. "We don't work at weekends if we can avoid it, we try to close the issue by Friday," says the editor – with the result that weekend topics can appear in the newspaper almost a week later. "They count the lines of our articles and the editor-in-chief gives points for the articles as a judgement of quality, but they are not openly discussed at the editorial meetings. This judgement affects our remunerations," explains a journalist.

The uncertainty and failures of responsibility are the hardest for the editor, who although she has experience, lacks confidence, and waits for the decision of the editor-in-chief: "I wait for the editor-in-chief who decides about front pages and edits them. And these are the 'sitting, waiting and wasting time' moments that I don't like." Even though the editor-in-chief trusts her and says about her: "What we would do without her!", his corrections of her work crush her: "He always fixes something after me. At first, I sometimes cried, but I got used to it. In the end, I always tell him: it's your newspaper." On the other hand, she receives the manager's criticisms not with humility, but anger: "I'll get too *furious at some point and just quit. If the editor-in-chief is not here for once, the manager immediately starts interfering."*

Intra-organisational relationships also affect inter-organisational dynamics. Although external actors don't see behind the curtain of internal processes, the latter have a negative impact on the organisation's reputation. What appears to its readers and sources is a newspaper which once had the habit of being successful – a sense of self-importance, irreplaceability and therefore superiority. Journalists expect that the readers must love the newspaper because it is about them. However, the reader's point of view is seldom part of the discussions about what items should be covered. Sometimes journalists pretend that they are away from the newsroom when they are visited by a reader or a source they don't care about: "We've already had him everywhere in the newspaper, even on the title page, and he still comes here and now he's bothering us. I can't get rid of him," said one journalist. These people, some of them visibly poor, are labelled "homeless" by the newsroom and their visits, perceived as disagreeable, are handled and rejected mainly by the editor-in-chief.

In what appears to be a pragmatic approach, the organisation does regular surveys of its readers, the last one a year ago. However, when I ask about the results they cannot be found, only a copy of the article which reported them. It contains a finding that the readers would like to move the publishing day in order to keep the content more current, but it never happened. "Don't ask me, it was the manager's decision not to do it," shrugs the editor. This decision, which is probably motivated by relationships with advertisers, acquires an even broader context when it emerges that the problematic topicality of the news is partly the fault of the Czech Post, which distributes the newspaper to subscribers. "We don't speak about it publicly because it's terrible. How can we compete with the dailies?" asks the editor-in-chief.

The organisation's reputation as an achiever encourages other newspapers on the periphery to try to cooperate with it. However, in struggling to deal with its internal tensions and in underestimating the smaller actors, this organisation, while apparently at its peak, is both isolated and trapped in a vicious circle of its own making.

The relational construction of internal organisational dynamics

To immerse oneself in the flow of the organisational dynamics of newspapers is to focus on how a survivor-organisation differs from other agents in the field and why it is not as successful as an achiever-organisation.

Being merely a "survivor" doesn't mean that the individuals in such an organisation do their job without enthusiasm. In difficult times their zeal manifests itself in an *esprit de corps*. "Those were stormy times, yet we stayed. We were a bunch of people who cared," recalls manager Anna. Nevertheless, in these organisations the journalists' interest in their job is seen as rather individualistic.

> The most important thing for me is that they are interested, and they have to enjoy it, they have to want to do it. (...) But not everyone is good for every topic ... in the end you just have to follow their preferences. (journalist-entrepreneur Pavel)

The fact that newsrooms in these organisations are made up of a group of individuals rather than a team is related to a problem which usually bothers newspapers on the periphery: stability. Anderson (2013, p. 162) refers to this as *institutional fragility* and notes that it "can be attributed to the pulverized condition of traditional news institutions". It is a complex progression – from the broader context of the organisation's economic insecurity (Nielsen & Levy, 2010); through staff lay-offs, significantly lower salaries, and a fluctuation in the number of journalists (Ekdale et al., 2015); to a limited number of potential new employees and the training of newcomers which is a secondary burden on the newsroom (Cohen et al., 2019).

> There are two of us in the newsroom, so not many people are left, and we have been here for a long time. But it is true that some young people came in. They didn't like the paycheque, so they looked for something else. (journalist Tom)

> I have people who have been with me for ten years or more. But when newcomers arrive, the pace is murderous for them. When I look at the town hall, the press spokesperson, the press department, they're all my former colleagues (laughs). (...) I've taught so many people that I don't even enjoy it any more (laughs). (journalist Eva)

> There is nowhere to recruit round here, these people have to be trained up. And if we did teach someone, he often ended up somewhere in the big media. (journalist-entrepreneur Karel)

Stability is also related to the position of journalists within the organisation – whether they are employees or freelancers of various types ranging from contractual workers to external contributors paid by an honorarium – and their position determines their security and loyalty. As Ekdale et al. (2015, p. 384) sum up, economic downturn brings challenges which lead to "reduced staff through layoffs and buyouts". "[As] a result, news organizations increasingly rely on freelancers"; "at the same time, the expectations of working journalists have increased. News organizations are trying to do more with less, meaning journalists are asked to work harder and more efficiently to compensate for smaller newsrooms." Other scholars (Cohen et al., 2019, p. 819) confirm that journalists are increasingly "in precarious forms of work such as part-time, contract, and freelance, working for lower wages, and fewer hours per week".

> We thinned out a lot ... a lot. And we switched from employed to self-employed, contractual workers, because of course the newspapers can't feed these people any more. So they started earning extra money elsewhere and now they just lend a hand with the

newspaper. And because they are experienced and know the routine, we can fill the newspaper quickly. (journalist-entrepreneur Lucie)

I'm the only employee here, the others work as self-employed persons on contracts. When the new owner bought us, he wanted everyone to be self-employed. He didn't want any employees, but I miraculously managed to convince him that I wanted to be an employee and the others became self-employed. (journalist David)

We have [freelancers] but we use our employees more. There are many fewer freelancers than in the 1990s. Hard to say why, the money is a big problem, but they probably don't even want to write. (…) Of course we can't pay them the way we did. (manager Anna)

In addition, relations between the individual actors in the newsroom are marked by the fact that in most survivor-organisations, the physical newsroom no longer exists. Usher (2015, p. 1007) stresses that "interior newsroom objects are loaded with symbolic meaning that give cues to journalists about the security, safety, and stability of their jobs". Moreover, newsrooms are sites of the journalists' socialisation (Cornia et al., 2020) and the newsroom is a meeting point between journalists and other actors in the field (Milliken, 2020).

We don't even have our own newsroom any more, we only have a contact point for advertisers. I work from home, I'm not [from the district town] and all my colleagues work from home too. We are such a "virtual" newsroom that we only meet once a year. (journalist David)

We meet three times a year, we call it the reunion, I make snacks and we chat about what's new. It's not a business meeting, it's kind of a family meeting. We are in touch with colleagues, we have transferred everything to the Internet, to emails and phones. (entrepreneur-journalist Dan)

Finding a reporter here is impossible, journalists don't exist. My journalist lives and works in [a town about 60 kilometres distant from the newsroom and in a different region]. He works from home. I send him the tasks and he writes the stories. Today the phone is good enough. (journalist Eva)

The intra-organisational hierarchy of survivor-organisations resembles that of the achiever-organisations owned by journalist-entrepreneurs and entrepreneur-journalists. But there are two visible differences: the entrepreneurs are often "lone wolves" who are the sole occupants of the newsroom (Beck & Beck-Gernsheim, 2001); and among the survivor-organisations are a bigger group of newspapers owned by local businesspersons or politicians (Jenkins, 2019). The journalists who are working in the newsrooms of these engaged entrepreneurs feel alienated from their bosses and try to keep their journalistic autonomy (Örnebring, 2013).

> The strange thing is that the businessman who owns us is not really interested in the newspaper at all, he is glad that it works the way it works and that we don't bother him when we need something. We've got used to him not giving us anything anyway (smile), so we arrange it ourselves. (journalist David)

> [The owner-businessmen] basically let us function independently, but there is a certain economic control (laughs). Newspapers whose owners are journalists are, in my opinion, more stable and better. (manager Anna)

An organisation's cultural capital is based on tradition, norms, knowledge, development, and learning. In the case of survivor-organisations, the tradition which is built on longevity and brand maintenance is somehow in conflict. Newspapers are published for decades, sometimes they even follow the tradition of a previous title. It is often the case that local newspapers "have a brand that's been established over decades in their community" (Ali et al., 2020, p. 464). "To this day readers call us by the name of the previous title," says journalist Eva. Journalist-entrepreneur Filip adds that his weekly still has the previous name on a nameplate next to the new one. Other interviewees confirm the importance of the immutability of the newspaper's name as part of the organisation's brand and tradition (journalist-entrepreneur Ivo; journalist Emil; journalist-entrepreneur Lucie).

Nevertheless, part of brand maintenance is the impression created by individual actors, which is related to the symbolic capital of both the organisation and the individual. As journalist-entrepreneur Pavel points out, "every journalist has to win her own place somehow, someone is recognised, someone else is an absolute jerk". One must also take into account the specifics of a locality where most people know one another: "Once you make a bad name for yourself, they will finish with you," adds journalist Radim.

For survivor-organisations, brand maintenance is not without its problems. These can be understood as a conflict between the individual and the organisational. As Erzikova and Lowrey (2017, p. 922–923), paraphrasing Siapera and Spyridou, point out: "brands or individuals who manage to successfully convert cultural capital – meaning journalistic excellence – into economic capital – meaning good ratings and advertising revenues – tend to increase their symbolic capital – wide peer recognition and high reputation levels – and thus to dominate the field."

> It's scary how visible we are, we have to realise that when we make a mistake, the mistake reaches our readers at lightning speed. (journalist Eva)

> The former owners did not agree among themselves, and we had about a year of crisis management. Of course, we were all constantly aware of it, but I think we all tried not to let it show in the newspaper, and I believe that the reader did not know about it. (manager Anna)

> The reputation of the weekly is crazy because basically we've always investigated everyone, no matter what kind of person they are, so you can imagine in this small district how much they love us. (entrepreneur-journalist Dan)

As with achiever-organisations, internal norms and rules are part of the survivor-organisations' cultural capital, but they are seldom formulated, they are rather part of doxa (Bourdieu, 2005). With exceptions, my interviewees don't consider it a problem for journalists to be politically active. Some claim that there are no explicit rules in the newsroom (journalists Tom; David; journalist-entrepreneur Ivo). As journalist Tom sums up: "I don't know if we'd ever talk about any barriers. It's just ad hoc." Some even consider rules as the opposite of freedom (journalist Eva). Others, after some thought, name several partial rules: "We don't publish anonymous texts or slander – that's our ethical rule" (journalist-entrepreneur Dana); "The borders are in decency, in ethics, in factuality. Journalists must not just invent things and write subjectively. They must collect the facts and put them together and they are responsible for the truth of what they write" (journalist Eva).

In one newsroom, the ethical code is part of the journalist's contract (and similar to those used by some of the achiever-organisations); in another newsroom, the ethical code of the professional journalistic organisation, the Czech Syndicate of Journalists is considered the obligatory internal document. Nevertheless, while in the first newsroom it is a standard requirement not to mix the work of a journalist and a politician, in the second newsroom such mixing still occurs.

> Everyone who writes for us signs a code of ethics, and in some meetings, I hammer the basic principles into their heads – the need to keep a clean conscience, and so on, the importance of the rule of law and suchlike. Sometimes someone just makes a mistake, but it's quite exceptional. (journalist-entrepreneur Karel)

> We adhere to the code of ethics of the Syndicate of Journalists. Everything can be described in terms of specific examples, it's the best and it has already happened that I've said in the newsroom: what do you think about this, give me your opinions, so they told me their opinions and I said, so we'll do it like this. (journalist-entrepreneur Pavel)

Due to the less stable economic condition of the survivor-organisations and the fact that journalists more often work for them as freelancers or contractors, the fact that a journalist will have a parallel job elsewhere is openly tolerated. Scholars consider these forms of work precarious – "such as part-time, contract, and freelance, working for lower wages, and fewer hours per week" (Cohen et al., 2019). Some newsrooms have a rule that journalists can't work for a competing medium (journalist-entrepreneur Pavel; journalist-entrepreneur Karel) but there are no other restrictions: for example, a journalist can at the same time be a company's spokesperson or a PR writer. As journalist-entrepreneur Cyril sums it up: "Everyone has some side jobs, but I don't mind. They make extra money, and they feel that this is a bonus, because it is mostly not tolerated. But I have no problem with it. Plus the more they write, the better."

The same reason – economic circumstances and the limited number of people in the newsroom – leads to the collapse of the wall between the editorial and commercial parts of the newsroom and thus to a breach of its unwritten internal rules, doxa (Bourdieu, 2005). As Artemas et al. (2018, p. 1004) explain, "the norm, articulated as a metaphor of a wall, is embedded in the symbol system or rhetoric of the institution. Institutional norms are a source of institutional stability as they guide individuals and organizations in their thinking, speaking, and doing. However, norms are also subject to contestation and change."

Scholars increasingly view "the walls as less rigid, silos less confining, and collaboration and teamwork as preferred"; and use metaphors such as "a shorter wall, a wall with holes, a line, a blurred line" (Artemas et al., 2018, pp. 1016–1018). It is in line with Alessio Cornia's et al. (2020, p. 173) findings, that "the traditional norm of separation no longer plays the central role that it used to. In their rhetorical and normative discourses, both editors and managers stress the need to adopt what they see as more integrated and efficient organisational solutions." Moreover, they find a new emerging norm, "which we call the norm of integration", "based on combining established editorial values with values such as collaboration, adaptation, and business thinking, and it is already playing an important role in legitimising new practices that are based on frequent exchanges between editorial and the commercial teams".

Journalist-entrepreneur Filip admits that he is at the same time a journalist, entrepreneur, and advertising worker: "Basically, I take care of everything. Well, of course it's a problem, it's not the way it should be. It's also not okay that the director and editor-in-chief are one, but otherwise it can't be done. I don't see any other solution in the reality of the regional medium." Scholars point out, that these changes in professional norms "are presented as being necessary to survive in an increasingly challenging media environment", showing "that journalists are now expected to develop new skills (e.g. business thinking), to change their working practices (e.g. collaborating with marketing professionals to promote their stories), and to fulfil new roles (e.g. that of subscription sellers)" (Cornia et al., 2020, p. 186).

In a similarly grey zone is, as in the case of the achiever-organisations, the rule on the (in)activity of journalists in local politics, which reveals it as a part of the nomos of the sub-field (Bourdieu, 1995). The zone extends from advocates of a strict ban on combining these roles, through those who tolerate such a combination, to entrepreneurs who either have experience as local politicians or understand as unavoidable the interconnection of journalism and politics at the local level. Therefore they can be seen as members of more interpretive communities (Jenkins, 2019).

> In my newspaper no politics is allowed if there is no payment. Politicians can buy an advertisement or a PR text if they wish, so long as it doesn't insult anyone. If they pay the money, they can boast as much as they want. (entrepreneur Mirek)

> The editor-in-chief must not be part of politics. Because these writers are not my employees, I make sure that they don't figure in politics at all, or if they do, that they write things that have nothing to do with politics. (journalist-entrepreneur Karel)

> I would really consider [being a journalist in politics] a conflict of interest now. (...) I was in [a political party] for a while, but I was so upset that I left, and I said to myself: never again. (journalist-entrepreneur Dana)

> Those were wild times. Today's standards are different, and an age must always be viewed through contemporary eyes. When I was on a city council, I didn't see it as a conflict of interest, but I perceived it as a conflict of interest when I became the editor-in-chief, because at that moment I was supposed to be the guarantor of the truth and I felt that it was a problem, so I resigned from my political functions. (journalist-entrepreneur Pavel)

But deeper analysis reveals a subliminal difference between the newsrooms of the achiever-organisations and those of the survivor-organisations. In the former, the breach of professional journalistic norms is discussed openly, and solutions are sought: in the latter, the approach to (non)compliance with these standards is rather passive and ad hoc. Or in other words, the less powerful agents just reflect the underlying law of the field, the nomos (Hovden, 2008).

> A fellow journalist is a member of a town council, and it is not a problem. (journalist-entrepreneur Ivo)

> Here we have had, and maybe still have, journalists who serve on the local councils. It's a problem but we just let it go, because forbidding them from going to the council in a tiny village where there is nothing seemed pointless. (journalist-entrepreneur Pavel)

> We don't have any such rules here. When a colleague, a cultural journalist, entered politics and rose high enough, the owner talked to him, and he left. (journalist David)

> We had a rule that no one could be a member of the party, which was enforced until 2009, when my colleague secretly joined [a particular political party]. That was one of the reasons he left. (journalist-entrepreneur Cyril)

In the case of survivor-organisations which are owned by politicians or explicitly collaborate with a local municipality, the connections with local politics are more common. These can be seen as a potential breach of a professional journalistic autonomy, which is understood to be "the degree of self-governance within the profession, and the extent to which the profession is independent of other societal institutions" (Örnebring, 2013, p. 39). But at the same time, it can just reflect the specifics of relationships with the political field incorporated in the nomos of the peripheral journalistic sub-field.

> Yes, our owner is very active in local as well as national politics. Some responded by not liking it because for them he was controversial, but others didn't care. (journalist Radim)

> The previous owner probably bought the newspaper to gain political influence, but then it somehow came to an end and that was probably the reason why he got rid of it. (journalist-entrepreneur Filip)

> We have contracts with the town for publicity. They order advertising and it's more convenient for us because they contract to pay a certain amount and then they choose what they need. Of course, the deal is that I won't throw dirt at them. [*Given its history, do readers perceive you as an independent newspaper?*] You see, I don't even think the question arises because there are no independent newspapers today. You can't be independent when companies give you money, when the municipality gives you money. (journalist-entrepreneur Lucie)

Regarding the product, the newspaper's actual content, the rules that influence decision-making on topics and genres have also been conditioned by the economic situation of the survivor-organisations. The lack of operational money is related to the lack of employees, and also to the lack of journalists who would like to embark on more complex and inevitably more demanding topics and genres. These newsrooms, unlike those of the achiever-organisations, are widely resigned to their inability to do investigative topics (Jenkins & Nielsen, 2020b). Although they realise that it is wrong, they take the attitude that there is nothing that can be done about it. This resignation and passivity, which can be understood as a manifestation of actors' illusio, are what most distinguishes this group of journalists from their more successful counterparts (Goyanes & Rodríguez-Gómez, 2021).

> We've got a little bit tamer. (laughter). (…) Well, I'm not completely reconciled to that … (journalist Tom)

> We don't have the strength to do any investigative things, I don't even think we're here for it. When someone calls me and wants to do something like that, I just refer them to Czech Television or to someone who has the staff for it. (journalist-entrepreneur Filip)

> We did investigative journalism for a long time when there were more of us, but now I'm basically alone on it. (…) When we did investigative articles, it was a bomb, the

> politicians were done, everyone was terribly scared because they were thieving like magpies and suddenly it was all over the newspaper. So people thanked us, but later on, it all came back. [*Can it be seen in the sales of copies?*] When it increases, for example by ten or by twenty issues, it's nothing. Everyone watches American movies and thinks that we're just doing it to sell a thousand copies more (laughs). (entrepreneur-journalist Dan)

> When we wrote such pieces and we were very critical and we had a lot of such cases, we got a lot of other tips. And when we stopped writing the pieces, the tips stopped as well. (journalist-entrepreneur Pavel)

The newspapers of the survivor-organisations are more focused on the standard topics, which according to my interviewees are the most read and receive the biggest feedback: local history (journalist Tom; manager Anna); sport (entrepreneur Mirek; journalist-entrepreneur Filip); obituaries (manager Anna). Nevertheless, some interviewees admit dissatisfaction with the newspaper's content because "the topics don't appear on their own", nevertheless they don't reflect their own passivity. Conversely, Jenkins and Nielsen (2020a, p. 250) report that their respondents-journalists prefer "investigative reporting, in-depth features, and coverage which reflects the identities of their communities, all serving a public-service function"; and to "reconstitute established news values, such as localizing national issues, identifying resolutions to a conflict, highlighting locally prominent sources, covering the unusual or unexpected, and prioritizing human-interest stories".

> It's such a weekly sifting of the leftovers to find the peg we can hang a story on. (journalist Emil)

> I'll tell you bluntly, we put everything in, everything that's happened here, because there is no selection … (entrepreneur-journalist Dan)

> We were hard pressed to cover the whole region, but now that is almost never the case. Everything essential we take from the agency because we can't get it for ourselves, but it's not good. (journalist-entrepreneur Pavel)

Moreover, activities that will attract both readers and advertisers are often interpreted in the newsrooms of survivor-organisations as a step towards sensationalism. Julie Firmstone (2016, p. 4) finds local media "in a difficult position where it is hard to strike a balance between producing news that appeals to their audiences and covering issues that are in the public interest", and her interviewees (local journalists and council communicators) point out that "local news has become increasingly sensational in order to retain the attention of fragmenting audiences". My interviewees similarly tried to justify such a move as consistent with the readers' interest, that may be reminiscent of Bourdieu's criticism: "this is an effect typical of the field: you do things for competitors that you think you're doing for consumers" (Bourdieu, 1996, pp. 24–25).

As my communication partners see it: "The biggest response was when someone shot someone here" (journalist-entrepreneur Filip); "The car crash is ideal, four dead, unfortunately it happened here. It's guaranteed to raise sales" (journalist Tom); "People just like crime news, the most ordinary topics that give you the least work people like the most, and when you publish a bomb and expect it to explode, nothing at all happens" (journalist David). Clyde Bentley (2001, p. 14) regards popular topics as part of the success of local newspapers, "due to the mixture of 'legitimate' news and community gossip that allows readers to fulfil their politically incorrect desire to be 'nosy' in a way that is not only accepted but lauded by society". Journalist-entrepreneur Cyril states, "we are serious, only sometimes we allow ourselves to be more tabloid" and recalls that the biggest readers' response in the history of the newspaper was caused by the report of a visit to a local brothel.

The passivity of the survivor-organisations towards thematic diversity is related to other integral parts of their cultural capital – enthusiasm, a desire or encouragement to learn, the possession of knowledge and a striving for innovation. While achiever-organisations were active and tried to develop, though they could not always see how to exploit certain innovations, this activity was missing in the case of the survivors. The reason may be the more unstable state of the newsroom. Some interviewees complain that they lack educated and experienced journalists – individual actors with cultural capital. As journalist-entrepreneur Pavel who remembers, that "a graduate journalist has never come to us".

> The team has been the same for a long time, they are mostly high school graduates, with few exceptions. Now we have an editor who is older, a university graduate and experienced. (manager Anna)

> I've been learning this job for ten years. I say it quite honestly, this would no longer be possible today. Tomorrow, I would give you this chair, show you where everything is and say goodbye. (journalist Eva)

The effort to learn and develop innovations is evidently lower among these interviewees, or else, as can be seen in the introductory story of the survivor-organisation, it encounters hierarchical resistance. While the achievers see new trends as an opportunity to learn new things and develop, the survivors try it but mostly give up. The main reason is that they have to help fund online content from the printed edition of the newspaper, which is itself in financial difficulties.

Conversely, other scholars (Siegelbaum & Thomas, 2016, p. 400) see journalists' embrace of nostalgia as an excuse for not embracing innovation: "[W]e ought to take a detour away from nostalgia for the future (…) and examine how journalists make sense of the ethos of their work at a time of economic tumult." They add that one of their respondents said that "he approaches his work the same way he always had, but that the quality of the newspaper is not what it used to be, a statement echoed by multiple newsworkers at each publication" and "a columnist expressed concern that the relentless focus on technology was distracting journalism from its core duties" (Siegelbaum & Thomas, 2016, p. 398). Similarly, interviewees often speak about their print and web editions as enemies.

> We have a web page, but it's a poor one. We keep it deliberately trimmed. (journalist Tom)

> I admit that I don't like web news. We do it because we have to, and you can see it for yourself. I think money is being thrown at it. It's the paper newspaper that makes the money, so we have to take care of that. (manager-entrepreneur Ema)

> We built a website, which was not a happy idea because of course it takes readers away from the print medium. We basically keep it alive because of the contacts and if, let's say, the printed paper doesn't survive and there is still a desire to do something, we would revive it. (journalist-entrepreneur Karel)

Only one interviewee, entrepreneur-journalist Dan, is willing to devote energy and money to the online news. He is the one who from the beginning of his entrepreneurship came up with (mostly technological) innovations. As scholars recall (Ali et al., 2018, p. 2), "closer investigation reveals a rich tapestry of innovative techniques, frustratingly slow websites, and passionate journalists and editors who have been overlooked in conversations about the newspaper industry that tend to focus either on the large metros or the digital start-ups". The entrepreneur-journalist is at the same time the only one of all my interviewees who is able to make money from an online edition (Jenkins & Nielsen, 2020b): "We have had websites and custom software since 2004. There have been pressures: why don't you give the news for free? But I've always explained: it can't be free. I wouldn't appreciate my own work, if I gave it away for free when I've worked hard on it." Other interviewees similarly embrace innovations which will bring immediate financial returns:

> We use Facebook for advertising, we say yes, you have an ad in the newspaper, we will put it for free on our Facebook. And advertisers are really interested. (manager Anna)

One of the key characteristics of the survivor-organisations' performance is their economic condition, which is problematic for various reasons. Interviewees and communication partners from the participatory observation admit some degree of economic instability and financial results hovering around the profit-and-loss threshold. Broadly speaking, it can be understood as a result of deviating from the law of the field, the nomos. However, there is a certain hierarchy of economic conditions in this class of organisations. There are recognisably large ones, chains and "one man" newsrooms, all of which have somehow failed to succeed. As Neil Fowler (2011, p. 32) describes: "the simple view is that the internet has been the sole cause of the industry's ills. But it is a much more complex problem than that. Regional and local newspapers have faced a perfect storm of factors that have been developing over decades to bring them to their knees."

The biggest organisations were never in the red, but their financial stability was significantly disturbed. For example, journalist-entrepreneur Cyril says that when advertising declined, it hit the company hard. "But we never went into the red, either we were on the border or just in the black." For him the secret of survival is simply to treat money wisely, which doesn't mean save money on the newspaper's operation: "Managing money, and not wasting it, is a multifactorial matter. Trimming doesn't work, but when we made a profit, it was put into a savings account in case we hadn't enough for salaries." This newspaper would appear to be one of the achiever-organisations, except that it now has to repay the loan that one of the owners took out to fund the outgoing co-owner's share. "I have to pay creditors and think about how to stabilise it all economically," adds Cyril. Another newsroom is economically "self-sufficient", but again there is a catch: "We can't go into the red. Our owner wants a profit from us, which we give him. To make a profit, we unfortunately have to save on wages, on people. I'd say we're at the limit of what we can handle," sums up manager Anna. Another big newspaper has run into economic problems because of declining advertising and increasing competition. This resonates with Ulrika Andersson and Jenny Wiik's (2013, p. 706) findings that "competition grows tougher and economic considerations become increasingly central". Large organisations then find it much more difficult to cope with the financial downturn (manager-entrepreneur Ema).

As a result, the commercial part of the newsroom usually gains a stronger voice in the organisation, which crumbles "the wall" (Cornia et al., 2020), upsets the balance and continues slowly and almost imperceptibly to disturb organisation's stability (journalist-entrepreneur Pavel). In contrast, a chain owner, journalist-entrepreneur Ivo, evaluates the economic development of his company optimistically: "Every man is the architect of his own fortune. We know how much we have to get from the sale of newspapers. The less we get from it, the more we have to gain from advertising or some other activities, so we just have to secure the budget." And adds: "Of course, we can talk about adjusting costs, but certainly not about the end of newspapers. We are still in the black, even if it is not so good. If we could not generate a profit, newspapers would no longer be published." However, his subordinate, journalist Jana, notes that within the company the owner talks about earning so little that he can't give his employees any Christmas bonuses or pay rises.

The smaller newsrooms have already fought economic problems more openly. As journalist Radim points out: "When people start saving, you have to save too."

> If someone had told me ten years ago that I had to issue a weekly on these numbers, I would have told him he had gone mad, so now it is simply misery. We were in good health, economically independent, we made profits, we distributed dividends. When we fell, we sold the stake and now we're hiding under the wings of a large publishing company. I expect them to help us financially. (journalist Eva)

> How do I know if it will all work out, I don't even know if we'll get through this year. So far we don't have a big problem but the economy is really, as I would say, tense. It has to be watched and we will need to take some steps to attract new advertisers. (journalist-entrepreneur Dana)

> I was wondering for a while if I would have to close the newspaper. (…) We now distribute some copies free of charge and this improves our position with the advertisers. (journalist-entrepreneur Lucie)

The third group are the newsrooms which are on the edge of survival and whose circumstances resemble those of the leaver-organisations. As Ekdale et al. (2015, p. 384) confirm, the economic challenges "have been particularly hard on newspapers, which have seen circulations drop and advertisers disappear. A few well-known newspapers have shut down, some have discontinued print products, others have scaled back print operations from daily to semi-weekly, and many have reduced staff through layoffs and buyouts." Entrepreneur-journalist Dan admits, "it is not enough for surviving, we are at zero. I pay all the costs, I pay all the people, and I have nothing left, so I make a living from something else. It would be easier if some advertising remained, but it has all moved to the Internet, it's all gone." Journalist David and journalist-entrepreneur Filip speak about the newsrooms' economic situation as the sword of Damocles hanging over their heads.

> The newspaper is small, and this is a poor region so there are few advertisers, therefore the economic package has to be limited. If you wish to employ two people full time, you'll have to close it tomorrow. Basically, we haven't always been in the black. There have been such fluctuations, at times we were only a month away from going under. I borrowed money from my family to pay salaries, and in two months I returned it. (journalist-entrepreneur Karel)

There was a slight loss last year, but somehow, we can ride it because we have a good relationship with the printing house, and that may help us. It was in the tens of thousands of Czech crowns. I think we can keep our head above water for a while. We had to save through personnel cuts; there were sixteen pages and we cut it to twelve. And then we tried to gain money in other things, for example graphics. (journalist-entrepreneur Filip)

It didn't work economically from the beginning and the owner was losing money here which he had put into it from elsewhere. Then in some years, when there were elections, there was some political advertising, but otherwise he put two million Czech crowns into the business, and he never get it back. (journalist Tom)

The survivor-organisations also build on the traditional business model of income acquired from advertising and the sale of newspapers (Jenkins & Nielsen, 2020b). As the volume of advertising decreases on the periphery, the interviewees are looking for other ways to maintain their organisations' income. Hess (2016, p. 522) calls it "the rivers of gold that once flowed for the traditional press from classified advertising" and later "have become a competitive online pool for independent start-ups and companies providing advertising platforms for everything ... The births, deaths and marriage notices are gradually attracting the attention of new competitors beyond the news media in online space." As journalist Eva sees it: "When I don't have subscribers, I don't have revenue from sales, so I'll close it, because if advertising revenue falls, I have to get money from the readers."

According to the interviewees' experiences, there are different ways to maintain the business model: "My policy is an expensive newspaper at the newsstand and a cheaper subscription" (journalist Eva); "Money from the sale of the newspaper covers production costs, printing and distribution, the money for salaries should be earned from advertising. Previously, four Czech crowns remained from the sale of each newspaper, but not any more because we decided to support the sale with a supplement, a television magazine" (journalist Tom); "I completely changed the philosophy of distribution because we still had copies left. I said, we have to get the newspaper among the people. An issue cost only eight Czech crowns, we have nothing from the sale. So we have made a network of collection points and we deliver the newspaper there for free" (journalist-entrepreneur Lucie); "We still manage to pay all the costs. We have risen in price by two Czech crowns, so if it works, it means that at least some money will be left. If not, then it's no longer worth it, basically it means that people don't want us. Now it's genuinely financed from sales alone" (entrepreneur-journalist Dan).

The traditional business model is shifting to that of financing newspapers primarily, or solely, from readers (Olsen et al., 2020) – not by choice, but because the organisations would otherwise have to seek alternative income. Some of the entrepreneurs have taken this approach for years, as journalist David recalls: "Our owner doesn't care about advertising revenue, he says that the newspaper must make a living from its readers, so we've never had an ad-man. We tried to convince him we should, but he doesn't want to pay extra for it, but years ago it could have made us a lot of money." As Jenkins and Nielsen (2020b, p. 477) see the situation, "local journalism has to adapt to a structural change from a world in which local media users had low choice and local media had high market power over advertisers to a world in which local media users have high choice and local media have low market power over advertisers". This shift also changes the nomos and should be related to the attention which the organisations give to their readers.

> We do a so-called road show for our readers every year. We look for different villages, we try not to go to the same ones every year and cooperate with local companies that support us. We actually tour these villages, organise a competition there, for beer and lemonade, and our partners contribute prises, introduce themselves and we present the newspaper. People come to us, they have competition coupons from the newspaper, they can ask about anything they are interested in. It has a tradition going back ten years, so it gets a response. It increases the sales, because people get to know us, and they know how to contact us. (manager Anna)

> I figured I'd put the newspaper in everybody's mailbox for free. So for the whole year, I went round the mailboxes across the region. I gave them a sample edition and a silly card with it which said: order four free editions and see how beautifully we work. And then we made follow-up calls and fifty per cent of the people became subscribers (laughs). (journalist Eva)

The interviewees I spoke with understand the importance of this contact, that this relationship is not purely economic but also about the social and cultural capital of the organisation. Bentley (2001, p. 14) suggests, that "there is something beyond the news alone [which] attracts readers. It is an aura, an ambience, a special feeling of comfort that is ripe for additional research. The field is ripe for a search for that 'something special' that continues to keep newspapers popular." And journalist-entrepreneur Pavel agrees: "As a newspaper we try not only to publish news but to influence the locality socially and culturally. For example, we publish books by local authors. The newspaper is much more than just paper covered with writing."

Nevertheless, the survivor-organisations often no longer have the staff or the energy to support such a relationship, which scholars consider important: "holding events to discuss community concerns, hosting local awards to celebrate their community, organizing roundtables to discuss what readers want from the newspaper, and opening editorial meetings to the public" (Ali et al., 2020, p. 464).

At the beginning of the millennium, we started doing competition shows. (…) People wanted competitions, they wanted to have fun, but as the years went by, fewer and fewer people applied, and you could see that they just didn't want to show off any more. People began to envy them (…) The last thing we did was to publish a book [on local traditions and identity] which was a great success. (journalist Radim)

We've done it before, though not much recently. (…) For example, we published postcards and books about local history and held discussions over wine in the cellar. Now, since there are only two of us in the newsroom, it's not possible. (journalist Tom)

Nothing happened here, so for 18 years we organised a ball and handed out prises at it. Since we criticise people the whole year, we also wanted to praise some people here. But I am alone here now, and I can't do it any more. (entrepreneur-journalist Dan)

The relational construction of the organisation's position in the journalistic field

The inter-organisational dynamics on the margins of the journalistic field require us to consider the relations of the survivor-organisations with actors who are both cooperative (audience, sources, advertisers, organisations involved in the newspaper's production) and competitive (other media), along with the related symbolic capital of organisations (Berkowitz & TerKeurst, 1999; cf. *the extra-media level*, Jenkins, 2019).

Thinking about the relational position of individual actors in the journalistic field, interviewees consider the position of their own organisation in terms of size rather than success and power. That this view is irrelevant and misleading can be illustrated by the position of a group of the smallest newspapers (in terms of geographical coverage). These newspapers, covering an area smaller than a district, confirm that bigger does not necessarily mean more successful and powerful (Napoli et al., 2018). They sprang mostly from the negative emotion of rivalry. The second largest town in the area often, and usually unsuccessfully, fought for the title of district town, thus creating animosity between individual towns in the district. One consequence of the rivalry was a strong relationship between the citizens of these "peripheral" towns and their own newspapers (journalist-entrepreneur Dana; journalist Jana; entrepreneur-journalist Dan). As journalist-entrepreneur Dana adds, "being a non-district newspaper is ambivalent: on the one hand we're closer to people, we say that we are more like a family newspaper. But on the other hand, we are so close that when they want to hurt us, they can." Maintaining the newspapers' existence in a small area with a limited number of readers and advertisers is difficult (Abernathy, 2018). Nevertheless, these newspapers are successful as long as they remain active, otherwise their relationships with other actors will fail.

> Even though it is a non-district town, I knew that newspapers were published here in the past, that historically speaking this was a district town. (journalist-entrepreneur Karel)

> Such is the rivalry between [the two towns] that if we wanted to break through in one of them, we would have to have a title that looked as if it were intended for that town alone. (…) Our philosophy is that regionalism is the only trump card that can work today, because all those national and regional-looking titles always try to go into regionality at the start, but then they find out that the market is too small, that they can't make it work, and they start centralizing again. And so I realised that a local newspaper like us, without an oligarch-owner or municipal backing, is the only way to make it work. (journalist-entrepreneur Ivo)

> I think there are already three titles in one district, so it brings an even greater connection to the inner community. You can really write in great detail about everything that people are interested in. I see it as their advantage. From the point of view of the journalists, it is of course a disadvantage, because even in the whole district we have a problem to find out something that is worth publishing. (journalist Emil)

Even though an organisation's relationship with such individuals as readers, sources and advertisers is inevitable and generally considered as advantageous (Jenkins & Graves, 2019), among the survivor-organisations it is a far more complicated and controversial topic. First of all, the interviewees don't have a clear idea of who their readers are. As Ewart (2000, p. 3) confirms, "regional journalists (like journalists in general) know very little about their readers or publics" and he proposes a term *presumed readership:* "That is, journalists make a number of presumptions, based on their own experience and that of their friends and colleagues, about the readership, and by extension, the public."

Although the interviewees usually respond to a question about their readers by referring to a newspaper questionnaire which regularly examines the structure of the readers and their preferences, more detailed inquiries reveal that they know nothing accurate, current, or relevant about their audience: "Who are our readers? We just assume …" (journalist-entrepreneur Dana); "Readers? Mostly older people … We did surveys about ten years ago, we did them regularly every year and the results were the same. But we could revive them" (journalist Eva); "We did a survey once, twice. (…) It's been a long time … We think that we almost know … Ehhhm, so we know … we assume that our readers are older folks, but we want young ones as well" (journalist-entrepreneur Pavel); "Readers? We did a survey once that just confirmed what we thought!" (journalist-entrepreneur

Cyril); "We have no idea. We didn't do surveys, but of course we see who goes around town with the newspaper" (journalist-entrepreneur Ivo); "We did surveys with readers, but that's a matter of five years ago ... it would have to be renewed" (journalist-entrepreneur Filip).

Similarly, the interviewees don't take into account the specifics of, and differences between, their print audience and their online audience:

> That's what advertisers ask me: what kind of target group do you have? So I always say: layered ... The readers, I can't even determine who reads us, because even though I see the people who take the newspaper and those who call us, the readership is very broad. (...) [*Do you have different audiences for print and web?*] Definitely not. (journalist-entrepreneur Lucie)

> We used to do surveys. These people are more like older retirees. Otherwise, we assume that printed newspapers are simply for people who do not go online or get news on their mobile phones, and they are mostly seniors ... If it is already changing, I do not know how it will continue. (journalist David)

This unclear relationship with the audience is also related to the decreasing willingness of survivor-organisations to strive harder for readers which has impact on the nomos of the sub-field. As Hanusch (2015, p. 818) sees it, "recent evidence suggests that local journalists may not actually be as much in tune with their audiences as they like to proclaim". Other scholars (Hermans et al., 2014, p. 642) who see a gap between journalists and audiences propose "both from a legitimacy and an economic perspective (...) to reconnect" with "rethinking professional performance and re-establishing the relationship with the public by adopting citizen-centred practices". The exception that confirms the rule is the one newsroom that has a feedback system for the readers:

> We do surveys (...) so we form quite an accurate idea about the readers. I cannot say that they come exclusively from the older generation, we are also read by young people – less, but they do read us. Because when the customer dies, the children keep the newspaper, so it stays in those families where they're used to it. (manager Anna)

More often than actively pursuing the audience, the interviewees mention the criticism they receive from the readers, and resignation and fatigue resound in their views. The criticism is a disruption of the symbolic capital of the survivor-organisations: "We have feedback, people swear at us. When they don't like something, they call" (manager-entrepreneur Ema); "Readers today are more afraid to talk, they are more scared, but at the same time they are angrier, more vindictive, they just come to vent their anger ... I'm surprised when someone calls to praise us, it completely throws me" (journalist-entrepreneur Cyril); "As interestingly as I can,

I ask people what they think of the newspaper and, equally interestingly, they are unable to say anything" (journalist-entrepreneur Pavel).

Being mostly in their fifties and upwards, journalists also often think of their readers as either their contemporaries or their elders and underestimate the younger generation, whom they do not regard as their target group. It is in line with scholars' findings, that journalists "typically construct an audience based on a small, select group of individuals, including their supervisors, friends, neighbors, family members, and journalism colleagues" (Wolfgang & Jenkins, 2018, pp. 14–15) and dismiss others.

> We are the last generation that still reveres the written word, that's a fact. The generations that are younger than us live more in the world of fake news, because they've already grown up with the yellow press and know very well that not everything that is written is true. (journalist Radim)

> These young people live in a bubble. They've no experience, don't encounter real life, but they believe they have it all figured out … They work in groups that consist of no one but young people, they know nothing at all about the world, there is no one who will tell them that what they are doing is bullshit. (entrepreneur-journalist Dan)

There is one more important reason for the problematic relationships that exist between survivor-organisations, their readers, and sources, and that is the invisibility of newsrooms and journalists in the field they cover. As Bowd (2014, p. 66) points out, "continued emphasis on direct and personal contact with news sources and audiences is highly valued". Mostly for economic reasons some of the newsrooms are no longer based in the localities (journalist-entrepreneur Filip; journalist David), while other organisations are considering closing newsrooms, and yet others maintain a newsroom, but no longer have journalists sitting in it (entrepreneur Mirek).

> I wondered why I should pay for a newsroom when we could all do it from home. But my colleagues convinced me, so for now we are keeping the newsroom, even though we have cut the official hours. (journalist-entrepreneur Karel)

> We regard the newsroom as important … but of course a publishing house has to finance itself, so the economic aspect is still important to me. I still pay twenty thousand Czech crowns a month in rent, so I need to draw at least the same amount in revenue from the newsrooms. (journalist-entrepreneur Ivo)

But survivor-organisations and their journalists are also invisible in other ways and therefore erode their social and related symbolic capital (Bowd, 2014). They themselves observe that, again mostly for economic reasons, they spend vastly less time in the field and with their sources (journalist Tom; journalist Ben; journalist David; journalist Jana; journalist-entrepreneur Filip). Maggie Rivas-Rodriguez (2011, p. 111) depicts this "gap between journalists and their communities" as *the community gap*. As journalist-entrepreneur Pavel recalls: "There used to be more field work because there was no other way of doing things, that's one thing. The other thing is that when you're looking for savings, you stop going out into the field." Entrepreneur-journalist Dan adds: "I am in the field definitely less than before ... I do all the administration, it's crazy. We used to have a secretary, but not anymore because we just have no money." Firmstone (2016, p. 6) paints a similar picture of "an increase in desk-based journalists reliant on press releases and unable to invest time to attend council meetings, court hearings, or [to] get out into the community".

The survivor-organisations' former close relationship with their readers has been replaced, but it has taken on a more problematic form, especially within their relationship to sources, and specifically those members of the local field of power (Hájek et al., 2015). Nevertheless, it can further disrupt the symbolic capital of these organisations: some interviewees reflect that the criticisms made by newspapers may result in the refusal of municipalities to communicate with them (journalist-entrepreneur Karel; journalist-entrepreneur Filip); others speak of "better than ordinary relationships" and "financial support from some municipalities" (journalist-entrepreneur Dana); "contracts with the town hall" (journalist-entrepreneur Lucie); or "you have to be fine with those people" (journalist-entrepreneur Ivo). However, such accounts suggest that the professional integrity of the journalists and journalistic doxa may have been compromised.

Significantly stronger than their relationships with individuals is the cooperation of the survivor-organisations with other peripheral newspapers (Hatcher & Thayer, 2017). They were probably led to this by long-lasting production problems which they shared with others in the field. Nevertheless, even though they spoke of some other publishers and journalists as colleagues or friends, for various reasons there was no real inter-organisational cooperation. One reason is that the ties that depended on individual relationships have faded away over the past thirty years, which reminds us of fragility of newspapers on the margins (Anderson, 2013): "Our former publisher befriended a newspaper publisher in the neighbouring district" (journalist Tom); "We knew each other even before 1989. But everything has changed, those people are no longer there" (journalist-entrepreneur Cyril); "We know about each other, of course, but I don't even know how they're doing now. We've been in touch a lot, but completely different people are running it now" (journalist-entrepreneur Dana); "I used to be in contact with the nearest foreign newsroom, the editor-in-chief was a friend of mine" (entrepreneur-journalist Dan).

Another reason that hinders potential cooperation is that journalists from the survivor-organisations lack the time to keep in touch: "I met a man from a similar newsroom in another district, he communicated for a while and then it went completely dead. I must say that when the crisis came, everyone had different worries and stopped talking to one another" (journalist Radim); "I have often wanted to contact someone and swap experiences, but it never happened" (journalist-entrepreneur Filip); "The cooperation is rather random, because I'm not looking for it, I'm overwhelmed with work … Everyone is struggling in various ways, so we cut it off" (entrepreneur Mirek).

Further reasons for failing to cooperate include the persistent feeling that the newspapers were competitors, if "only a little". Hatcher and Thayer (2017, p. 1286) suggest that "one of the biggest roadblocks to success for organizations considering a partnership could be that the ideas of competition are so ingrained in many journalists that they find it difficult to agree to, or enjoy, working with other journalists", explaining it "as a trust issue". My interviewees think similarly: "They are a bit of a competition for us … so there has always been such careful cooperation, we watch each other warily" (manager Anna); "When we had distribution problems, we called each other. But they didn't like us very much because we interfered with their newspapers" (manager-entrepreneur Ema); "We were friends and then they surprised me a little. They came up with a proposal to add my newspaper to their chain. And I said, don't be angry, but I won't get involved. And they said: so we'll destroy you … (laughs). But they couldn't" (entrepreneur-journalist Dan).

Hence, the only real matter on which the parties agreed was the joint reduction of costs and the solution of common production problems. But even this didn't last long. Hatcher and Thayer (2017, p. 1286) describe sources of friction, "a tension when one organization is perceived to be doing more work or giving more than they get out of the partnership".

> We had problems with the Czech Post who were increasing the cost of distribution. I talked to my lawyer, and he said call a meeting with them, ideally after you have spoken to someone who is in the same situation. So we asked how a couple of other newspapers would deal with it, particularly [two newspapers from neighbouring districts], and they told us there was no way of solving it … (journalist-entrepreneur Cyril)

> More than ten years ago we had a joint project built on cooperation. I initiated it and invited representatives of other district newspapers. I said to them, let's exchange crossword puzzles, and do a single TV supplement between us so we can save money on it. (…) Well, I was the only one who did the work on it, everyone else took it (laughs) and no one gave me anything back. So that was that. (journalist Eva)

As with the achiever-organisations the most problematic cooperation is with those who work in production, for the latter is no longer conducted in the locality by those with equal power but by national and monopolistic partners. The interviewees are happiest when their organisations are self-sufficient. One of the bigger newspapers boasts significant recognition because it owns the house in which its newsroom is located. As manager-entrepreneur Ema recalls: "It was a coincidence that this house was offered to us to buy and I said to myself, I don't want to pay rent any more. We went to see it, we liked it, especially that it came with parking space, and we bought and repaired it." Similarly, most of the survivor-organisations aim to arrange their newspapers' distribution for themselves (journalist-entrepreneur Filip; journalist David).

> Distribution is self-distribution, we have about fifty points of sale, to which we carry the papers ourselves sometimes using buses, some stuff goes by mail, but we deliver most of it. Distribution gives the best feedback, because you meet dozens of people in two hours, who in turn get feedback from the readers, who swear at it or praise it. (journalist-entrepreneur Karel)

> We always have our own distribution system using our own car. My colleague only works for two days – she brings the newspaper from the printing office and then she delivers to the town. And in the meantime, I prepare the rest of the distribution, the part which is helped by my local network of friends. I was just an idiot in not working it out before because we were delivering everything ourselves, it was crazy. We were trying to do it fast, so we always had one foot in trouble. (entrepreneur-journalist Dan)

> We distribute ourselves, only a negligible part goes via the distribution company, and then we have a company that supplies to the subscribers. We actually started by distributing everything through the company, but that would have led us to total bankruptcy within the first year. (journalist-entrepreneur Dana)

Nevertheless, some consider self-distribution unmanageable now, or after calculating the costs they didn't even try it. The main reason is the size of a district combined with the small number of distributed issues (manager Anna; journalist-entrepreneur Cyril; entrepreneur Mirek). As manager-entrepreneur Ema puts it, "it is no longer possible to deliver to the villages, because you could find yourself driving twenty kilometres to deliver just one newspaper".

When the survivor-organisations can't manage the newspapers' production on their own, they form strong partnerships with other businesses on the periphery. Here, relationships are long-term, contracts are still being fulfilled, and their power, professional recognition (and thus symbolic capital) is mutual. These partners are mainly local printing houses (journalist-entrepreneur Karel; journalist-entrepreneur Filip; manager Anna) and sales outlets – newsstands and grocery stores in villages. However, in recent years they have been declining (journalist-entrepreneur Dana; manager-entrepreneur Ema).

> We print in one of the last small newspaper printing houses in the country, but qualitatively it's a horror. I get offers from [a printing house which is part of a chain], they do a beautiful job. But they can't swallow everything, they've already got most of it. (entrepreneur Mirek)

> There are no longer small newsagents, and the big newsagents are tied to [certain companies], so even if the saleswomen wanted to put our newspapers there, they're not allowed to. (journalist-entrepreneur Ivo)

> We rely on traditional and local partners. We print in a small printing house, one of the last which is not [part of an ownership chain]. (...) A local company of friends helps us with the distribution. They have a bakery, so they deliver newspapers with their pastries. (...) We have contracts with shops in the villages. (...) The number of newsstands is decreasing. We used to sell the newspaper in pubs, but that's all finished. (entrepreneur-journalist Dan)

Cooperation with national, monopolistic companies – which for survivor-organisations indicates a dependence on stronger players rather than a genuine business partnership – becomes a decisive factor in the newspapers' struggle for survival (Waschková Císařová, 2023b). Newspapers on the margins cannot profit from the distinctiveness of the large companies, they possess no symbolic capital in this relationship and must fully adapt to the unpredictable conditions that undermine the very existence of the newsrooms and influence the field's nomos (Bourdieu, 1995). They depend on two key components of newspaper production: distribution and sale.

The state monopoly, the Czech Post, does not consider the peripheral newspapers worth distributing, but is at the same time the only available distributor to subscription readers. The interviewees complain about repeated price increases in the service and at the same time about its poor quality (manager Anna; journalist Radim; journalist-entrepreneur Cyril; journalist Eva; journalist-entrepreneur Filip; entrepreneur-journalist Dan; journalist-entrepreneur Ivo).

Czech Post also disrupts the newspapers – for example, by changing the issue or delivery day (manager Anna; journalist Emil; journalist-entrepreneur Ivo) or by postponing deadlines (manager-entrepreneur Ema). But the most difficult thing is that the survivor-organisations feel trapped. As manager-entrepreneur Ema sees it: "We have no choice, because no one else does it"; and journalist-entrepreneur Cyril adds: "They increased the price of distribution by fifty per-cent. It's no joke for us, because that will cost me a quarter of a million more in a year!"

> The Czech Post does things that are deadly to us. But there is nowhere else to go. And if we do anything against them and they take a dislike to us, we could probably expect a shock: the service could become even more expensive. (journalist Radim)

A similar situation prevails with the over-the-counter sale of newspapers. While the local shops close, the chains of newsstands and shops in big department stores only cooperate with the large distribution companies, not with individual, small publishers.

> The largest press distributor is the company owned by the largest national newspaper publishers, and they of course favour their own titles. (...) In the big stores, no one talks to us. Fortunately, we have a long tradition, so we sell in some of them for historical reasons, but we are not able to get into the new ones unless we pay the distribution company. (journalist-entrepreneur Ivo)

> All we have left is [a chain of village shops], so today we put most of our papers into petrol stations and village shops, because we can't get into the big shops. Fortunately, some convenience stores have started to sell our newspaper. (journalist Radim)

More problematic for survivor-organisations than competition from other peripheral media is a lack of cooperation in the field of newspaper production. More precisely, some interviewees see the problems of distribution and sales that they have with monopolistic organisations as essentially those of competition. Manager Anna sums up: "The big newspaper publishers have stakes in distribution companies, they own printing houses. Where there are strong independent regional newspapers, these national publishers lag behind. And that could be the cause of the problem."

Competitive struggles between small organisations on the margins were more relevant in the 1990s, when the survivor-organisations were also in much better shape. These struggles, often in districts with two other competing newspapers, meant concessions for certain organisations, and in the end, they were the ones who came out on top and most of their competitors were killed off. It was about adjusting publication days; poaching journalists; slowly attracting extra readers (journalist Tom); or stealing ideas to improve content (journalist Radim). Having a strong, stable, and competitive newspaper means, according to journalist Ben, that one has to have a strategy: "When we are pressed by competitors, we have to take a different approach, we have to explain it to the readers, justify it, market it to them correctly and give them something extra."

Conversely, in the recent past certain short-term publishing projects have appeared that have unfair advantages and different goals. Yet according to the interviewees, they undermine the stability of the peripheral journalistic sub-field and don't bring the satisfaction of defeating the competition when they end. The important point is that these competitors cream off advertising money and obscure the environment for the readers. They are mostly the free press (entrepreneur Mirek); or advertising sheets (journalist-entrepreneur Cyril).

> They hurt for a few months or two or three years, and then disappear again because they didn't pay off, it was just some political move … because at this time, when someone starts a newspaper, it's about as successful as trying to run against a train. (journalist Radim)

> When someone sees you publishing a newspaper, they think it's a piece of cake. The attempts sprang from that mentality. (journalist-entrepreneur Lucie)

Like those who represent the achiever-organisations, those from the survivor-organisations have an ambivalent relationship with the municipal press (Hájek & Carpentier, 2015). The interviewees from the more stable and stronger organisations regard it as unfair competition which is funded from local people's taxes yet still competes with them for advertising revenues in a small market.

> When the municipality publishes newspapers, I have an opinion on that. I don't think there is any other field in which the municipality competes with private individuals using public money. I perceive the municipal press as our only real competition, because for public money they offer what I am trying to sell. But the problem is not that they offer the information but that they also offer advertising. And there are situations where they just print something for free that I would sell. I have a problem with the fact that I basically pay the competition from my money, which I pay into the town budget. It became widespread when politicians discovered that they could tell their "truth" using public money. Ordinary people don't think about it, they're happy, they have information from the city for free in their mailboxes. (journalist-entrepreneur Ivo)

Nevertheless, others regard the municipal press as offering cooperation rather than competition. Some entrepreneurs earn extra money just by publishing such titles to order for several municipalities (journalist-entrepreneur Filip; journalist-entrepreneur Pavel). Yet others, such as journalist-entrepreneur Dana, have created a "synergy" with the municipal press: "I have now established friendly relations with them, so they promote us and we promote them, even though it seems meaningless. I created a synergy when the two opposites came together, one plus is created." This can be understood as another manifestation of a specific nomos of the peripheral journalistic sub-field that allows close relationships with the political field.

Online local news sites are not considered by my interviewees to offer any kind of competition, which is in line with their general attitude to technology and innovation. They don't even have an overview of these actors on the journalistic periphery. As manager Anna puts it: "There's probably something like that here, but it's no competition for us."

Surprisingly enough, and despite the different types of problems that the interviewees identified, some representatives of the survivor-organisations consider themselves to be "unrivalled" (journalist Eva; manager-entrepreneur Ema; journalist-entrepreneur Pavel; journalist-entrepreneur Filip; journalist-entrepreneur Karel). They represent organisations who prefer to consider themselves as achievers, the powerful ones. In their environment, which is devoid of competition, they are likely to succeed in hiding their true situation. More often they win recognition from members of the local field of power and thus acquire symbolic capital there.

> We have no competition here on our level ... Rivals would have little chance because we are already here. So it makes us happy that we always rule the roost here. (manager-entrepreneur Ema)

> I think that both the politicians and other major figures know who is important here. They know that we can sway public opinion better than the other newspapers because we are still the most read and largest here. (journalist-entrepreneur Pavel)

The survivor-organisation is caught in a vicious circle arising from its passive and nostalgic attitude towards incoming challenges and unavoidable changes. Its balance and stability is disturbed, and its acquired capitals are crumbling. The survivors can be divided into two groups. First there are those organisations which from an inter-organisational point of view could be considered as achievers. Their symbolic capital and peer recognition remain high, but they cannot adapt to a changing journalistic field and the nomos of the sub-field. Then there are the organisations which are drifting slowly but steadily downstream with the general trends in the journalistic field and approaching the point where they might be considered leaver-organisations. What the survivor-organisations illustrate is that whether they are big regional bi-weeklies on one hand or small-town fortnightlies on the other, size does not mean success and power.

Disposition and position of an unsuccessful newspaper on the margins

Story of an organisation: The Leaver

The story of the leaver-organisation is an account of the demise of a specific type of medium – the newspaper on the margins. But because such an organisation no longer exists, the account is by no means pointless. On the contrary, knowing about its gradual disintegration in the journalistic field can help us to understand those organisational dynamics that are necessary for success or survival on the periphery.

The story of this particular leaver-organisation was acquired, symbolically enough, at the moment the last edition of the more than twenty-year-old newspaper was published, during the collection of the last issue from the printing house and its delivery to the sellers. It was therefore on the borders of being and not-being.

The editor-in-chief had for a long time been the only journalist in the newsroom, hence all the necessary professions for the functioning of the newspaper met in him. He produced content, organised production, picked up the issue from the printing house and distributed the copies for sale. Unsurprisingly, it was quite challenging – "I never have free time during weekends. I can take a holiday only during one week in the summer and one in winter, when there is a 'company-wide holiday', and the newspaper is not published." Being in his forties, he saw this as a problem that disrupted his private life and his relationships with family and loved ones.

When the editor-in-chief spoke about the team, he mainly meant the owners, whom he considered close and spoke of as family. However, when we got below superficial conversation, he admitted that he was not part of the circle in which decisions about the organisation were made. The owners presented as proud people who wanted to solve all their problems unaided and create the newspaper to a certain standard. Yet the money they had to invest in it from another business gradually grew until the losses were unsustainable. The bad financial situation brought everyone together: "I think the newsroom functioned only on ordinary enthusiasm and a self-denial on the part of all the workforce. This maintained the driving force of the newsroom and perhaps that's why the newspaper survived so long. If it weren't for those qualities in these people, I think it would have ended much, much sooner. Everyone had to be restrained," recalls the editor-in-chief. But at the same time this situation put the main player in a difficult situation. The editor-in-chief himself had a company car but was only allowed by the owners to drive a certain number of kilometres per month, which they calculated. "However, they forgot to include my weekend trips to events. So during distribution, on which I spent about twelve hours a week, I had to stop fifty meters from the shops to save on kilometres. But these were only the small annoyances," adds the editor-in-chief.

He was also burned out as an author and journalist, a situation exacerbated by the fact that he didn't have the same voice as the owner when deciding about suitable topics for the newspaper.

It is hardly surprising, then, that he was not minded remaining in the industry after the newspaper closed. The main problem, however, is that he cannot find a suitable post in a small town. "All the political parties in a town would definitely try to grab me now, but I know a lot about the politics here, so I don't even contemplate working for them," he smiles. However, his emotional relationship with the newspaper and the organisation was evident on the last day he spent delivering the newspaper. He was disorientated, repeating several times over the duties he had that had suddenly become difficult for him. "That's weird. I have to get used to talking about the newspaper in the past tense," he repeated.

Considering inter-organisational relations, the editor-in-chief was no longer convinced that the newspaper would meet the readers' expectations – either because it failed to address sufficiently subtle topics or because it reacted passively to innovations. Although the decisions were up to the owners, he himself felt that they were stuck and stagnant.

The formerly increasing recognition of the organisation by the readers and local notables had weakened – gradually and invisibly. As the editor-in-chief remembers, "the newspaper gained a reputation and name quite quickly, not only with the readers but the employees of public institutions. The newspaper had a voice, such that even mayors were afraid to make a mistake, which I think contributed to a fairly spectacular growth of printed and sold numbers of copies in the first years." But with the declining number of journalists in the newsroom, the scope for investigative journalism significantly decreased. The owners became important figures in the locality. Later, however, their other business and political activities complicated their position in the locality, along with that of the newspaper. Moreover, it generated a vicious circle of decline – from loss of financial stability to the disappearance of the brand: "Unfortunately the newspaper lost even the colour it had: it was named [after the colour they used in the header]. Even readers used to call it that, and the vendors knew what they meant," recalls the editor-in-chief.

Rather than seeing it as a prominent player in the locality, people began to take the paper for granted. Although in the last two issues the newsroom announced the end of the paper, other actors seemed taken aback. The saleswomen in the stores where the editor-in-chief was loading the last issue were shocked: "They don't read us, so they don't know we're finished. They asked, as usual: See you again after Christmas? And I say: No, we're done. And they replied: Right, of course, but after the holidays … ? And I said: No, this really is the last issue. Then they were shocked." Similarly, during the distribution of the last issue, the lady who witnessed the conversation about the end of the newspaper enthusiastically suggested that she get up a petition against the closure. "And where will you take it? They won't do anything about it now."

The remembered pride of the owners probably led to the fact that many outsiders did not know about the real problems of the publishing house. Regarding external agents, the organisation fought, for example, for the freedom to supply newspapers to large supermarkets: "The big distribution companies discovered that we ourselves were distributing the newspaper to some of the supermarkets that they considered to be 'theirs', and so they threatened us. Either they would distribute our paper everywhere or they would distribute it nowhere." *Cooperation with other newspapers also failed when they attempted to offer advertising space together.* "It worked for about two years. The effort was considerable, but we couldn't reach the big advertisers, and in the end, it wasn't a viable project. Unfortunately, it didn't bring much economic benefit to the newsroom," *recalls the editor-in-chief. Small wonder, then, that he rather lost interest in any cooperation with peers:* "[T]here was no time, and no one saw the point in meeting and discussing."

Towards the end, he became more of a pessimist and saw no place for local newspapers in the system: "I don't foretell a good future for them, I think that the information they offer will increasingly be shifted to the municipal press. Some of them are, I must admit, of good quality and they make quite a good impact. Leaflets in mailboxes still draw a response." *Despite his pessimism there are certain actors whom he will miss, not the organisations but the people whom he saw every week and over so many years. The director of the printing house sighs that although he has a rotary press, there are almost no newspapers left which he can print on it. But he and the editor-in-chief agree that they will visit each other and go for lunch together. Similarly, when the latter finds out that the employees of the distribution company, whom he met every week, are no longer on the shift, he is saddened.* "I will never see them again in my life," *he says as he drinks coffee from the vending machine just as he has routinely done every week. And for the last time he lights a cigarette with his coffee.*

The relational construction of internal organisational dynamics

The intra-organisational dynamics of the leaver-organisations' newsrooms look similar to those of other organisations and shows trends that are observable in the others. That which is mentioned most by the interviewees is the disappearance of employed journalists and the related closure of newsrooms (Goyanes & Rodríguez-Gómez, 2021). Their newspapers rely increasingly on freelancers and eventually only one person is responsible for all of production, typically the editor-in-chief (journalist Milan; journalist Alena).

In response to the question about relations in the newsroom, journalist-entrepreneur Barbora laughs sadly: "We ended up not even having employees. We have just one girl in the newsroom who runs the advertising, the others have already dispersed, but they work for us as freelancers." Similarly, journalist Robert describes how the changes in the newsroom took place gradually in response to adverse economic circumstances: "Once every few years a journalist was always fired or the newsroom moved to smaller premises, and then the secretary was fired ..." As he points out, the social capital inside the newsroom is fading away.

> It's funny that I'm the editor-in-chief and I don't live in [the town] we've covered for 35 years (laughs), and I go there once every fortnight for the town hall's press conference. (...) Today, thanks to all the Facebook groups, where there are fifteen thousand people, I am more in the picture than if I walked around [the town]. It is such an oddity that the newspaper is created without any physical contact. (journalist Robert)

However, this internal arrangement of the organisation is not without its problems. For example, the editors-in-chief can't find suitable co-workers (entrepreneur-journalist Max; journalist Robert); they do a lot of work for free because they have no money for salaries (entrepreneur Petr); they can't rely on the freelancers: "For the fees we can offer, no one cares, and those capable people who can do it are usually busy with something else," adds journalist Robert. The other choice is that they can either have people without a newsroom or a newsroom without people: "The place is very important. The advertisers go there all the time, but I already thought I would change the newsroom, it's our house, but we need to move to something smaller, because that's a huge space with just one woman sitting there," states journalist-entrepreneur Barbora.

As scholars have pointed out: "[The] ongoing job loss in journalism, and journalists' consequent exit from the profession, suggest there is likely to be a shrinking pool of people able to participate in journalistic work" (Cohen et al., 2019, p. 818). This means that the newspaper's operation depends entirely on one person who is typically middle-aged, overworked and burnt-out. Moreover, if she isn't also the owner, the person often has no motivation to stay in the newsroom. For example, MacDonald et al. (2016, p. 42) show that "a profile of the kind of journalist most likely to be at risk of burnout and therefore to have low levels of job commitment can be constructed". These are "young females with fewer years of journalism experience, working in small circulation size newspapers"; while "editors and reporters seem to experience higher levels of burnout than those in other roles, as do journalists in non-management positions".

> Other work-related factors associated with levels of burnout include increased work-family conflict and workload, reduced capacity for innovation and autonomy in the workplace, low levels of perceived organisational support, income, involvement, peer cohesion, task orientation, and physical comfort in the workplace. (MacDonald et al., 2016, p. 42)

When such a person decides to quit, the newspaper usually ends, as in the cases of journalist Anna and journalist Robert, who decided to leave their position, and the owner subsequently stopped publishing the newspaper. Moreover, being alone in the newsroom, the journalist has no feedback, doesn't communicate with other colleagues, and has no team and manager. Stacy Spaulding (2016, p. 218) emphasises that this impacts on a journalist's morale: "Mentors, friends, and teachers are suddenly gone, along with the paper's institutional memory"; "survivors are left behind saying goodbye to friends and hello to additional work". Spaulding quotes Weiss, that "this led one writer to imagine 'what it must have felt like to be on the deck of the crippled Titanic, watching the too few lifeboats drift out of sight as I awaited my inevitable fate'".

Either the owner is at the same time the sole journalist, or the owner trusts the journalist and lets him do the job. As journalist Robert explains, "I see the publisher once a year. (…) The nice thing about it is that basically he doesn't care, he's so obliging that he doesn't interfere." Journalist Alena adds: "I was really left alone, it was pretty hellish because I didn't know how to put the issue together. It just didn't work, so I said that if nothing changed, I'd pack up. Well, nothing much did change, so I sat down with [the owner's deputy] and told him, I can't do this any more. And he said: I've been expecting this for a while."

A similar decline can be seen in the cultural capital of the leaver-organisations. Their newspapers may be just as long-lived as those published by the achiever-organisations. However, over time they have for various reasons lost credit and trust in the eyes of the other actors in the journalistic field. In terms of the newspaper's content, the interviewees from the leaver-organisations often felt implicated in its loss of face. They had plans which later faded away because of a lack of money, for example, to cover the smallest villages and their problems (journalist-entrepreneur Barbora; journalist Alena; entrepreneur-journalist Jan); to do investigative journalism (journalist Robert); to offer content over 54 pages (entrepreneur Petr); or give a voice to everybody (journalist-entrepreneur Barbora; entrepreneur-journalist Max). As Max adds, he planned "to feature the opinions of the most absurd, the most marginal, to air views that are unusual and extreme and provoke discussion".

Moreover, the interviewees regretted the choice of a newspaper's name which did not refer to the locality and thus weakened their identification with it (journalist-entrepreneur Barbora). Or they changed the format of the newspaper only to discover that the readers did not welcome the changes (entrepreneur-journalist Max; journalist Milan). Or they perceived the closure of the newsroom as signifying the disappearance of a newspaper's identity from the town: it was no longer anywhere to be seen (journalist Robert). The gradual loss of a leaver-organisation's relevance is detailed in the story told by journalist Alena:

> The former owner was a perfect guy, a really good journalist, and I worked with him, but only occasionally. Then he died and for a while it was managed by his relatives. But to make it profitable they went after the money and the journalistic standards went down. (…) There was interest in buying the newspaper from various entrepreneurs, but family demanded so much money that no one bought it. And then suddenly, out of the blue, they stopped publishing the newspaper in the September, even though people had a subscription for three more months which they couldn't recover. Later, an entrepreneur came to start the newspaper again, changed its name slightly, and asked me if I wanted to do it. I decided to take it because I was sorry that it had ended. However, I had no idea that the man didn't understand the business, it turned out that he didn't pay anybody but just ran up debts, and eventually the newspaper went bankrupt. And again, the subscribers were left high and dry and desperate for information. The printing house had the biggest claim on it, so they took the newspaper over. I stayed, but people demanded that someone pay them for the lost issues, and it was a terrible problem to explain to them that the latest publisher simply had nothing to do with what had happened. It was just very difficult to regain trust. I had to rebuild it, and I think I succeeded. It had potential, but for financial reasons it failed a third time. (journalist Alena)

Newsrooms have no explicit rules or norms about how to do the job, and the interviewees I engaged with understood rules as the opposite of freedom (journalist-entrepreneur Barbora). Journalist Robert recalls the 1990s as a period when anything was possible: "It was an absolute wild west. I took on one issue of the newspaper for which I would now be jailed for fifteen years and pay fifteen million in fines. The paper was like a loaded weapon! It established itself as a model at that time, so it didn't really seem strange to anyone." Interestingly enough, while my interviewees from the other kinds of organisation either directly prohibit the linking of journalism and politics or have learned from their simultaneous careers as journalists and politicians that such a practice is no longer possible or at least problematic, this breach of normative expectations is sometimes regarded as a benefit in the leaver-organisations and part of their nomos (Bourdieu, 1995).

> Print is totally going to hell, but an absolutely crucial thing happened eight years ago: a publisher entered local politics. The publisher felt very cleverly that even if it's in the red, having a newspaper is an amazing power tool. Everyone is afraid of you, and you have a different influence when you come to negotiate. Because you're a publisher, you can make different offers: we will praise you in the newspaper or we will give you an advertisement for free. (journalist Robert)

The digital transition and the innovations didn't gain trust in the newsrooms, even if the newspaper ended and continued as an online news page. Most of the individual actors in the newsroom were exhausted and frustrated at the time that although they often planed continuing online, most eventually resigned. They still retain nostalgia even at the cost that the newspaper ceased publication (Usher, 2010).

> The web platform cost half a million, everything remained there, and it works perfectly. But we haven't used it yet. (entrepreneur Petr)

> We were considering continuing online, [the boss] said he would prepare it ... that was two months ago. (journalist Alena)

From the perspective of economic capital, it is quite clear why the leaver-organisations either ended or were approaching the end or are still heading towards the end (Abernathy, 2018). In every case, the simple equation, as formulated by the manager Josef, does not balance: "I can only spend as much as I have in my pocket." For various reasons, these newspapers have been in debt for a long time; they are on the verge of economic collapse; or they cover their debts from other businesses (journalist Robert; entrepreneur-journalist Jan; journalist-entrepreneur Barbora; entrepreneur-journalist Max). However, in all organisations of whatever kind the same situation emerges: economic problems arise and increase where passivity dominates. The group of leaver-organisations was successful when they began business in the 1990s. However, they merely *followed* the changes in the field rather than *reacting* to them (Hess, 2016). Interestingly, the interviewees' memories of this do not differ.

> In the beginning the advertising worked well, we didn't even have to look for it. It flowed into the newsroom, and we had a lot of correspondents. You know, in our first year we attracted half as many readers again. The turning point in sales occurred five years ago, today we are almost down to a third of our highest numbers. The decline started with the Internet, it destroyed it, we had a lot of competition – newspapers started up, but they never lasted, but the Internet cannot be overcome. (journalist-entrepreneur Barbora)

Another group of leaver-organisations had economic problems from their inception, and these continued to grow. These were newspapers that stopped publishing for a while, and/or changed owners, and then tried to regain their position.

> When I bought the newspaper, people wanted it, but we couldn't make a profit from the demand. We printed extremely cheaply but delivery to subscribers was expensive. And, of course, what with the newsroom's rental, computers, cars, and so on, the loss was at first about half a million, and then it increased by about three hundred and fifty thousand Czech crowns every year. In addition, my business partner subsidised the paper by doing the graphics for free. We went into the red from the beginning, but I thought, well, if we do it properly, when we can print colour issues, we will succeed. (entrepreneur Petr)

Hence some of these organisations were already in such straits that they began to consider any form of support, whether from local economic or political elites, and this raised concerns about compliance with journalistic ethics, part or organisations' nomos (Bourdieu, 1995).

> If there was a donor who would pour money into it every month, it could continue, but we didn't get one. The longer a paper stops publishing, the harder it is to restart it. (journalist Alena)

Moreover, what contributed to the organisations' economic problems was a distrust of the traditional business model (Olsen et al., 2020). As the interviewees searched for scapegoats, the business model was something that could be blamed for the newspapers' failure. By the end of the newspapers' existence, some staff came to believe that the only way to maintain a newspaper was to turn it into a freesheet. But they did not come up with a sustainable way to fund it when there wasn't enough advertising in the region (entrepreneur-journalist Max; journalist Milan).

From the opposite point of view, it is fascinating to see how these organisations survived for such a long time when they did not meet the basic premise of business, to generate profit, or at least cover costs. To the question why they did it, the entrepreneurs answered: because of the influence we could exert (entrepreneur Petr; entrepreneur-journalist Jan) and/or the passion we felt for the job (journalist-entrepreneur Barbora; entrepreneur-journalist Max), which can be understood as illusio (Lamour, 2019).

The relational construction of the organisation's position in the journalistic field

Regarding inter-organisational dynamics, the leaver-organisations do not differ in size from the other types of organisations. In all types there are bigger and smaller newsrooms, newspapers that cover a large district or just a smaller town and its surroundings: size has no bearing on success. Like their more successful counterparts, the less successful organisations depended for their position and operations on peripheral structures and cooperative organisations. The leaver-organisations show other similarities to their more successful rivals: for example, none of the interviewees have any relevant information about their readers, moreover some tend to look down on them. The exception is entrepreneur-journalist Max, who understands that the journalist must neither patronise nor flatter the reader.

> We have a significantly greater number of older readers, the young ones are abandoning us, they only use the Internet. (journalist-entrepreneur Barbora)

> When you have readers in the fifty-plus age range, a hundred of them will leave you every year by natural mortality alone, and no matter what you do no new ones replace them. For the under-forties, papers are something they hardly know how to handle, plus they're used to free content. And let me leave aside my age-old opinion that ninety percent of the population are stupid, so why make them a clever newspaper? (…) So I've just decided that I'll produce a newspaper no matter what the readers are like. (journalist Robert)

Similarly, contacts with other actors, such as sources, are hampered by a lack of funding. Journalists no longer go out into the field, they report from their desks (journalist-entrepreneur Barbora; journalist Robert; journalist Alena), hence the close relations between journalists and (such living people as) sources which are expected on the periphery have been disrupted or replaced by official spokespeople (Firmstone, 2016). And again, this passivity is not considered a disadvantage but an advantage (Goyanes & Rodríguez-Gómez, 2021).

> A lot of villages have up-to-date web pages and put stuff on them, so I just look at the pages and call the mayor: I've read your news, can you tell me something else or can I use this information? They're mostly happy to give it to the newspaper. (journalist Alena)

With respect to those with whom they have to cooperate in order to achieve a functioning publishing structure – the printers, the distributors and the retail outlets – the leaver-organisations struggle with the same obstacles as the other organisations. But while for the latter this is a partial complication, for the former it becomes a matter of survival: "It was the Czech Post alone, no one else finished us. We were in the red just on the production only" (entrepreneur Petr); "The newspaper was distributed by a company, but it was a catastrophe, I would not recommend it to anyone" (entrepreneur-journalist Max); "Our problems were very much related to how the points of sale disappeared … there are only three newsagents in the town. The other copies went to petrol stations and grocery stores, which were served only by the [large distribution company]" (journalist Robert); "It hurt us that the shops started to fall off, mainly in the villages" (journalist-entrepreneur Barbora).

The entrepreneurs tried to solve their problems by conducting their own distribution or by achieving it in unusual ways – e.g. by getting bakeries to deliver the paper with their pastries (entrepreneur Petr; journalist-entrepreneur Barbora). But even these did not always have the desired results.

> For example, we delivered the newspapers in a hearse. We didn't have a big enough car, so we went to borrow one and a colleague appeared in front of the newsroom with a

funeral car and pulled out two coffins into the street. I was in a cold sweat. I asked: Are we going to deliver the newspaper by hearse? So we always pulled out the coffin and took the packages round to the sellers. Everyone was horrified, but we sold all the copies (laughs). (entrepreneur-journalist Max)

The interviewees didn't see much sense in collaborating with other newspapers, either because, like other organisations, they had had a bad experience of this (journalist Milan; journalist-entrepreneur Barbora) or because they were afraid of losing control over their newspapers. As entrepreneur-journalist Jan frankly explains: "Cooperation? No, I wouldn't be able to influence it." Nevertheless, another interviewee, while not wanting to lose influence by cooperating, was at the same time not discouraged from considering possible collaborations which he had never actively sought. At the same time, he had no idea that similar newspapers existed in the surrounding areas. The proverbial "roadblocks" which stand in the way of cooperation (Hatcher & Thayer, 2017, p. 1286) consist largely of interviewees fearing to lose influence over their own newspaper: but the real problem is simple inertia.

> It would simply be worthwhile, for example, to make the municipalities take care of it as they care for the transport services in the region. (entrepreneur Petr)

Entrepreneur Petr's suggestion rests on a belief shared by all the interviewees in this group of organisations, that the municipal press is at the same time the biggest competitor of the local newspapers and the key obstacle to their economic viability. He himself sees this competition as "the last straw" that brought his newspaper to an end: "All those town halls have their own press and publish with taxpayers' money. We published an independent newspaper using my money," he adds. Journalist-entrepreneur Barbora agrees and believes that the competition "is getting worse". Entrepreneur-journalist Jan adds: "The municipal press charges for advertising at a quarter of the price that we do, but you can't do anything about it because if they don't have the money, they just ask the town for more. How can you fight it?"

Some of the interviewees were convinced that their newspapers had significant symbolic capital, mainly gained from the local field of power and/or their journalistic peers. Nevertheless, none of them is published anymore due to a loss of several capitals and not merely the symbolic one.

> I think that the town will suffer a significant intellectual loss from the closure of our newspaper, because it gives some awareness of context, which is the most precious thing today. The present is connected to what happened twenty, thirty years ago, and the newspaper kept reviving that awareness of context. (...) The newspaper should

be 'noble' if I can exaggerate it a bit. By growing up with it and reading it the townspeople understand the standard. And it is a standard we have raised and maintained. Of course, the newspaper in this form is read by the powerful of the town, by teachers, officials, politicians, intellectuals. But I think we are exceptional, specific. (journalist Robert)

Actors in the leaver-organisations either illustrate the way in which these organisations decline and die, or they represent organisations that were destined never to prosper. They became members of the field with an already insufficient set of operating rules, doxa, and kinds of capital; or they possessed capitals but fell victim to a worsening imbalance between internal and external dynamics. As in the case of the survivor-organisations, passivity played a part but also a lack of self-reflection and self-preservation.

To conclude, having analysed the stories of my communication partners and information from participatory observations, I have focused on selected elements of *organisational dynamics*, particularly on its internal relational construction and on the relational construction of the organisation's position in the journalistic field (Benson, 1999). The findings show that an organisation's capitals are a better indication of success than an organisation's size. It has been helpful to consider both the micro level of an individual organisation, its internal dynamics, and relations (Schultz, 2007), and the macro level of the inter-organisational field (Willig, 2016), both of them viewed through the lens of acquired capitals (Bourdieu, 2005).

There were two main factors which complicated the achievement of my aim. The first was the wide range of communication partners from all the organisations on the periphery: while providing a lively general picture, they were less able to cover in detail the relationships which exist within any organisation. The second was a neglect of the individualistic tendencies not only of journalists but newspaper organisations (Wiik, 2009). These behave like fragile islands in the journalistic archipelago, lacking contact or cooperation with other organisations (Anderson, 2013). Nevertheless, it was still possible to identify shared characteristics and divide the analysed organisations into three discrete classes, which usually corresponds to the degree of their power, their activity/passivity, the coherence of their rules, and compliance to the nomos of the peripheral journalistic sub-field. To finish my overview of the field on the margins of journalism, I must now connect it, in the words of Benson and Neveu (2005, p. 11), to "the entire universe of journalists and media organizations acting and reacting in relation to one another". This is the aim of the next and final chapter.

References

Abernathy, P. M. (2018). *The expanding news desert*. Hussman School of Journalism and Media: Center for Innovation and Sustainability in Local Media. www.usnewsdeserts.com

Ali, C., Radcliffe, D., Schmidt, T. R., & Donald, R. (2020). Searching for Sheboygans: On the future of small market newspapers. *Journalism, 21*(4), 453–471.

Ali, C., Schmidt, T. R., Radcliffe, D., & Donald, R. (2018). The digital life of small market newspapers: Result from a multi-method study. *Digital Journalism, 7*(7), 1–24.

Anderson, C. W. (2011). Blowing up the newsroom: Ethnography in an age of distributed journalism. In D. Domingo & C. Paterson (Eds.), *Making online news – Volume 2: Newsroom ethnographies in the second decade of internet journalism* (Vol. 2, pp. 151–160). Peter Lang Publishing.

Anderson, C. W. (2013). *Rebuilding the news: Metropolitan journalism in the digital age*. Temple University Press.

Andersson, U., & Wiik, J. (2013). Journalism meets management: Changing leadership in Swedish news organizations. *Journalism Practice, 7*(6), 705–719.

Artemas, K., Vos, T. P., & Duffy, M. (2018). Journalism hits a wall: Rhetorical construction of newspapers' editorial and advertising relationship. *Journalism Studies, 19*(7), 1004–1020.

Beck, U., & Beck-Gernsheim, E. (2001). *Individualization: Institutionalized individualism and its social and political consequences*. Sage.

Benson, R. (1999). Field theory in comparative context: A new paradigm for media studies. *Theory and Society, 28*(3), 463–498.

Benson, R., & Neveu, E. (Eds.). (2005). *Bourdieu and the journalistic field*. Polity Press.

Bentley, C. (2001). No newspaper is no fun – Even five decades later. *Newspaper Research Journal, 22*(4), 2–15.

Berkowitz, D., & TerKeurst, J. V. (1999). Community as interpretive community: Rethinking the journalist-source relationship. *Journal of Communication, 49*(3), 125–136.

Bourdieu, P. (1995). *The rules of art: Genesis and structure of the literary field*. Stanford University Press.

Bourdieu, P. (1996). *On television*. The New Press.

Bourdieu, P. (1998). *Practical reason: On the theory of action*. Stanford University Press.

Bourdieu, P. (2005). The political field, the social science field, and the journalistic field. In R. Benson, & E. Neveu (Eds.), *Bourdieu and the journalistic field* (pp. 29–47). Polity Press.

Bowd, K. (2009). "Did you see that in the paper?": Country newspapers and perceptions of local "ownership". *Australian Journalism Review, 31*(1), 49–61.

Bowd, K. (2011). Reflecting regional life: Localness and social capital in Australian country newspapers. *Pacific Journalism Review, 17*(2), 72–91.

Bowd, K. (2014). Eroding the connection?: Web 2.0 and non-metropolitan newspaper journalists. *Australian Journalism Review, 36*(1), 57–68.

Cestino, J., & Matthews, R. (2015, May 27–30). *Cultural norms and path dependence in business model innovation dynamics: The case of legacy provincial newspapers* [paper presentation]. European Media Management Association Conference EMMA, Hamburg, Germany.

Cohen, N. S., Hunter, A., & O'Donnell, P. (2019). Bearing the burden of corporate restructuring: job loss and precarious employment in Canadian journalism. *Journalism Practice*, *13*(7), 817–833.

Cornia, A., Sehl, A., & Nielsen, R. K. (2020). "We no longer live in a time of separation": A comparative analysis of how editorial and commercial integration became a norm. *Journalism*, *21*(2), 172–190.

Deuze, M., & Witschge, T. (2018). Beyond journalism: Theorizing the transformation of journalism. *Journalism*, *19*(2), 165–181.

Ekdale, B., Tully, M., Harmsen, S., & Singer, J. B. (2015). Newswork within a culture of job insecurity: Producing news amidst organizational and industry uncertainty. *Journalism Practice*, *9*(3), 383–398.

Erzikova, E., & Lowrey, W. (2017). Russian regional media: Fragmented community, fragmented online practices. *Digital Journalism*, *5*(7), 919–937.

Ewart, J. (2000). Capturing the heart of the region – how regional media define a community. *Transformations*, *1*, 1–13.

Firmstone, J. (2016). Mapping changes in local news. *Journalism Practice*, *10*(7), 1–10.

Fowler, N. (2011). Regional press challenges promote calls for new ownership forms and legal bases. In D. A. L. Levy & R. G. Picard (Eds.), *Is there a better structure for news providers?* (pp. 31–54). Reuters Institute for the Study of Journalism.

Goyanes, M., & Rodríguez-Gómez E. F. (2021). Presentism in the newsroom: How uncertainty redefines journalists' career expectations. *Journalism*, *22*(1), 52–68.

Hanusch, F. (2015). A different breed altogether?: Distinctions between local and metropolitan journalism cultures. *Journalism Studies*, *16*(6), 816–833.

Hatcher, J. A., & Thayer, D. (2017). Assessing collaboration in one media ecosystem. *Journalism Practice*, *11*(10), 1283–1301.

Hájek, R., & Carpentier, N. (2015). Alternative mainstream media in the Czech Republic: Beyond the dichotomy of alternative and mainstream media. *Continuum: Journal of Media & Cultural Studies*, *29*(3), 365–382.

Hájek, R., Vávra, J., & Svobodová, T. (2015). Threats to mutual trust: Czech local politicians and local journalists in the era of professional political communication. *Media Studies*, *6*(11), 36–50.

Hermans, L., Schaap, G., & Bardoel, J. (2014). Re-establishing the relationship with the public: Regional journalism and citizens' involvement in the news. *Journalism Studies*, *15*(5), 642–654.

Hess, K. (2013). Breaking boundaries: Recasting the "local" newspaper as "geo-social" news in a digital landscape. *Digital Journalism*, *1*(1), 48–63.

Hess, K. (2016). Ritual power: Illuminating the blind spot of births, deaths and marriages in news media research. *Journalism*, *17*(4), 511–526.

Hess, K., & Waller, L. (2016). River flows and profit flows. *Journalism Studies, 17*(3), 263–276.
Hess, K., & Waller, L. (2017). *Local journalism in a digital world.* Palgrave.
Hovden, J. F. (2008). *Profane and sacred. A study of the Norwegian journalistic field* [Unpublished doctoral dissertation]. University of Bergen. https://bora.uib.no/bora-xmlui/bitstream/handle/1956/2724/Jan%20Fredrik%20Hovden.pdf?sequence=1
Jenkins, J. (2019). Elevated influences: The construction of journalistic identities at a city magazine. *Journalism Studies, 20*(8), 1069–1087.
Jenkins, J., & Graves, L. (2019). *Case studies in collaborative local journalism: Digital news project.* Reuters Institute for the Study of Journalism.
Jenkins, J., & Nielsen, R. K. (2020a). Proximity, public service, and popularity: A comparative study of how local journalists view quality news. *Journalism Studies, 21*(2), 236–253.
Jenkins, J., & Nielsen, R. K. (2020b). Preservation and evolution: Local newspapers as ambidextrous organizations. *Journalism, 21*(4), 472–488.
Lamour, C. (2019). The legitimate peripheral position of a central medium. Revealing the margins of popular journalism. *Journalism Studies, 20*(8), 1167–1183.
Lindgren, A., Jolly, B., Sabatini, C., & Wong, C. (2019). *Good news, bad news: A snapshot of conditions at small-market newspapers in Canada.* Local News Research Project, National NewsMedia Council.
MacDonald, J. B., Saliba, A. J., Hodgins, G., & Ovington, L. A. (2016). Burnout in journalists: A systematic literature review. *Burnout Research, 3*(2), 34–44.
Marchetti, D. (2005). Subfields of specialized journalism. In R. Benson, & E. Neveu (Eds.), *Bourdieu and the journalistic field* (pp. 64–84). Polity Press.
Milliken, C. (2020). The case for local news journalism professors use innovation to revitalize a struggling industry. *Northwestern Magazine.* https://magazine.northwestern.edu/exclusives/the-case-for-local-news/
Napoli, P. M., Weber, M., McCollough, K., & Wang, Q. (2018). *Assessing local journalism: News deserts, journalism divides, and the determinants of the robustness of local news.* DeWitt Wallace Center for Media and Democracy.
Nielsen, R. K., & Levy, D. A. L. (2010). Which way for the business of journalism? In D. A. L. Levy & R. K. Nielsen (Eds.), *The changing business of journalism and its implications for democracy* (pp. 135–147). Reuters Institute for the Study of Journalism.
Olsen, R. K., Kammer, A., & Solvoll, M. K. (2020). Paywalls' impact on local news websites' traffic and their civic and business implications. *Journalism Studies, 21*(2), 197–216.
Örnebring, H. (2013). Anything you can do, I can do better? Professional journalists on citizen journalism in six European countries. *The International Communication Gazette, 75*(1), 35–53.
Paulussen, S., Geens, D., & Vandenbrande, K. (2011). Fostering a culture of collaboration: Organizational challenges of newsroom innovation. In D. Domingo, & C. Paterson (Eds.), *Making online news – Volume 2: Newsroom ethnographies in the second decade of internet journalism* (pp. 3–14). Peter Lang Publishing.

Raviola, E. (2012). Exploring organizational framings: Journalism and business management in newspaper organizations. *Information, Communication & Society, 15*(6), 932–958.

Reinardy, S. (2011). Newspaper journalism in crisis: Burnout on the rise, eroding young journalists' career commitment. *Journalism, 12*(1), 33–50.

Rosenlund, L. (2009). *Exploring the city with Bourdieu*. VDM Verlag Dr. Müller.

Rivas-Rodriguez, M. (2011). Communities, cultural identity, and the news. In W. Lowrey & P. J. Gade (Eds.), *Changing the news: The forces shaping journalism in uncertain times* (pp. 102–117). Routledge.

Russo, T. C. (1998). Organizational and professional identification: A case of newspaper journalists. *Management Communication Quarterly, 12*(1), 72–111.

Schultz, I. (2007). The journalistic gut feeling: Journalistic doxa, news habitus and orthodox news values. *Journalism Practice, 1*(2), 190–207.

Siegelbaum, S., & Thomas, R. J. (2016). Putting the work (back) into newswork. *Journalism Practice, 10*(3), 387–404.

Smethers, S. J., Bressers, B., & Mwangi, S. C. (2017). Friendships sustain volunteer newspaper for 21 years. *Newspaper Research Journal, 38*(3), 379–391.

Smethers, S., Bressers, B., Willard, A., Harvey, L., & Freeland, G. (2007). Kansas readers feel loss when town's paper closes. *Newspaper Research Journal, 28*(4), 6–21.

Spaulding, S. (2016). The poetics of goodbye: Change and nostalgia in goodbye narratives penned by ex-Baltimore Sun employees. *Journalism, 17*(2), 208–226.

Usher, N. (2010). Goodbye to the news: How out-of-work journalists assess enduring news values and the new media landscape. *New Media & Society, 12*(6), 911–928.

Usher, N. (2015) Newsroom moves and the newspaper crisis evaluated: Space, place, and cultural meaning. *Media, Culture & Society, 37*(7), 1005–1021.

Wahl-Jorgensen, K. (2019). Challenging presentism in journalism studies: An emotional life history approach to understanding the lived experience of journalists. *Journalism, 20*(5), 670–678.

Waldenström, A., Wiik, J., & Andersson, U. (2019). Conditional autonomy: Journalistic practice in the tension field between professionalism and managerialism. *Journalism Practice, 13*(4), 493–508.

Waschková Císařová, L. (2013). *Český lokální a regionální tisk mezi lety 1989 a 2009* [Czech local and regional press between 1989 and 2009]. Masarykova univerzita.

Waschková Císařová, L. (2015). Comparing Czech and Slovak council newspapers' policy and regulation development. *Media and Communication, 3*(4), 62–75.

Waschková Císařová, L. (2023a). We were innovators, but we gave up: The muted digital transition of local newspapers. *Digital Journalism, 10*(3), 1–18.

Waschková Císařová, L. (2023b). Backed into a corner: Structural changes that lead to local news deserts. *Media and Communication, 11*(3), 1–9.

Wiik, J. (2009). Identities under construction: professional journalism in a phase of destabilization. *International Review of Sociology, 19*(2), 351–365.

Willig, I. (2016). Field theory and media production: A bridge-building strategy. In C. Paterson, D. Lee, A. Saha, & A. Zoellner (Eds.), *Advancing media production research: Shifting sites, methods, and politics* (pp. 53–67). Palgrave Macmillan.

Wolfgang, D. J., & Jenkins, J. (2018). Crafting a community: Staff members' conceptions of audience at a city magazine. *Community Journalism, 6*(1), 1–20.

CHAPTER 6

The margins of journalism revisited: Alongside journalism

I now turn to add the finishing touches to my picture of the margins of journalism and its actors by summarising their characteristics. I shall focus on three related matters: first, and in line with my ground-up approach and path-dependent focus, based on the self-understanding and self-definition of my communication partners, I will start with the individual actors and organisations in the field of peripheral journalism, summarising their habitus, capitals, and practices. Second, I will sketch the full picture of this peripheral sub-field, the positions of the agents within it and their relations with other fields and agents. Third, I will address the questions I formulated in the introduction and outline other directions in which the topic may be pursued in the future.

The margins of journalism from the ground up

From the outset, I intended to develop this analysis of the margins of journalism by building out from the strength of the stories of the individual and organisational actors, in order to give them voice. With that in mind, I present a summary of findings that focus on the individual agents below. I describe in particular the habitus, capitals and practices of the individual journalistic workers and the capitals and practices of the classes of organisational actors. This approach follows

Bourdieu's paraphrase of Pascal (1998, pp. 12–13): "[T]he social world embraces me like a point. But this point is a point of view, the principle of a view adopted from a point located in social space, a perspective which is defined, in its form and contents, by the objective position from which it is adopted." And with that in mind, I now summarise all the points made by the journalists on the margins.

I explored the suitability of the field theory for my aim, and I recap my framework here. Bourdieu (1984, p. 114) summarises the definition of *habitus* as "a space whose three fundamental dimensions are defined by amount of capital, composition of capital, and change in these two properties over time (manifested by past and potential trajectory in social space)". With respect to the capitals (see Table 1) an individual in the journalistic field can possess, there is the *social capital* manifested by relationships with colleagues, competitors, audiences and sources; *cultural capital* as the sum of knowledge, skills, education, rules and norms, potentially convertible to *economic capital*, an individual's income or revenue; and the *symbolic capital* which legitimises and derives prestige from the recognition of their peers and other actors (Erzikova & Lowrey, 2017).

As I pointed out earlier, habitus itself does not embrace all social practices, therefore, Bourdieu proposes an equation: *[(habitus) (capital)] + field = practice* (1984, p. 101). For journalists, their *practice* – where and how they work, the nature of their position with respect to resolving important dilemmas – depends on the specific structure of their habitus, the amount and composition of capital and the dynamics of the specific field in which the social practice takes place (Hovden, 2008). At the same time, it is important to recall that although I treat the actors individually, I am referring to the class of actors and/or a fraction of the class, and I take into account that

> when the trajectory effect concerns a whole class or class fraction, that is, a set of individuals who occupy an identical position and are engaged in the same collective trajectory, the one which defines a rising or declining class, there is a danger of attributing to the properties synchronically attached to the class, effects (e.g., political or religious opinions) which are in reality the product of collective transformations. (Bourdieu, 1984, p. 112)

During speaking with my communication partners, I realised, that the analysis is complicated by the fact that some members of the class fractions decided to embark on individual trajectories running in the opposite direction to the fraction as a whole (Bourdieu, 1984).

To paint a fuller picture of this sub-field as it develops, my analysis took into its considerations that the peripheral journalistic sub-field is relatively autonomous, with its own definable law; its own underlying *nomos* (Hovden, 2008). The practical schemes, implicit tacit presuppositions in the field represent the *doxa* (Bourdieu, 2005), which is intertwined with the *illusio*, the belief, emotional investment, or strong feeling for the journalistic mission (Lamour, 2019).

To explore how the habitus and the capitals of peripheral actors in the journalistic field are constructed, and through it their practices, I sum up my research findings in a table (see Table 4) which divides them into two classes of individual agents (journalist, entrepreneur) and their fractions (journalist, freelancer; journalist-entrepreneur, entrepreneur-journalist). The table sets out not only the forms of acquired capital but also, in the cases where it is necessary to create an overall picture and possible trajectory, their sources, reasons and ways in which they are obtained.

Although I would argue that the boundaries between the classes of agents in the peripheral journalistic sub-field would be permeable, it emerged from the analysis of habitus, capitals, and practices that their differences could still be clearly identified according to the distribution of their forms of *capital*, their *doxa* and their *illusio*.

Speaking about the class of journalists, I recognised two class fractions: journalists and freelancers. The *habitus* of a *journalist* on the margins entails a close but ambivalent relationship to the job. On the one hand, a journalist understands journalistic work as a passion and is fully dedicated to both the profession and the newspaper. She understands the work as an opportunity to feel free, to be visible and recognisable, and that is more important than money. On the other hand, the closeness of the relationship means that the job is precarious, causing burn-out and problems with work-life balance, and over a longer period of time brings passivity and weariness. *Journalistic capital* is in effect a combination of the capitals a journalist possesses. They are typically based on relatively high social capital, average cultural capital and low economic capital and reflect a significant decline of social capital over time and a related decline of symbolic capital. Regarding distinctive *practices*, the journalist still works in a newsroom; she substitutes in other journalistic roles; and she devotes less time to the more expensive work associated mainly with investigative journalism.

Being a *freelancer* on the journalistic margins means having a *habitus* based on the relationship to work but involves only a loose relationship with the newspaper. Doing the job as a hobby creates for a freelancer a sense either of local recognition/ visibility in a locality or of acquiring money as an honorarium. As both of these feelings weaken over time, the freelancer's passivity increases. *Freelancer's capital* is uniquely acquired in that specific social capital (close networking with sources and readers) is turned into economic as well as symbolic capital. The *freelancer's practices* are based on working from home; substituting in journalistic roles as

Table 4: Habitus, forms of capital, and practices of the class fractions of individual agents

	Journalist	Freelancer	Journalist-entrepreneur	Entrepreneur-journalist
Habitus	Journalistic work as a passion/Dedication to the profession and the newspaper

Work as precarious/Risk of burn-out from acting as a substitute

Problems maintaining a work-life balance

Work as an opportunity to feel free and acquire visibility | Journalistic work as a passion/Dedication to the profession rather than the newspaper

Work as a hobby/One of several jobs

Work as an opportunity to be visible

Insecure and ambivalent position: not regarded as a journalist, and being underestimated, by colleagues/Considered a journalist by readers and sources

Increasing unwillingness to work as a freelancer due to deteriorating financial conditions/Tendency to passivity | Journalistic work as a passion/ Journalistic work as a relaxation from entrepreneurial responsibilities/ Frustration when doing something different from journalism

Entrepreneurial work is a must and a burden/ Increasing passivity towards managerial performance

Stronger identification with the role of journalist than with that of entrepreneur

Doing things their way is a must/ Desire to be autonomous and in control as a journalist

Busy-ness and new projects as a solution to burn-out/ Burn-out from multi-tasking and weight of responsibility | Journalistic work as a hobby

Entrepreneurial work as a passion

Doing things their way is a must/Gives entrepreneurial freedom

Wishes to buy a newspaper as a profitable business and/or a tool of influence

Decreasing interest in profit connected to growing interest in journalism |

Increasing passivity in conduct of work/ Alertness to easier ways of doing the job	Saviour of a newspaper		Increasing identification with journalism risks burn-out/added pressures/responsibilities	
The dedicated journalist is indifferent to money	Feeling a responsibility for colleagues		Feeling a responsibility for the entire business	
	Difficulty of balancing two roles, and both these with a private life/ Achieving a balance brings satisfaction and reduces burn-out		Managerial responsibility as a reason to enter local politics	
	Discrepancy between ideals for the job and actual organisational practices		Freedom understood as independence from municipality/ state support	
	Growing status in the locality/ Member of the local field of power/ Journalistic responsibility as a reason for entering local politics			
	Solving the problem with a handing over the newspaper to a successor			

Capitals

Cultural capital

No journalistic education	No journalistic education	No previous managerial or business skills or experience	No previous journalistic knowledge	
Journalistic talent(s) and skills (creativity)	Journalistic talent(s) and skills (creativity)	Acquiring entrepreneurial skills by trial and error	Acquires journalistic skills by trial and error/through socialisation in the newsroom	
Work as a calling	Work as a calling	Motivated to become an entrepreneur by a certain type of crisis or uncertainty		
Relatives (parental example) or friends (dissident past) in the profession	Acquiring journalistic skills through socialisation in the newsroom			

(*Continued*)

Table 4: *Continued*

	Journalist	Freelancer	Journalist-entrepreneur	Entrepreneur-journalist
	Acquiring journalistic skills through socialisation in the newsroom	Lower professional self-confidence	Understanding of ways to combine journalistic and entrepreneurial roles as normatively problematic	Entrepreneurial experiences gained gradually in other businesses
	Journalistic norms and rules taken for granted/ Unconventional approach to active participation in local politics/ Rules affected by the proximity of audiences and sources	More relaxed approach to journalistic normative and ethical expectations/ Willingness to help/ Activism	Values public service and socially responsible roles of the newspaper	Growing emotional attachment to the newspaper
			Involvement in local politics as a way to make changes in the locality/ compromises impartiality	Journalistic rules and norms declared rather than practised/ Rules and norms apply to subordinates/ Refusal to take any money or support from municipality/state
Social capital	Network of relationships from the dissident past	Distance from colleagues	Balance in the relationship between the editorial and commercial elements of the newspaper	Understands readers as customers and consumers
	Social network that gives entry to the profession	Proximity to sources and readers	Collegial authority/Peer recognition	Relationship with other actors seen as a power relationship
	Knows nothing relevant about readers	Lack of collegial and organisational support/ Distance from the newsroom/relative autonomy	Declining knowledge of readers	"Lone wolves" or with a less powerful partner
	Declining relationships with colleagues in the newsroom		Developing relationship to individuals with economic and/or symbolic capital in a locality/to members of the local field of power	Underestimates journalists if they are non-entrepreneurs
				Close relations to businesspersons in a locality/ to members of the local field of power

	Spokespersons understood as an obstruction to genuine sources		
	Proximity to sources seen as a double-edged sword		
	Declining status in the locality/Outdated and irrelevant role		
Economic capital	Brings own equipment to the newsroom	Financial motivation to enter the field	Economic motivation to own a newspaper
	Organisational economic decline perceived as the Sword of Damocles	Saving newspaper without considering its economic viability	Assesses the reader and product from a business/profitability perspective
		Maintaining the traditional business model of the newspaper	Relationship to the newspaper based on profitability/Struggle for the survival can grow deeper
		The more numerous the jobs, the greater the independence from individual sources of income	Supports the newspaper with income from other business(es)/Thinking about synergies between the businesses
		Understood as cost-savers and potential competitors for full-time journalists	Refusal to take any financial support from municipality/state

(Continued)

Table 4: Continued

	Journalist	Freelancer	Journalist-entrepreneur	Entrepreneur-journalist
Symbolic capital	The "face" of the newspaper/Recognised in the locality as a journalist	Job as a way of gaining a position in a locality	Being renowned in the locality for the cultural capital acquired in becoming an entrepreneur	Being renowned in the locality for economic capital and business experience
	Diminishing credibility caused by growing distance between journalists and readers/sources	Diminishing credibility when breaking down normative and ethical walls for money	Activity in local politics brings both the benefits and problems of recognition	Journalistic identity/financial problems as obstacles to recognition in the locality
		Of questionable reliability in the eyes of colleagues and bosses	Part of the local field of power because a newspaper owner	Activity in local politics as a next step to entrepreneurial responsibility
				Membership in the local field of power despite owning a newspaper

Practices	Proposing, confirming, and writing stories	Proposing, confirming, and writing stories	Editorial responsibility for the content	Making a profit
	Talking with ordinary people as sources	Decline of investigative journalism because of lack of organisational backing	Entrepreneurial responsibility for the survival of the newspaper/for colleagues and their socialisation	Financially supports the newspaper from other businesses
	Copying press releases as unprofessional work	Mostly works from home	The recurrent duty of appointing and training new colleagues	Uses the newspaper as a power lever
	Still works in a newsroom	Working as a substitute for internal journalists in the newsroom/Acquisition of other, various jobs	Aversion to managerial work, bureaucracy and administration	Entrepreneurial responsibility for the profitability and survival of all owned businesses
	Working as a substitute in other journalistic roles in the newsroom		Working as a substitute on any of the jobs in the newsroom, whether journalistic or entrepreneurial	Does not draw a salary for working for the newspaper
	Decline of investigative journalism because of lack of money			Bureaucracy and administrative chores are part of the job
				Working as a substitute on any of the jobs in the newsroom, whether entrepreneurial or journalistic

Credit: The Author.

well as performing non-journalistic roles in the newsroom; and working on non-conflicting topics because the freelancers lack organisational support.

The class of *entrepreneurs* consists of two fractions: journalist-entrepreneurs and entrepreneur-journalists. The *habitus* of a *journalist-entrepreneur* on the margins conflates two distinct identities whose relationship develops over time: journalistic work transformed from a passion into a guilty pleasure, and entrepreneurial work degraded from a necessity to a burden consequent upon the fact that the journalist-entrepreneur identifies more with her journalistic than with her entrepreneurial identity. As an active initiator of changes and an individualist in this endeavour, and at the same time feeling responsible for both paper and colleagues, the journalist-entrepreneur is often burnt-out from multi-tasking, lonely in her role and frustrated because she must manage but prefers to write. On the one hand there is the difficulty of balancing these roles, and then of balancing both with the rest of her life; on the other the growing recognition and status in the locality, entering into the local field of power and the related option of entering into local politics. *Journalistic-entrepreneurial capital* is based on a strong and colourful network of social relationships, while a journalist's social capital is built mainly on relations with colleagues and the freelancer's social capital on readers and sources. The journalist-entrepreneur's social capital consists of the widest spectrum of social networks – with colleagues, readers, and members of the local field of power. At the same time economic capital, the ability to earn money, impacts on her only when it disrupts other capitals. Recognition in the locality as well as in the journalistic field represents a social and cultural capital acquired over years of experience. The recognisable *practices* of a journalist-entrepreneur are: taking overall responsibility for editorial content and administrative matters, and ensuring the economic survival of the newspaper. She is responsible for her colleagues' professional experiences and therefore for building their cultural capital, and she is able to act as substitute in all the jobs in the newsroom, whether journalistic or administrative.

Being an *entrepreneur-journalist* on the margins means having a *habitus* built first from the entrepreneurial role and then from the journalistic, which suggests that entrepreneurial work is a passion and journalistic work a hobby. The original motivation to run a newspaper as a profitable business has yielded to a growing relationship with journalism. Nevertheless, business success is a core part of the entrepreneur-journalistic habitus, the individual gains recognition from it and managerial responsibility prompts her to become more active in a local field of power, perhaps by entering politics. *Entrepreneurial-journalistic capital* is based on a network with a whole spectrum of actors, nevertheless, the person who has it despises many of them. There is a large part of economic capital which does not need to come from the newspaper but could be derived from other businesses, such as real estate agency. The recognition of an entrepreneur-journalist is gained to a greater degree from business than from journalism, moreover financial problems in the newspaper business can pose a threat to her symbolic capital. Activity in local politics is understood as the next phase of entrepreneurial responsibility. The distinctive *practices* of an entrepreneur-journalist focus mainly on making a profit, either from the newspaper or other businesses, and using the newspaper as a lever.

The next step was to characterise the organisation as an agent within the peripheral journalistic sub-field. This approach offers an understanding of the local newspaper organisations' capitals and practices, assembled and performed in the process of *organisational dynamics*, through both an intra-organisational focus on how individual actors and their interplay build the organisation's identity from within, and an inter-organisational focus on their relations with other actors in the field (Bourdieu, 1995).

Capitals (see Table 3) and related practices are as important for organisational agents as for individual ones. They are based on the same essence of the four kinds of capital and practices but take on specific forms based on organisational dynamics: *social capital* reflects the relations of individual actors inside the organisation as well as the organisation's relations with other actors in the peripheral journalistic field; *cultural capital* refers both to that of the individual actors within the organisation and the organisation's institutional rules and norms, knowledge, traditions, associated experiences and the brand it has cultivated. Cultural capital can be converted into *economic capital* – property holdings, size of circulation, subscriptions, advertising revenue and the organisation's overall financial condition. Any of these kinds of capital can be converted into *symbolic capital* through legitimisation and recognition (Benson & Neveu, 2005). Moreover, an organisation's *practices* encompass the work it performs, how it approaches key dilemmas, which roles it plays in the field, the amount and composition of capital and the dynamics of the specific field in which the social practice takes place (Hovden, 2008). My findings relating to the capitals and practices of the three classes of organisational actors – achievers, survivors, and leavers – are summarised in the following table (Table 5).

At the organisational level I consider three classes: achiever-organisations, survivor-organisations, and leaver-organisations. The *capital of an achiever-organisation* is built on a strong and wide network of social relationships, a stable position in the journalistic field and locality, and on a sound economic position. The *practices of an achiever-organisation* are characterised by proactivity and self-sufficiency. The *capital of a survivor-organisation* reflects relationships succumbing to individualism, crumbling social capital, a reputation for instability, and a declining economic condition. The *practices of a survivor-organisation* are characterised by a growing passivity and the newspaper's reliance on external

Table 5: Forms of capital and practices of classes of organisations

	Achiever-organisation	Survivor-organisation	Leaver-organisation
Capitals			
Cultural capital	Individuals emotionally attached to their work	Attachment to work and organisation varies with individuals	Organisation relies on only one full-timer and external freelancers
	Individuals emotionally attached to the news organisation	Lack of skilled and experienced journalists/The frequent socialisation of newcomers hampers the newsroom	Deterioration of credit and trust due to various causes/Weakened brand/Loss of newspaper's "face"
	The organisation's publishing tradition and brand maintenance	Operational problems disrupt the brand	
	Nostalgia for the "good old days"/Willingness to take an active approach and learn continuously	Nostalgia for the "good old days"/Passive approach to problems/Little effort to learn and develop innovations	Nostalgia for the "good old days"/Indifference to innovations and new knowledge
	Journalistic rules and norms mostly tacit and implicit	Journalistic rules and norms rarely formulated	Journalistic rules and norms rarely discussed
	Wall between the editorial and commercial parts of the newsroom	Crumbling of the wall between editorial and commercial parts of the newsroom	Collapse of the wall between the editorial and commercial parts of the newsroom
	Involvement in local politics an acceptable "tradition"/Openly discussed	Involvement in local politics an acceptable "tradition"/Passively accepted	Involvement in local politics seen as an advantage
	Slow pace of digital transition	Digital transition halted	Resignation to digital transition

Social capital	Team of colleagues who stick together	Group of individuals rather than a team of colleagues in the newsroom	Only single operators in the newsroom/Fragility of newspapers, which mostly shut down when that operator leaves
	Team-spirit built during hard times	Fluctuation in number of journalists/Limited number of potential new employees on the periphery	Lack of teamwork or leadership
	Existence of newsroom as a meeting point for colleagues/readers/sources	Alienation of workers from entrepreneurs	
	Superiors lead by example, with clear demands	Closures of the newsroom and introduction of home offices/Gradual loss of contact between colleagues/Loss of a meeting point with readers and sources	No relevant information about readers/Attempts to rise above the readership
	Organisations as individual players/Lack of intra-organisational or journalistic cooperation	Lack of people and/or energy to support a relationship with readers/ Declining relationship with sources	Loss of contact with sources
	Tighter social relationships of smaller newspapers/Proximity to other actors	Lack of relevant information about audience	
	Relevant information about the readership	Especially close relationships with, and financial support from, municipalities	Dysfunctional inter-organisational cooperation
	Resistance to competition/Competition seen as a spur to improvement	Attempts at inter-organisational cooperation fail through inertia and fear of competition	Other news and/or printing, distribution and selling organisations are seen as competitors rather than allies
	Cooperation with local printers, distributors, and sellers	Problematic cooperation with national and monopolistic printers, distributors, and sellers	
		Competition undermining the stability of an organisation, particularly from municipal press	

(*Continued*)

Table 5: *Continued*

	Achiever-organisation	Survivor-organisation	Leaver-organisation
Economic capital	Seldom treating people or operations as a means of making economies	Staff lay-offs	Reluctance to spend money on people
	Journalists as employees or internal self-employed persons	Journalists as freelancers, contractual workers, external contributors paid by honorarium	Long-term debts or on the verge of economic failure
	Money not regarded as the main motivation	Partial economic problems and financial uncertainties	Financial problems arise and increase where passivity prevails
	The tabloid appearance of the newspaper aims to attract readers	Dwindling budget for newsgathering attributed to lack of employees	Distrust in the traditional business model/No idea about any other sustainable means of existence
	Economic stability and profitability	Temporary economic instability and occasional economic results hovering between profit and loss	
	Costs and revenues balanced		
	Ability to overcome temporary economic problems	Traditional business model shifting to a model of financing newspapers mainly or wholly from readers	
	Traditional business model/Inability to imagine another which would be viable	Dependency on outsiders for production and distribution, creating financial vulnerability	
	Self-sufficient production prevents financial vulnerability		

Symbolic capital	Title and team visible in the locality	Decreasing visibility of the title and of the journalists in the locality	Invisibility of the title and journalists in the locality
	Strong brand or strong individual who embodies it	Decline in the brand or individual who embodies it/Decline in the readers' recognition/Criticism from the readers	Loss of brand and relevance of the title or the individual who embodies it
	Stable financial situation	Unstable/Declining financial situation	Financial instability
	Decline of relevance due to missing innovations and slow-paced digital adoption	Declining preconditions for quality journalism	Loss of preconditions for quality journalism
	Fulfilling the preconditions for quality journalistic work	Close relationships with members of the local field of power	Economic problems attract support from local economic and/or political elites
	Loneliness at the top of the organisation		
	Maintaining a balanced relationship with relevant co-dependent organisations in the locality		
Practices	Willingness to learn/Active approach to new ideas and topics	Problems with finding topics: they no longer present themselves	Reliance for news on official sources and press releases/Abandonment of self-originated or investigative topics
	Newspaper production is in-house	Newspaper dependent on outside printers, distributors and sellers	Dependence on outside printers, distributors and sellers
	The newsroom is maintained		

(*Continued*)

Table 5: *Continued*

Achiever-organisation	Survivor-organisation	Leaver-organisation
Publishing locally relevant topics/ Maintaining investigative reporting	Closure of the newsroom	Closure of the newsroom
Slow digital transition	Abandonment of investigative reporting/ Moving towards sensational topics/Resignation to thematic diversity	Moving online as the last resort
		Abandonment of digital transition
	Digital transition halted	Closure of the newspaper

Credit: The Author.

organisations for production and distribution. The *capital of a leaver-organisation* is the most depleted of all. It is built on individuals rather than a network of relationships, is recognisable only to a few, and is hampered by serious economic problems with no idea how to devise a sustainable means of existence. The *practices of a leaver-organisation* are characterised by a passivity of attitude, a loss of relevance to public needs and tastes, and a dependency on external production organisations.

It turns out that the cultural capital of these various agencies does not significantly distinguish between them. Its only meaningful characteristic is that it increases over time as the agents acquires experience. With respect to symbolic capital, participation in local politics is recognised as a logical part of the agents' progression into the local field of power. It shows a tighter dynamic in the exercise of power within the locality, the specifics of the nomos of the peripheral journalistic field and a greater permeability between the journalistic and political fields, but at the same time a loss of cultural capital in terms of what people understand to be journalistic norms. We might assume that these actors would appear in a locality and vie with each other for the prestige expressed by symbolic capital. Yet interestingly enough this is not the case because with one exception these newspapers are the sole operators within their respective localities. The competition comes more from something else, notably the municipal press, which by the nature of its propaganda should not pose a threat to independent media. It is thus another example of the overlap between the journalistic, political, and economic fields and the local field of power and the specifics of the nomos. In the fight for power the players in the latter cannot be defeated: it is less of a genuine conflict than a tilt at a windmill. Yet no matter how futile the struggle, it affects the agents in the field of peripheral journalism.

The margins of the journalistic field

Having summarised the dispositions of the agents, I turn to sketching the full picture of the peripheral journalistic sub-field, the positions of the agents within it and the relations with other fields and their agents. This further interconnect the analysis of individuals and organisations within the framework of the journalistic field. As Bourdieu reminds us, distinction is,

> a certain quality of bearing and manners, most often considered innate (one speaks of *distinction naturelle*, "natural refinement"), is nothing other than *difference*, a gap, a distinctive feature, in short, a *relational* property existing only in and through its relation with other properties. (1998, p. 6)

He adds (1998, p. 6) that this difference, "or a gap, is at the basis of the very notion of space, that is, a set of distinct and coexisting positions which are exterior to one another"; "which are defined in relation to one another through their mutual exteriority and their relations of proximity, vicinity, or distance, as well as through relations of order, such as above, below, and between".

The findings confirm the existence of a relatively autonomous *peripheral journalistic sub-field* formed by the local newspapers' journalistic workers as individual agents and the local newspapers as organisational agents (Bourdieu, 1984, 2005), and their mutual struggles (Carlson & Lewis, 2015) and boundaries (Bourdieu, 1995). This sub-field is particularly based on a specific group of media (local newspapers) and the path-dependent context (Benson & Neveu, 2005) of the Czech post-socialist and post-transitive media system. On the one hand, then, I focus on the interplay of these actors over time (Benson & Neveu, 2005) and on the other hand on the relations of this field with other, adjacent fields and with the local field of power (Hovden, 2008). This sub-field is a relatively autonomous social world, unique and distinguishable, a world with its own nomos, characteristics, and processes within which there are power relations, interests, a struggle for hierarchy and relevance; the broader context of the rules, conventions and values implicitly adopted by actors, the doxa and illusio. The agents have identifiable positions and dispositions within it and the boundaries between their classes and fractions are quite clear. Nevertheless, the sub-field is at the same time heteronomous in its relations to other fields (the national journalistic field, the political field, the economic field, the local field of power) and in the permeability of its boundaries with them. The interlocutors from other fields are important in the development of the sub-field, they affect it and therefore change its nomos (Marchetti, 2005).

The diagram (see Figure 7) shows how the peripheral journalistic sub-field is created by the agents and their positions according to the relative weight of their social and economic forms of capital, together with their actions and reactions. Moreover, it captures the trajectory of the agents (Benson & Neveu, 2005). There are two axes, social capital, and economic capital (Hess, 2013b), and two positions are assigned to each agent.[1] The first (in grey) is the agent's past position, based on the interviewees' memories of the situation and data from the surveys of 2009 and 2014; the second (in black) is the present position of the agent based on the same data from 2019. In addition, practices are shown which relate to each class or class fraction.

There are four distinguishable quadrants in this diagram. The first is of agents with large amounts of both social and economic capital – the journalist-entrepreneur, the achiever-organisation, and a former position of the survivor-organisation. The

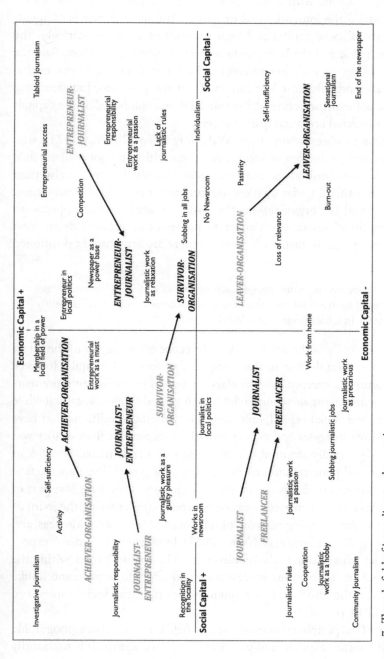

Figure 7: The sub-field of journalism on the margins
Credit: The Author.

second cluster is of agents with a large reserve of social capital but low reserve of economic capital – the journalist and freelancer. The third cluster is of agents with low amounts of social capital and high amounts of economic capital – the entrepreneur-journalist and the later position of a survivor-organisation. And the fourth cluster is of agents with low reserves of both social and economic capital typifying the leaver-organisation. We can see from the positions, practices, and relationships the coherent structure of the sub-field and confirm that the capitals which have been selected are suitably distinctive.

This is similar to observations from Wahl-Jorgensen (2019b, p. 673), who finds "journalists occupy distinctive subject positions within the journalistic field (…). These positions not only shape their engagement with change, but also their ability to adapt and thrive under challenging circumstances." At the same time, "some journalists, and the organizations they work in, are better equipped with material and emotional resources to adapt to processes of 'creative destruction' currently shaking up the industry", "whereas others are structurally positioned to fail":

> responses to change cannot be understood as occurring in a vacuum but are instead profoundly shaped by structural conditions and power relations which have frequently remained invisible in scholarly accounts. (Wahl-Jorgensen, 2019b, p. 673)

Above all, the trajectories of the agents reflect the economic struggles of the actors in the field and a general decline in the amount of all forms of capital. However, there are two interesting exceptions – the class fraction of journalist-entrepreneurs and the class of achiever-organisations, which both gained economic capital while they lost part of their social capital, reflecting the changing conditions that have occurred after power struggles and victory over the competition. This victory was in turn a result of gradually acquired self-sufficiency or a constructed network of cooperative actors and penetration into the local field of power. The class fraction of entrepreneur-journalists shows a remarkable trajectory: they have lost part of their economic capital but increased their social capital after entering the journalistic profession, building a strong network of relationships with acquaintances, and gaining social recognition (Benson & Neveu, 2005). In line with Bourdieu's expectation, we can relate this to other scholarship on local journalism's space within the field, where "social capital requires endless time and effort to acquire and unlike economic capital, if the effort and investment ceases then the social capital can dissolve" (Hess, 2013, p. 120).

My diagram of the peripheral journalistic sub-field is the result of ethnographic insights into the habitus, capitals, and practices of selected agents. It is necessarily selective, but the aim of my approach from the ground up was to capture those agents fully and from their self-reflective positions (Schultz, 2007; Zelizer, 2017). I was thus able to depict a relatively autonomous sub-field of local newspapers within the larger national journalistic field (Duval, 2005; Marchetti, 2005). The distinctive features of the sub-field turned out not to be the cultural capital which is usually identified but the social and economic capitals of the agents. This is in line with the author's expectations of local newspapers. To understand social capital with Bourdieu as "the sum of the resources, actual or virtual, that accrue to an individual or a group by virtue of possessing a durable network of more or less institutionalized relationships of mutual acquaintances and recognition" (Benson & Neveu, 2005, p. 21) is to understand the local newspaper as an embodiment of local social relations. Kristy Hess (2013, p. 113), for example, suggests "viewing social capital as a specific resource of power/advantage that commercial news organizations can consciously invest in and develop for their own gain"; and proposes reconceptualisation of social capital to *mediated social capital* "to consider the small newspaper's ability to connect people as a resource of advantage which it may utilise to build or maintain its position of power" (2015, p. 482). Similarly, Kathryn Bowd (2011, p. 75) discusses local newspapers primarily in terms of social capital: "If social capital helps to hold communities together, institutions that foster its growth may make valuable contributions to life in regional areas. Local news media – including local newspapers – are one such institution." The potential of social capital emerged from my focus on the life histories of the individual actors. Wahl-Jorgensen observes that

> individual lives do not unfold in isolation but are deeply embedded within and shaped by particular communities, cultures and professions (…). They are part of collectivities that experience and react to sweeping change. (2019b, p. 672)

There are several *interlocutors* (Marchetti, 2005) we need to consider in relation to this sub-field; that is, agents with which those in the sub-field interact, such as the readership, the sources and those organisations supplying production and logistics. These impact on the sub-field, which is, moreover, heteronomous since it intersects with the economic field (on the side of entrepreneurs) and also overlaps with the political field and the local field of power. Jenkins (2019, pp. 1070–1071) emphasises the importance of the extra-media level, of external institutions "such as advertisers, sources, and other media organizations".

Nevertheless, it is inappropriate to assume that all types of local media simply mirror the experiences of the actors who have been represented here. Scholars remind us that they "argue for a more nuanced vocabulary to speak about newspapers and local news. Grouping all newspapers into a monolithic industry – as general sector analyses often do – suggests a homogeneous experience. This is not the case" (Ali et al., 2020, pp. 454–455). To consider the distinctive potential of social capital for other agents in the journalistic field, further research steps are needed to broaden the picture and avoid the errors which Bourdieu (1996, p. 68) terms: the illusion of the "never-been-seen-before" and its counterpart, "the-way-it-always-has-been".

Journalism – and alongside journalism

Finally, I will now address the questions I posed at the beginning and suggest some future avenues of inquiry. At the beginning I entered virgin territory labelled *Hic sunt leones* and in the pages between then and now, I have tried to explore this territory and place it clearly on the map. My aims were focused both on individuals and organisations in the margins of the journalistic field: I wished (1) to contribute to a wider understanding of what it means to be a journalist, analysing the identities of these peripheral journalists through the way they understand their occupational boundaries, their attitude to the job and the reflection of their everyday practices in the timespan of their life histories; (2) to set out the peripheral journalistic sub-field of local newspapers – to investigate the journalists from their habitus(es), capitals and practices, the position of local newspapers as media organisations, and the situation of these peripheral players within the journalistic field; (3) to develop my arguments from the ground up – from the individual actors to the broader field – in order to lend an openness to the concept of the margins and ensure that all actors and processes are included in the research; (4) to argue for the feasibility of an overarching theory to study this journalistic sub-field.

In order to understand the journalistic identities, I developed a typology of the agents, drew distinctions between types and dispositions and plotted positions within the peripheral journalistic sub-field. The structure of the book reflects my inductive approach, with its focus on journalists and organisations and discussions of these agents as peripheral agents in relation to Bourdieu's conception of the journalistic field. First, and based on my interviews and participant observations, I set out the habituses, capitals, and practices of my communication partners, particularly the journalists and entrepreneurs. Then I turned my attention to media organisations as actors in the journalistic field. Based on the interviews, observations, and survey data, I have emphasised the capitals and practices of organisations within the peripheral sub-field of local newspapers. At the last and most general level, I analysed the particular characteristics of local newspapers and summarise them in a thematic diagram of the sub-field.

My findings suggest that a theory for studying the actors in this field is eminently feasible. And, although the findings are site- and time-specific, they can serve as a framework of reference for further empirical investigation. Those which I consider to be the most important and unique, reflect: (1) the specificity of the actors' doxa and illusio – the acceptance of the involvement of journalists in local politics; the extent to which precarious working conditions discourage initiative and replace it with passivity and the growth of a negative individualism; and therefore (2) the causes and consequences of changes in the sub-field's nomos: the influence of the local political field and local field of power; the disintegration of local structures of production and distribution; the termination of digital transition; and a resigned attitude on the issue of cooperation (Goyanes & Rodríguez-Gómez 2021; Wiik, 2009).

The next logical step for research would be to explore in more detail the relationships between this sub-field and the national journalistic field, and to more closely analyse both the internal agents of the field and its permeability with other fields, along with the influence of interlocutors (Marchetti, 2005). Another avenue would be to adopt my own ground-up approach and map another autonomous area of the journalistic field.

My overall aim was to define the *margins of journalism* by analysing its dynamics, including the unorthodox actors and practices which are less visible from above and difficult to capture (Wahl-Jorgensen, 2019a, 2019b) but which, I argue, have always existed not so much "beyond" journalism as *alongside* it. I have interviewed and observed peripheral journalists in order to uncover not only the obvious but to find out "What are journalists *not* talking about – and why not?" (Usher, 2010, p. 913). I have heard and witnessed both cheerful and sad stories and events, but my first impression, that the attitudes of journalists on the margins are either absolutely optimistic or totally pessimistic, was not confirmed (Ali et al., 2020).

A second look revealed a subtler, more colourful spectrum of findings and, even after thirty years of existence, of constant development and change. Hence, I cannot endorse the judgement of Anderson (2013, p. 159) who sees local media as in a "stasis" and "journalistic evolution as a long, slow, hard slog". Good practices can encourage, the arrival at dead ends can inspire ways of escaping them. Opportunities and threats turn outliers into role models and trendsetters. The microcosm of peripheral newspapers can generate practices, ideas, and experiences from which the macrocosm of the mainstream media can learn. In mapping the margins of journalism, not only its familiar terrain but the blank spots that lie alongside it, I hope I have made my own small contribution. And that I made the journalistic field a more inclusive, complex, colourful, and less blurred space.

Note

1 Seven agents are selected: agents as class fractions of individuals – journalist, freelancer, journalist-entrepreneur and entrepreneur-journalist, and agents as class of organisation – achiever-organisation, survivor-organisation, and leaver-organisation. They are set out in capital letters and italics.

References

Ali, C., Radcliffe, D., Schmidt, T. R., & Donald, R. (2020). Searching for Sheboygans: On the future of small market newspapers. *Journalism, 21*(4), 453–471.

Anderson, C. W. (2013). *Rebuilding the news: Metropolitan journalism in the digital age.* Temple University Press.

Benson, R., & Neveu, E. (Eds.). (2005). *Bourdieu and the journalistic field.* Polity Press.

Bourdieu, P. (1984). *Distinction: A social critique of the judgement of taste.* Harvard University Press.

Bourdieu, P. (1995). *The rules of art: Genesis and structure of the literary field.* Stanford University Press.

Bourdieu, P. (1996). *On television.* The New Press.

Bourdieu, P. (1998). *Practical reason: On the theory of action.* Stanford University Press.

Bourdieu, P. (2005). The political field, the social science field, and the journalistic field. In R. Benson, & E. Neveu (Eds.), *Bourdieu and the journalistic field* (pp. 29–47). Polity Press.

Bowd, K. (2011). Reflecting regional life: Localness and social capital in Australian country newspapers. *Pacific Journalism Review, 17*(2), 72–91.

Carlson, M., & Lewis, S. C. (Eds.). (2015). *Boundaries of journalism: Professionalism, practices and participation.* Routledge.

Duval, J. (2005). Economic journalism in France. In R. Benson, & E. Neveu (Eds.), *Bourdieu and the journalistic field* (pp. 135–155). Polity Press.

Erzikova, E., & Lowrey, W. (2017). Russian regional media: Fragmented community, fragmented online practices. *Digital Journalism, 5*(7), 919–937.

Goyanes, M., & Rodríguez-Gómez E. F. (2021). Presentism in the newsroom: How uncertainty redefines journalists' career expectations. *Journalism, 22*(1), 52–68.

Hess, K. (2013). Tertius tactics: "Mediated social capital" as a resource of power for traditional commercial news media. *Communication Theory, 23*(2), 112–130.

Hess, K. (2015). Making connections. "Mediated" social capital and the small-town press. *Journalism Studies, 16*(4), 482–496.

Hovden, J. F. (2008). *Profane and sacred. A study of the Norwegian journalistic field* [Unpublished doctoral dissertation]. University of Bergen. https://bora.uib.no/bora-xmlui/bitstream/handle/1956/2724/Jan%20Fredrik%20Hovden.pdf?sequence=1

Jenkins, J. (2019). Elevated influences: The construction of journalistic identities at a city magazine. *Journalism Studies, 20*(8), 1069–1087.

Lamour, C. (2019). The legitimate peripheral position of a central medium. Revealing the margins of popular journalism. *Journalism Studies, 20*(8), 1167–1183.

Marchetti, D. (2005). Subfields of specialized journalism. In R. Benson & E. Neveu (Eds.), *Bourdieu and the journalistic field* (pp. 64–84). Polity Press.

Schultz, I. (2007). The journalistic gut feeling. Journalistic doxa, news habitus and orthodox news values. *Journalism Practice, 1*(2), 190–207.

Usher, N. (2010). Goodbye to the news: How out-of-work journalists assess enduring news values and the new media landscape. *New Media & Society, 12*(6), 911–928.

Wahl-Jorgensen, K. (2019a). The challenge of local news provision. *Journalism, 20*(1), 163–166.

Wahl-Jorgensen, K. (2019b). Challenging presentism in journalism studies: An emotional life history approach to understanding the lived experience of journalists. *Journalism, 20*(5), 670–678.

Wiik, J. (2009). Identities under construction: Professional journalism in a phase of destabilization. *International Review of Sociology, 19*(2), 351–365.

Zelizer, B. (2017). *What journalism could be*. Polity Press.

Appendix

Nickname	Function	Gender	Age	Years of experience	Education
Marie	Journalist-entrepreneur	Female	50–65	30+	University
Josef	Manager	Male	50–65	10–15	University
Ema	Manager-entrepreneur	Female	50–65	30+	High school
Pavel	Journalist-entrepreneur	Male	50–65	25–30	University
Jan	Entrepreneur-journalist	Male	50–65	25–30	University
Anna	Manager	Female	50–65	20–25	High school
Petr	Entrepreneur	Male	50–65	5–10	University
Tom	Journalist	Male	50–65	25–30	High school
Robert	Journalist	Male	50–65	25–30	High school
Radim	Journalist	Male	40–50	20–25	High school
Milan	Journalist	Male	40–50	25–30	High school
Artur	Entrepreneur-journalist	Male	50–65	25–30	University
Cyril	Journalist-entrepreneur	Male	50–65	30+	University

Nickname	Function	Gender	Age	Years of experience	Education
Ben	Journalist	Male	20–30	1–5	University
Eva	Journalist	Female	50–65	20–25	High school
Dan	Entrepreneur-journalist	Male	50–65	25–30	University
David	Journalist	Male	30–40	10–15	High school
Filip	Journalist-entrepreneur	Male	30–40	10–15	University
Jana	Journalist	Female	30–40	15–20	High school
Emil	Journalist	Male	50–65	30+	High school
Ivo	Journalist-entrepreneur	Male	40–50	30+	High school
Monika	Journalist	Female	20–30	1–5	University
Ota	Journalist-entrepreneur	Male	50–65	30+	High school
Lucie	Journalist-entrepreneur	Female	50–65	25–30	High school
Karel	Journalist-entrepreneur	Male	50–65	25–30	High school
Dana	Journalist-entrepreneur	Female	50–65	25–30	High school
Max	Entrepreneur-journalist	Male	50–65	25–30	High school
Mirek	Entrepreneur	Male	50–65	5–10	High school
Leo	Journalist	Male	20–30	5–10	University
Marta	Journalist	Female	50–65	25–30	University
Martin	Entrepreneur-journalist	Male	20–30	1–5	University
Alena	Journalist	Female	65+	20–25	High school
Barbora	Journalist-entrepreneur	Female	65+	25–30	High school

Credit: The Author, similarly used in Waschková Císařová (2023a, 2023b).

Index

Abernathy, Penelope Muse 4, 115, 136, 163, 180
achiever-organisation 116, 122–144, 201, 202–206, 208, 209, 210, 214
activism (journalistic) 62, 196
activity (of agents) 54, 98, 138, 157, 184, 198
agent/agents 5–8, 10, 17, 21, 22, 23, 50, 63, 79, 86, 87, 105, 106, 111, 112, 114, 121, 143, 148, 184, 191, 193, 194, 201, 207, 208, 209, 210, 211, 212, 213
Ahva, Laura 17, 28, 53
alongside journalism 2, 10, 24, 113, 212, 213
Anderson, Christopher William 9, 18, 20, 44, 52, 53, 75, 114, 127, 136, 149, 167, 184, 213
Andersson, Ulrika 134, 159
Artemas, Katie 131, 153
audience/audiences 23, 24, 39, 47, 48, 49, 51, 59, 61, 63, 68, 75, 76, 94, 124, 125, 137, 139, 140, 142, 156, 157, 163, 164, 165, 166, 192, 196, 203

autonomy (journalistic) 7, 17, 26, 46, 47, 61, 62, 99, 125, 127, 132, 150, 155, 177, 196

Belair-Gagnon, Valerie 17, 97
Benson, Rodney 5, 6, 16, 17, 21, 22, 23, 37, 40, 44, 57, 63, 99, 105, 106, 107, 111, 112, 113, 142, 184, 201, 208, 210, 211
Bentley, Clyde 157, 162
beyond journalism 2, 113, 213
boundary/boundaries 1, 2, 3, 5, 11, 15, 16, 17, 18, 19, 20, 25, 29, 57, 96, 97, 106, 112, 114, 115, 116, 125, 133, 193, 208, 212
Bourdieu, Pierre 3, 5, 6, 7, 8, 10, 11, 20, 21, 22, 23, 29, 40, 46, 57, 63, 72, 75, 79, 86, 100, 106, 112, 129, 130, 132, 139, 142, 144, 152, 153, 157, 170, 179, 181, 184, 192, 193, 201, 207, 208, 210, 211, 212
Bowd, Kathryn 31, 47, 48, 50, 131, 133, 139, 143, 166, 211
burn-out 39, 46, 55, 65, 71, 72, 91, 99, 122, 123, 147, 193, 194, 195

business model 75, 113, 115, 122, 137, 138, 161, 181, 197, 204

capital 7, 11, 21, 22, 23, 24, 30, 37, 40, 41, 54, 57, 62, 63, 79, 90, 97, 99, 105, 111, 112, 113, 116, 121, 126, 139, 144, 173, 183, 184, 191, 192, 193, 194, 201, 202, 208, 210, 212, 214
    cultural capital 23, 24, 29, 41, 42, 46, 58, 63, 67, 69, 73, 77, 85, 86, 90, 97, 99, 100, 112, 129, 131, 134, 135, 151, 152, 157, 162, 178, 192, 193, 195–196, 198, 200, 201, 202, 207, 211
    economic capital 23, 24, 29, 44, 45, 52, 54, 58, 63, 73, 74, 77, 81, 89, 90, 94, 97, 112, 113, 129, 135, 138, 141, 151, 180, 192, 193, 197, 198, 200, 201, 204, 208, 209, 210, 211
    journalistic capital 8, 23, 26, 77, 193
    mediated social capital 211
    social capital 23, 24, 42, 47, 48, 51, 52, 54, 59, 60, 61, 62, 63, 67, 72, 74, 75, 76, 86, 90, 93, 94, 111, 112, 130, 138, 140, 177, 192, 193, 196–197, 200, 201, 203, 208, 209, 210, 211, 212
    symbolic capital 23, 24, 46, 49, 52, 54, 58, 63, 67, 72, 73, 74, 76, 79, 80, 88, 89, 90, 94, 97, 111, 112, 113, 116, 129, 135, 139, 141, 142, 143, 144, 151, 163, 165, 166, 167, 169, 170, 173, 183, 192, 193, 196, 198, 201, 205, 207
Carlson, Matt 6, 17, 208
Cestino, Joaquín 136, 137
Chadha, Monica 28, 30, 66, 69, 89, 93, 98
class 22, 23, 60, 64, 66, 84, 96, 100, 105, 116, 125, 139, 159, 184, 191, 192, 193, 194, 200, 201, 202, 208, 210, 214
class fraction 23, 64, 192, 193, 194, 208, 210, 214
competition 20, 23, 24, 26, 41, 48, 49, 50, 52, 53, 60, 63, 75, 92, 96, 98, 112, 113, 114, 122, 124, 125, 130, 131, 135, 136, 138, 139, 140, 141, 142, 157, 159, 161, 163, 168, 171, 172, 173, 180, 183, 192, 197, 203, 207, 210
community gap 167
cooperation 51, 58, 74, 84, 105, 112, 113, 123, 125, 127, 139, 140, 141, 142, 143, 144, 148, 163, 167, 168, 169, 170, 171, 172, 176, 181, 182, 183, 184, 203, 210, 213
Cornia, Alessio 129, 150, 153, 159
Cottle, Simon 10, 31, 113
creativity 1, 25, 43, 67, 113, 114, 124, 146, 195, 210
Cushion, Stephen 52, 60

Deuze, Mark 1, 2, 3, 11, 16, 18, 19, 26, 29, 30, 31, 37, 45, 46, 53, 54, 55, 62, 63, 77, 100, 113, 142
digital transition 115, 134, 179, 202, 206, 213
distinction 1, 5, 6, 9, 18, 28, 31, 86, 97, 106, 112, 207, 212
doxa 7, 8, 24, 40, 44, 45, 46, 47, 50, 51, 54, 58, 62, 73, 76, 77, 79, 80, 81, 92, 93, 96, 100, 112, 127, 128, 131, 133, 135, 152, 153, 167, 184, 193, 208, 213
Duval, Julien 73, 211

Eckert, Melissa 4, 11
Ekdale, Brian 26, 55, 62, 126, 129, 137, 138, 149, 160
Eldridge, Scott 1, 2, 17, 57, 60, 62
emotion in journalism 1, 3, 6, 8, 18, 19, 30, 37, 40, 41, 43, 44, 45, 51, 60, 62, 63, 70, 85, 86, 88, 91, 96, 97, 99, 113, 114, 126, 163, 175, 193, 196, 202, 210
entrepreneur 4, 10, 25, 28–31, 193, 194, 195, 198
entrepreneur-journalist 30, 52, 66, 82–99, 128, 158, 193, 194–199, 200, 201, 209, 210, 214
Erzikova, Elina 23, 46, 112, 113, 129, 134, 151, 192
Evetts, Julia 72, 86

Fauchart, Emanuelle 30, 98
field
   economic field 7, 97, 98, 207, 208, 211
   field of power 76, 79, 93, 94, 95, 97, 116, 143, 167, 173, 183, 195, 196, 198, 200, 205, 207, 208, 210, 211, 213
   journalistic field 2, 3, 4, 5, 6, 7, 8, 9, 10, 11, 15, 16, 17, 19, 21, 22, 23, 24, 25, 26, 28, 29, 30, 31, 37, 47, 52, 57, 59, 60, 63, 64, 66, 68, 72, 73, 75, 76, 77, 79, 85, 86, 88, 93, 94, 96, 97, 98, 99, 105, 106, 107, 111, 112, 113, 114, 115, 116, 121, 125, 127, 132, 133, 139, 140, 141, 142, 143, 144, 148, 150, 151, 154, 157, 163, 170, 173, 174, 178, 180, 184, 191, 192, 193, 200, 201, 207, 208, 209, 210, 212, 213
   political field 7, 155, 172, 207, 208, 211, 213
   sub-field 5, 7, 8, 9, 10, 19, 57, 92, 97, 112, 115, 153, 155, 165, 171, 172, 173, 184, 191, 192, 193, 201, 207, 208, 209, 210, 211, 212, 213
Firmstone, Julie 156, 167, 182
Fowler, Neil 159
fragility 9, 100, 105, 143, 149, 167, 184, 203
freelancer 6, 11, 25, 26, 31, 55–64, 84, 98, 99, 100, 126, 127, 147, 149, 150, 152, 176, 177, 193, 194–199, 200, 202, 204, 209, 210, 214

Gieryn, Thomas 9
Glück, Antje 40
Gollmitzer, Mirjam 25, 59, 61, 99
Gruber, Marc 30, 98

habitus 8, 10, 16, 21, 22, 23, 24, 25, 31, 37, 40, 41, 42, 43, 44, 45, 51, 54, 56, 57, 59, 61, 62, 63, 64, 68, 69, 71, 72, 81, 84, 86, 88, 96, 97, 98, 99, 100, 105, 112, 191, 192, 193, 194–195, 200, 210, 212
Hájek, Roman 132, 141, 167, 172
Hanusch, Folker 7, 8, 11, 23, 97, 165
Harlow, Summer 28, 30, 66, 69, 89, 93, 98

Hepp, Andreas 29, 30, 66, 67
Hermans, Liesbeth 31, 133, 140, 165
Hess, Kristy 9, 16, 133, 140, 161, 180, 208, 210, 211
Holton, Avery 17, 26, 57, 58, 60, 97
Hovden, Jan Fredrik 2, 6, 7, 8, 11, 15, 21, 22, 23, 24, 25, 40, 41, 99, 100, 113, 154, 192, 201, 208

identity 18, 22, 28, 69, 72, 86, 88, 89, 112, 125, 130, 132, 163, 178, 198, 200, 201
illusio 8, 24, 40, 41, 43, 44, 45, 46, 47, 51, 52, 54, 60, 61, 62, 63, 66, 68, 71, 79, 80, 81, 84, 85, 87, 90, 91, 95, 96, 97, 125, 135, 155, 181, 193, 208, 213
in-betweener 17, 18
individualism 10, 105, 148, 184, 201, 213
interlocutor 19, 47, 73, 99, 139, 208, 211, 213
interpretive community 15, 132, 154
intrapreneurial 26

Jenkins, Joy 9, 18, 49, 87, 90, 100, 113, 114, 125, 130, 132, 137, 142, 150, 154, 155, 156, 158, 161, 162, 163, 164, 166, 211
journalist 2, 3, 4, 5, 6, 7, 8, 9, 10, 11, 15, 16, 17, 18, 19, 23, 24–28, 29, 30, 31, 37, 38–55, 57, 64, 111, 112, 113, 114, 122, 123, 124, 125, 126, 132, 134, 143, 145, 146, 147, 148, 165, 166, 167, 174, 175, 176, 177, 178, 192, 193, 194–199, 209, 210, 212, 213, 214
journalist-entrepreneur 11, 21, 28, 29, 30, 52, 64–82, 84, 87, 89, 91, 92, 93, 95, 97, 98, 99, 100, 122, 128, 150, 194–199, 200, 208, 209, 210, 214

Lauterer, Jock 4
leaver-organisation 116, 201, 202–206, 209, 214
Lewis, Seth 6, 11, 17, 208
life histories 3, 16, 18, 19, 21, 22, 37, 40, 64, 86, 96, 98, 113, 211, 212
Loosen, Wiebke 29, 30, 66, 67

INDEX

Lowrey, Wilson 23, 46, 112, 113, 129, 134, 151, 192

Maares, Phoebe 7, 8, 11, 23, 97
MacDonald, Jasmine B. 43, 70, 71, 72, 91, 177
manager 30, 65, 73, 122, 146, 147, 148, 178
managerialism 128
margins of journalism 1–11, 17, 19, 21, 24, 28, 37, 52, 111, 184, 191–214
Marlière, Philippe 7, 11
Mathisen, Birgit Røe 1, 17, 26, 61
Matthews, Rachel 136, 137
media organisation 3, 5, 8, 9, 10, 19, 31, 59, 63, 99, 106, 115, 139, 212

Napoli, Philip M. 163
news deserts 4, 115, 116
newsroom-centric 4, 53
Nielsen, Rasmus Kleis 113, 114, 130, 134, 137, 149, 155, 156, 158, 161, 162
nomos 7, 8, 25, 26, 57, 73, 77, 92, 97, 127, 132, 139, 141, 143, 144, 153, 154, 155, 159, 162, 165, 170, 172, 173, 179, 181, 184, 192, 207, 208, 213
nostalgia 130, 134, 137, 158, 180, 202

O'Connor, Catherine 49, 50
Olsen, Ragnhild Kristine 137, 140, 161, 181
O'Neill, Deirdre 49, 50
organisational dynamics 111, 112, 113, 121, 122, 124, 125, 139, 144, 145, 146, 148, 163, 174, 176, 181, 184, 201
Örnebring, Henrik 46, 47, 59, 60, 86, 112, 127, 150, 155
owner 9, 11, 21, 26, 27, 29, 30, 31, 39, 45, 47, 48, 60, 63, 66, 72, 73, 74, 76, 78, 79, 81, 85, 86, 89, 90, 106, 107, 108, 110, 114, 122, 123, 124, 125, 126, 129, 130, 135, 137, 138, 146, 147, 150, 151, 154, 155, 159, 160, 161, 162, 164, 170, 174, 175, 176, 177, 178, 179, 180, 198

participants in the journalistic field 7, 9, 17, 24, 25, 209
passivity (of agents) 50, 51, 54, 55, 61, 68, 78, 98, 116, 147, 154, 155, 156, 157, 173, 175, 180, 182, 184, 193, 194–195, 201, 202–204, 207, 213
path dependency 6, 40, 105, 112, 137, 191, 208
Paulussen, Steve 137
Pauly, John 4, 11
peripheral actors 10, 11, 15, 16, 19, 24, 25, 37, 57, 144, 193, 105, 106, 114, 115, 126, 128, 129, 139, 143, 148, 149, 161, 169, 173, 174, 182, 184, 203
periphery 1, 2, 3, 4, 5, 6, 9, 15, 17, 18, 59, 81, 86, 105, 106, 114, 115, 126, 128, 129, 139, 143, 148, 149, 161, 169, 173, 174, 182, 184
pioneer journalist 29, 30, 66, 134
practices 1, 2, 5, 8, 15, 17, 18, 19, 22, 23, 24, 37, 40, 41, 49, 51, 53, 54, 57, 61, 62, 63, 64, 66, 71, 84, 86, 95, 96, 97, 98, 99, 100, 105, 112, 113, 123, 127, 129, 131, 137, 153, 191, 192, 193, 194–199, 200, 201, 202–206, 207, 208, 209, 2010, 212, 213
precarious 1, 4, 19, 26, 27, 43, 44, 46, 55, 60, 61, 62, 63, 72, 149, 152, 193, 194, 213
presumed readership 87, 164
pseudo-tabloid 132, 157, 204

Raviola, Elena 72, 85, 89, 113, 128
Reinardy, Scott 26, 43, 55, 71, 99, 125
Rivas-Rodriguez, Maggie 48, 167
Russo, Tracy Callaway 45, 99, 125, 126, 127
Ruusunoksa, Laura 52

Schapals, Aljosha Karim 2, 19, 43, 46, 63, 86
Schultz, Ida 7, 22, 23, 40, 131, 184, 211
Siegelbaum, Sasu 54, 62, 68, 81, 99, 158
Singer, Jane B. 18, 28, 29, 66, 67, 69, 77, 80, 97
Spaulding, Stacy 178

survivor-organisation 116, 117, 121, 145–173, 201, 202–206, 208, 209, 210, 214
Sýkorová, Lucie 115, 116, 117

tacit 6, 7, 44, 45, 46, 193, 202
teamwork 144, 153, 203
theory of action 5, 6
Thomas, Ryan J. 54, 62, 68, 82, 99, 158
trajectory/trajectories 7, 9, 10, 22, 23, 24, 37, 40, 62, 96, 111, 112, 192, 193, 208, 209, 210

Usher, Nikki 4, 11, 31, 49, 59, 99, 113, 130, 134, 150, 180, 213

Vos, Tim P. 15, 18, 28, 29, 46, 52, 66, 67, 69, 75, 77, 80, 97

Wahl-Jorgensen, Karin 1, 4, 16, 18, 40, 53, 59, 99, 113, 114, 125, 210, 211, 213
Waldenström, Amanda 11, 68, 88, 100, 127
wall of separation 18, 28, 29, 69, 73, 74, 144, 146, 153, 159, 202
Wiik, Jenny 16, 22, 41, 72, 100, 134, 159, 184, 213
Willig, Ida 5, 7, 8, 23, 184
Witschge, Tamara 1, 2, 3, 11, 16, 18, 19, 26, 29, 30, 31, 37, 46, 53, 55, 63, 113, 142
Wolfgang, David J. 9, 48, 87, 90, 166
work-life balance 46, 70, 71, 91, 193, 194

Zelizer, Barbie 1, 2, 3, 16, 18, 25, 31, 49, 114, 211

Frontiers in Journalism Studies

EDITOR: SCOTT A. ELDRIDGE II, UNIVERSITY OF GRONINGEN

The aim of the series Frontiers in Journalism Studies is straightforward: journalism as a field, and journalism studies as a way to make sense of it, both face the challenge of keeping pace with a range of developments. Buffeted by new, mostly digital, changes in content, journalistic production, media technologies, business models, political pressures, and audience interest, not to mention still unfolding questions around algorithms, data and privacy, and platforms, the challenges for making sense of journalism are many and the changes have been significant. But changes can be made sense of, and even the most novel developments come from somewhere.

The Frontiers in Journalism Studies book series embraces an opportunity to understand journalism's place in society anew. It does so in work that is:

- *Conceptually rich, abundantly clear.* This series provides a platform for a clear and approachable discussion of journalism's new frontiers, matching theoretical richness with accessibility.
- *Research for tomorrow.* The books in this series prioritize forward-looking research agendas that avoid being quickly 'outdated'.
- *Global and comprehensive.* Engaging theoretical and conceptual work that is being done across the world, this series aims to elevate a range of voices across its titles.
- *Provocative and ambitious.* This series provides scholars with the space to engage pressing questions with curiosity and boldness.